FROM OLD MAIN TO A NEW CENTURY:

a history of

PHI KAPPA TAU

from OLD MAIN
to a
NEW CENTURY:

A HISTORY OF PHI KAPPA TAU

By Charles T. Ball

Published by
Heritage Publishers, Inc.
1536 E. Maryland Avenue
Phoenix, Arizona 85014-1448
(602) 277-4780 • (800) 972-8507

Photo Credits:
Page 2, 3, 18, and 22 are from the Frank Snyder
Photograph Collection, Miami University Archives, Oxford, Ohio.
Page 58 and 77 are courtesy of Psi Chapter, University of Colorado.
Page 86 is courtesy of Lambda Chapter, Purdue University.
All other photos are from the archives of
Phi Kappa Tau National Headquarters, Oxford, Ohio.

ISBN: 0-929690-29-X
Library of Congress Catalog Number 96-75934

Printed and bound in the United States of America

DEDICATION

This book is dedicated to the memory of Jack L. Anson (Colgate, 1947)
whose groundbreaking book, The Golden Jubilee History of Phi Kappa Tau
was a constant source and guide to the author.
Beyond his written words, Anson freely shared his knowledge of,
and enthusiasm for, the fraternity's history with the author,
literally from the moment they met in 1982
until Anson's untimely death in 1990.

CONTENTS

FOREWORD

Even now I get a rush of adrenaline when I walk across the Miami campus.

Though it's been four decades since my own initiation into this fraternity, I still think about those early days of the Non-Fraternity Association and wonder what it was like being a student here in those times.

Criss-crossing the Miami campus two or three times a week on average as I do, I walk where the likes of Boyd and Douglass and Shideler and Borradaile walked. And I see some of the same things they saw. Several buildings are as they were then. Many of the same trees are still growing, trees which birthed their leaves in the spring and cast them to the ground in the fall as those men hiked past on their way to class.

"Things are working out just the way we planned them," Taylor Albert Borradaile used to say. I suspect he used that line often, but it was especially memorable when he said it during the 1972 convention in Miami at the Doral Country Club. He had outlived the other Founders and only had a few years left himself, but the magnetism he created when he walked up to a group of students was fascinating, contagious. He was the living, breathing personification of this fraternity, and he was right there in their midst. What merely had been a name to be memorized for a pledge test, suddenly had a face and an undeniable charm and wit.

My own passion for the history of our fraternity was given to me by Jack Anson (Colgate, 1947), who was initially my boss, forever my mentor and friend. Jack's *Golden Jubilee History*, published in 1957, doesn't look much like this current publication, but it carried his love for our fraternity's history and its personalities to countless generations of new initiates and alumni.

Now comes Charles Ball (Miami, 1982). Next to Anson, Charlie's passion for our history is unparalleled. That passion is spread over the following pages in a manner which will bring chuckles and misty eyes to those who can still recall many of the occasions he describes.

Maybe best of all, the new initiate, whose membership shingle has only recently arrived, will come to fully realize the heritage he now shares with thousands upon thousands of others.

What lies before the reader is both a labor of love and a celebration of our fraternity's past. Charlie has authored what is certainly going to be regarded as a treasure of treasures. He looks at our fraternity from a fresh perspective, and in so doing, he has created a collection of its memorable people and events for all to study.

Here in these pages, a truly memorable experience unfolds. Enjoy the passion of Charlie Ball's efforts. For those who have already lived much of the experience, and for those just embarking on the journey, Phi Kappa Tau will mean that much more. I guarantee it.

William D. Jenkins (Bowling Green, 1957)
Executive Vice President
Phi Kappa Tau Foundation

Old Main on the Miami University campus in 1907.
A hand drawn X indicates the location of the Miami Union Literary Society Hall

CHAPTER ONE

BENEDICTION

Author's note: The year listed in parenthesis is the brother's initiation year.

The old North Dorm's steam heat had been turned off in the chilly March weather of Miami University's 1906 spring vacation. Sophomore William H. Shideler, who was visiting his family in nearby Hamilton, Ohio, ended his vacation a day early and caught a train back to the dormitory. He planned to meet his friend Dwight I. Douglass, a senior who had remained in Oxford over the break rather than make the long trip home to Colfax, Illinois. Since their dormitory rooms were cold, the two decided to look for a warm place to discuss the outline of a constitution for the Non-Fraternity Association they had organized along with sophomores Taylor A. Borradaile and Clinton D. Boyd ten days earlier. They began their search in the twin-towered Old Main Building in the center of Miami's small campus, just a few yards west of their North Dorm rooms.

As Shideler remembered the day many years later, "We found all the doors along the main hallway locked until we came to the office of Dean Hepburn. This was unlocked, so we entered and took possession." Douglass, who was beginning his final term at Miami, immediately occupied the venerable dean's wooden swivel chair. At six feet two and two hundred pounds, Douglass cut an imposing figure, reputedly the largest man in the 202-member student body. Shideler pulled up a chair and sat across the desk strewn with the learned clutter of the Reverend Andrew Dousa Hepburn, dean of the College of Liberal Arts. The musty old building was silent except for the ticking of the dean's brass alarm clock.

"Looking into the dean's desk for some scratch paper, Douglass uncovered a box of cigars. Placing a couple in his vest pocket, and one in his mouth, Douglass lit up, leaned back in

Dean Andrew Dousa Hepburn in his Old Main office in 1906; Founders Shideler and Douglass discussed the Non-Fraternity constitution at this table.

of his tobacco. He really could have made an issue of the affair, but he was a good old sport in addition to being a fine gentleman of the old school, and at almost the age of eighty he still had an understanding and an appreciation of students' problems. He listened attentively, then finally he smiled and said, 'Well, boys, that's exactly how Beta Theta Pi [his fraternity] was founded. I wish you all the success in the world.' With this benediction and dismissal we eased through the door and got away from there—fast!"

Only in retrospect can one appreciate how profound was Dean Hepburn's "benediction," recalling the long and proud fraternity tradition at Miami University, the "Mother of Fraternities." For it was in that same Old Main Building that Hepburn's fraternity, Beta Theta Pi, oldest of the famous Miami Triad, became the first fraternity founded west of the Alleghenies in 1839.

Miami University's 1904 catalog advertised the college as the "oldest and most famous institution of higher education in the Miami Valley." The history of Miami University and her fraternities was well known to Phi Kappa Tau's Founders, and that history gives essential context to the fraternity's early development.

the dean's chair, put his feet up on the desk and said, 'Well Doc', my nickname even then, 'let's see what you have.' So we proceeded to discuss the draft item by item," Shideler later wrote.

Just as the smoke from the purloined cigars filled the office, Shideler and Douglass heard the door latch click, and in walked Dean Hepburn! As Shideler went on to recount, "It was difficult to say who was the more surprised. We bounced to our feet while Douglass undertook to explain just why we were there and what we were doing. The dean wrinkled his nose, of course recognizing the aroma

ORIGINS *of the* COLLEGE FRATERNITY

The first Greek-letter college fraternity was Phi Beta Kappa, founded in the Apollo Room of the historic Raleigh Tavern in Williams-burg, Virginia, on December 5, 1776. Since 1831 Phi Beta Kappa has been a nonsecret academic recognition society synonymous with the highest standards of scholarship in more than two hundred of America's leading colleges and universities; but for the first fifty years of that organization's history, it also was a general or social fraternity. Not only was Phi Beta Kappa first to adopt a Greek-letter name, it devised a secret ritual and grip and its members identified themselves by wearing a small silver badge engraved with the letters Phi, Beta, and Kappa, which represented its secret motto, "Philosophy is the guide of life." Almost every fraternity since Phi Beta Kappa has adopted similar ceremonies and insignia.

Phi Beta Kappa set another important precedent by placing chapters at several other colleges and universities. It was one of those chapters, Alpha of New York at Union College in Schenectady, that sparked the founding of the famous Union Triad fraternities. Shortly after Phi Beta Kappa entered Union in 1817, the college's faculty began to dominate the fraternity's governance. Groups of Union students who sought distinctly student-governed organizations formed Kappa Alpha Society in 1825, Sigma Phi Society in 1827, and Delta Phi in 1827, forming the triad.

Following Phi Beta Kappa's example, Sigma Phi established a second chapter at Hamilton College in Clinton, New York, in 1831. The following year, Samuel Eels, a member of Hamilton's class of 1832, founded Alpha Delta Phi. Eels had become concerned about the bitter rivalry between the two student literary societies at Hamilton. His efforts at Hamilton to establish "a society of a higher nature and more comprehensive and better principles" would become a familiar model for the founding of new fraternities and new chapters across the country.

Three years after accepting a position in the Cincinnati law office of the future U.S. Chief Justice Salmon P. Chase, Eels befriended William S. Groesbeck, who took a clerkship in the same office after graduating from nearby Miami University in 1834. Eels enthusiastically shared the Alpha Delta Phi story with Groesbeck and initiated him into the mysteries of Alpha Delta Phi right in the Chase office. Groesbeck quickly contacted two friends still in school at Miami about forming a fraternity; and in the fall of 1835, Alpha Delta Phi's new Miami chapter became the first fraternity chapter west of the Alleghenies and one of the first dozen fraternity chapters in America. Ohio became the third state to have fraternities (after Massachusetts and New York), and Miami became the fourth college to host fraternities following Union, Hamilton, and Williams colleges.

The Union Literary Society Hall, where the Non-Fraternity Association was founded on March 17, 1906

"YALE of the EARLY WEST"

By the time John Reily Knox founded Beta Theta Pi Fraternity at Miami in 1839, the young school with its 250 students was already the fourth largest college in America. Only Harvard, Yale, and Dartmouth were larger. Considering that college-level instruction had begun only

This photo of a North Dorm Senate "trial" appeared in Miami University's 1906 yearbook. Dwight I. Douglass is presiding, William H. Shideler (standing) reads a report, and Clinton D. Boyd and Taylor A. Borradaile sit to Shideler's left. This is the only photo in existence of the four Founders of Phi Kappa Tau together.

fifteen years earlier, the record of this institution in America's hinterlands was impressive.

Miami University's beginnings go back eleven years before Ohio became a state. An act of Congress signed May 5, 1792, by George Washington required Judge John Cleves Symmes to set aside a township to endow a college in the enormous tract of the Northwest Territory he had purchased between the two Miami rivers. Ultimately, no township was available within the Symmes Purchase, and Congress granted a township from unsold federal lands for the establishment of a college. On February 17, 1809, a decade before Thomas Jefferson founded the University of Virginia, the Ohio General Assembly passed an "act to establish the Miami University." Fourteen trustees were appointed to select a site and organize the university.

After trudging through the virgin forest for two days, a committee of five trustees chose 640 acres on the crest of a hill south and west of the

Tallawanda Creek for a college town to be given the academic name of Oxford. One hundred six acres on the eastern edge of the woodland tract were set aside for a "university square" and "botanical gardens." The pioneer spirit that could envision "botanical gardens" on a site without a single road, clearing, or building just six miles from the western boundary of the United States, now seems astonishing.

In 1810 settlers began to build simple dwellings along Oxford's new High Street (named for the main street in England's Oxford), which was still littered with tree stumps. By 1816 enough money was accumulated from land rents to build a three-story brick building on the Miami campus; and after two years of construction, Franklin Hall was opened as a preparatory school with one instructor and twenty-two students. As this small group of pioneer students prepared for college-level instruction, the Miami trustees continued their building campaign by erecting a much larger cupola-topped brick edifice that adjoined Franklin Hall directly to the east. This impressive Federal-style building, completed in 1824, would become the central portion of the Old Main Building that served Miami University for 134 years.

Miami finally opened for collegiate-level instruction in 1824 under the direction of President Robert Hamilton Bishop, who since 1804 had been on the faculty of Translyvania University in Lexington, Kentucky. Twenty male students, including some who had followed Bishop from Transylvania, began the winter term in November 1824. Enrollment swelled to sixty-eight students in the second

DWIGHT I. DOUGLASS

DWIGHT IRENEUS DOUGLASS was the oldest and most intriguing of Phi Kappa Tau's four Founders. He presided over the first meeting on March 17, 1906, just as he was entering his final term at Miami. He studied chemistry and graduated in June 1906 with an A.B. degree. Founder Douglass transferred to Miami in September 1904 after spending his freshman and sophomore years at Ohio Wesleyan University.

Nicknamed "Fat" because of his size (six feet two and two hundred pounds), Douglass was a football "M" man, playing right guard in 1904 and center in 1905. He was a member of the Erodelphian Literary Society, YMCA, Golf Club, and Tennis Club. He presided as judge over the North Dorm Senate, a kangaroo court where freshmen and academy students were tried for such trumped-up "offenses" as growing a bad mustache. As a senior, he was one of only three students elected to the Athletic Board of Control.

Soon after Douglass transferred to Miami, he began trying to organize the nonfraternity men and contributed articles to *Side Lights*, the publication of the Ohio University Union, as early as 1906. He and Taylor Borradaile were the primary organizers of the Non-Fraternity Association and were instrumental in arranging an alliance among the nonfraternity men, Phi Delta Theta, and Delta Rho.

Douglass was born June 6, 1884, in Colfax, twenty miles east of Bloomington in McLean County, Illinois, the second of four children of David T. Douglass, M.D., and Mary Louise Douglass.

From Miami, Founder Douglass went on to the Colorado School of Mines and earned a degree in mining engineering. He took an active interest in

the fraternity in those years, returning to Miami for reunions. The only national convention he attended was the landmark Champaign, Illinois, convention in December 1917.

Founder Douglass served with the 27th Engineers in World War I. He enlisted in April 1918 and embarked for Brest, France, June 30, 1918. He saw combat in the Aisne-Marne, Oise-Ainse, and Meuse-Argonne offensives in the final five months of the war and received a combat promotion to sergeant. According to a letter from his sister, Merriam Moore, "He was gassed once (he said *slightly*) which left him with a most distressing cough." He was discharged from the military in April 1919. His final contacts with the fraternity were two letters written to Dr. Shideler from France in the final weeks of the war. Douglass closes one letter, which is preserved in the fraternity archives, saying, "Believe me, I am very much interested in Phi Kappa Tau. I hope the Fraternity is growing and prospering." In early 1920, Founder Douglass bought a 160-acre farm near Cairo in the far southeast corner of Missouri.

The Douglass mystery begins in February 1922, when he disappeared. His family, his neighbors, and the fraternity lost touch with him. Past Grand President Edgar E., Brandon (Miami, 1906) and Grand Secretary R. K. Bowers (Mount Union, 1915) attempted unsuccessfully to help the family locate Founder Douglass in 1924. After several years, his family had him declared dead.

It was not until Jack L. Anson (Colgate, 1947) began research for the *Golden Jubilee History* in the early 1950s that the details of Founder Douglass' later life were discovered. In 1954 Founder *continued from p. 5*

Borradaile, who was then working for the Veterans Administration in Washington, D.C., learned from Douglass' sister (Emily Gilmer, in Maryland) that about 1930 Douglass had contacted his family for the first time since his disappearance. He had gone to New Orleans in 1922 and taken a job with a Veterans Administration hospital. It was there that he met his future wife, nurse Ruth Mathews. In 1925 he was transferred to the VA Hospital in Pittsburgh. Ruth Mathews later transferred to Pittsburgh, and she and Founder Douglass were married (coincidentally) on Founders' Day, March 17, 1934. Their only son, Donald Dwight, was born the following year. Forced to retire because of failing health, Douglass moved his family to Hammond, Louisiana, where he spent the remainder of his life writing short stories published under a pen name never revealed to his family. He died February 12, 1940, and is buried in Greenlawn Cemetery in Hammond.

For a number of years following Founder Douglass's death, his wife and son lived in San Marcos, Texas, where the son attended college. Phi Kappa Tau Field Secretary Bernie Scott (Nebraska Wesleyan, 1949) visited Mrs. Douglass and eighteen-year-old Donald in 1954. Until that time, they had not known that Douglass was one of Phi Kappa Tau's honored Founders.

term. As the new institution's enrollment grew, so did its reputation. An excellent faculty was assembled—most notable among them William Holmes McGuffey, a future president of Ohio University, who began work on his famous series of "Eclectic Readers" while a young member of the Miami faculty.

Following the tradition of the eastern colleges, two literary societies were formed at Miami in the college's second year. On the third floor of the Old Main Building, the Erodelphian Literary Society took up residence in the southeast room, and the Union Literary Society made its home in the southwest room, both with windows looking out over the rolling woodland south of the campus. In the years before fraternities entered Miami, the fellowship of the literary societies' Friday evening debates had been the primary social outlet for the all-male student body.

When they arrived, the fraternities had a tremendous impact on those societies. As Alpha Delta Phi badges began to appear on vests of members of both literary societies, the uninitiated became suspicious and fearful of this mysterious new secret society. These natural fears were fueled by the anti-Masonic and anti-secret society fervor, led by John Quincy Adams and others, that was sweeping the country in the 1830s.

BETA THETA PI

Curiously, one of the most vocal opponents of Alpha Delta Phi was the president of the Union Literary Society, John Reily Knox, a member of Miami's class of 1839. While he issued stinging antifraternity rhetoric from the Miami Union rostrum, he could not help but notice that Alpha Delta Phi had initiated some fine men and there was something attractive about their close-knit brotherhood. Inspired by the ideals of Masonic rituals, which were exposed in the early 1830s, Knox and seven others formed Miami's second fraternity, Beta Theta Pi, in August 1839. As Alfred Upham described in his 1909 book, *Old Miami*, "To the unprejudiced observer there is one feature about Knox's plan, novel enough in his day, that gets to be painfully familiar as time goes on. The new brotherhood was to have all the good qualities of Alpha Delta Phi and none of the bad ones."

Still, Miami's two young fraternities existed in the face of great faculty and student opposition. Members of Beta Theta Pi actually operated *sub rosa* for seven years, first publicly displaying their badges in 1846. It was not long before the "Alphas" and "Betas" were dealt a fatal blow following an 1848 college prank that is legend in Miami's history. "The Great Snow Rebellion" was orchestrated by

WILLIAM H. SHIDELER

By ALL ACCOUNTS, Founder William Henry Shideler was a remarkable man. He was born in West Middletown, Ohio, on July 14, 1886. His family moved to Hamilton, Ohio, twelve miles from Oxford, when he was quite young. In 1904 he graduated from Hamilton High School and entered Miami University in September of that year.

Along with Founder Boyd, he was a member of the varsity track team as a distance runner and was an organizer and member of the nonfraternity intramural teams, whose activities became important to the founding of the Non-Fraternity Association. He was an officer of the North Dorm Senate, serving as clerk of court when Founder Douglass presided as judge.

"Doc" (as he was known from undergraduate days on) was a member of the Erodelphian Literary Society and chaired the Athletic Board of Control in his final year. A member of the campus Democratic Club, he was an outspoken progressive as an undergraduate.

An ambitious student, Founder Shideler completed his undergraduate work in three years, receiving his bachelor of arts degree with the class of 1907. He earned his Ph.D. in geology at Cornell in 1910 and returned to Oxford as an eager young Darwinist to join the Miami faculty.

At first, he taught zoology and geology. He persuaded the Miami administration in 1920 to establish a geology department, which he would chair for thirty-six years.

As a paleontologist, he became an expert on the Upper Ordovician fossils and stratigraphy that are so magnificently revealed in the outcroppings and creek beds around Oxford. In geology circles, "Doc" Shideler was well known for his fossil collec-

tions, occasional publications, and professional activities. Scholars from around the world came to Miami to consult with him and study the specimens he collected. Though he was not a prolific writer, Shideler freely shared information and research, which led to many scholarly publications and Ph.D. theses. He amassed an outstanding collection of type specimens and Upper Ordovician materials for Miami. Thirteen species, three genera, one family, and one mountain in Antarctica were named for him as "a geologist's way of passing a compliment," he once said.

Shideler referred to Columbia University President Grayson L. Kirk (Miami, 1921), newspaper publisher J. Oliver Amos (Miami, 1928), and Gen. John Edwin Hull, supreme commander of U.S. forces in the Near East, as "some of my conspicuous failures—men I couldn't keep interested in careers as geologists at Miami." His "successes" were legend and included a long list of former students, who went on to academic positions in several of the nation's leading institutions.

In Phi Kappa Tau, Shideler held almost every national office, including a term as national president in 1913–14. He was instrumental in bringing the fraternity's National Headquarters to Oxford in 1930, and he was an almost daily visitor to the office, which was within a block of his home and campus office. The Shidelers lived in a historic Oxford home, which is now the home of Acacia Fraternity's Miami chapter. In his role as comptroller, he personally approved every fraternity expenditure for more than thirty years. And when National Secretary Richard Young (Miami, 1925) was in the service during World War II, he was acting national secretary and even janitor. In his last year, he *continued from p. 7*

conducted Phi Tau business from his hospital room during an illness and was in the office the day he fell ill for the final time.

Founder Shideler attended almost every national convention held between the time he was elected national president and the time he died.

Shideler married Katherine Hoffman, who was a student at Miami, during his first year. Katherine Shideler's student diary, now in the Miami University archives gives interesting descriptions of daily life at Miami in 1904–05. The Shidelers had two sons, William Watson (Ohio State, 1950) and James Henry (Miami, 1933).

He deferred his retirement from Miami three times, finally giving up the chairmanship of his department in 1956. When he retired the following year, he was the recipient of a John Hay Whitney grant to go to Hiram College to start a geology program there, much as he had done for Miami in 1920.

In 1967 Miami University named its new earth-science building William H. Shideler Hall in his memory.

PHI DELTA THETA

"Alphas" and "Betas," who, on their return from an off-campus prayer meeting, rolled enormous snowballs against the Old Main doors. The much-despised college president, Erasmus McMaster, derided the perpetrators at the next morning's chapel service, declaring that he was determined "to make Miami a decent college." This comment so infuriated the students that the next night they filled the Old Main corridors and barricaded the doors with piles of wet snow and all the scraps of wood, metal, and broken furniture that could be scrounged up.

When the temperature dropped later that night, the building solidified into an enormous block of ice. It was three days before the faculty members got into their offices at Old Main. The entire next week was devoted to determining the fate of each student which was decided in a trial with the Reverend Dr. McMaster presiding as judge and members of the faculty as jury. All the "Alphas" were expelled or left Miami in sympathy with their expelled brothers, and only two senior "Betas" were left to graduate in June. Whether or not it was President McMasters' intention to kill the fraternities will never be known, but kill them he did…temporarily.

Robert Morrison of Miami's class of 1849 kept a bottle of water from the melting snow of the "Great Snow Rebellion" in his room in the North Dorm. It served as a reminder of the vitality that was lost from the campus when the fraternities dispersed. In the chill of the evening after Christmas 1848, Morrison called together five friends in the candlelight of his second-floor North Dorm room to discuss forming a new fraternity, Phi Delta Theta. Since the members of Beta Theta Pi and Alpha Delta Phi had all departed Miami, the founding of Phi Delta Theta was unique in two significant ways: first, it was not formed in opposition to another secret society; and second, faculty members were favorably disposed to this organization, as several of them, including President McMasters' successor, were soon initiated.

Miami's fourth fraternity chapter was founded when a division occurred in Phi Delta Theta. In 1851, Benjamin Harrison, who later became the twenty-third president of the United States, was a serious and earnest president of the fledgling Phi Delta Theta Chapter. He led a movement in the chapter to enforce a strict oath of abstinence from strong drink. In spite of the pledges they had taken, Phi Delts Gideon McNutt and J. H. Childs were drunk on repeated occasions. In fact, it is recorded that the two were drunk on the night of their initiation but when confronted promised again to uphold the oath. After their repeated spills off the wagon of sobriety, the chapter, following long and painful deliberation, expelled McNutt and Childs. Four others left the chapter in support of their errant brothers.

Not long after that event, Jacob Cooper, a member of Delta Kappa Epsilon Fraternity's mother chapter at Yale, was visiting his family near Oxford when he met McNutt and the others in his gang. Along with another student who had not previously belonged to a fraternity, the group formed the Kappa Chapter of DKE at Miami.

SIGMA CHI COMPLETES *the* MIAMI TRIAD

To complete the Miami Triad, Sigma Chi was founded in 1855 after what today seems a trivial disagreement within the DKE Chapter. Whitelaw Reid, the Deke president in 1854, later the unsuccessful candidate for vice president of the United States on fellow Miamian Benjamin Harrison's 1892 ticket, was embroiled in a controversy over the election of a poet for the Erodelphian Literary Society. Reid wanted his brothers to support a fellow Deke for election as Erodelphian Poet, although the candidate apparently had little or no poetic ability. The four opposition Dekes supported another man, who was not a brother but was known to have considerably more talent as a poet. In the end, the controversy became a referendum on DKE loyalty; and although the chapter worked for a year to heal the wounds, it was not to be. Finally, in 1854 the six dissenters relinquished their DKE badges and left the chapter.

In 1855 the six former Dekes and William Lockwood gathered in a second-floor room on Oxford's High Street to form a new fraternity in a familiar attempt to maintain all of the advantages of the other fraternities but possess none of the evils. Sigma Chi's Miami chapter failed in 1857; but during its short life, chapters had been begun at Ohio Wesleyan, Western Military, and Mississippi, and expansion continued from those fronts.

Old Miami, which had for a time been the preeminent college in the early West, was on its last legs when Andrew Dousa Hepburn became president of the university in 1871. Hepburn tried to save the struggling school; but as the enrollment dwindled to eighty-seven students, the trustees had no choice but to suspend classes in 1873 "with a view to a full reorganization at the earliest practicable period." The reasons for its failure were many. The state legislature's refusal to provide financial support, the maintenance of an outdated classical curriculum, and its staunch opposition to coeducation were among the factors that brought about Miami's demise. The school was closed for twelve years until the legislature could be convinced to make some contributions and alumni could be rallied to their old college's cause.

"NEW MIAMI"

After securing its first-ever appropriation from the state of Ohio, paying all of the university's debts and accumulating a permanent endowment of more than $50,000, Miami reopened in 1885.

By 1892 Beta Theta Pi, Phi Delta Theta, Delta Kappa Epsilon, and Sigma Chi had all reestablished Miami chapters. A political "ring" consisting of the Betas, Dekes, and Sigma Chis immediately began to dominate campus athletic teams, politics, and social life. It was in this atmosphere at "New Miami" that the idea for an association of nonfraternity men began to crystallize.

Early histories of Phi Kappa Tau record that a nonfraternity organization called Independents was formed in 1894, but it existed only briefly. For the next ten years, occasional political alliances were formed to back candidates in student elections; but no lasting attempt to organize nonfraternity men took place until October 20, 1903, when a small group of them secretly founded a local fraternity, Delta Rho, which would become the Miami chapter of Delta Upsilon in 1908. This group was too focused on internal organization to have much impact on the "ring." In early 1905, an unsuccessful effort to organize nonfra-

ternity men was led by Arthur Harrison and Dwight I. Douglass. Harrison graduated with the class of 1905, but Douglass returned the next year with renewed fervor to organize the campus "barbarians," as nonfraternity men were commonly called. By the end of the 1905–06 school year, four men, including Douglass, his roommate Taylor A. Borradaile, William H. Shideler, and Clinton D. Boyd, would ultimately be successful in founding a lasting organization of nonfraternity men. It was this organization that evolved into Phi Kappa Tau.

CONDITIONS at MIAMI

Writing for Phi Kappa Tau's 1918 yearbook, William H. Shideler described the atmosphere at Miami in those days:

"A political combination of fraternities had taken charge of essentially all activities within the reach of the student body. A member of any fraternity not in the "ring," or a nonfraternity man, no matter how able or deserving he might have been stood absolutely no chance of winning any office within reach of the student body. Even membership on athletic teams was controlled in various dark and devious ways, and few but members of certain fraternities were able to make the teams."

Founder Shideler pointed to Miami's annual indoor track meet in March 1905 as the first real impetus for a nonfraternity association. A team of nonfraternity men was organized and coached by Boyd and Douglass. According to Shideler, "The 'Sigs' and 'Dekes' combined and so jockeyed in the trials, semi-finals, and finals, that the 'Dekes' were enabled barely to nose out the non-fraternity team. That night the 'Dekes' gave a dinner for the 'Sigs' as a token of appreciation for assistance given." The aftermath of that defeat was described by Shideler in the 1950s:

"After the defeat of the track team in the meet for which we had trained so long and so faithfully, it was quite natural that there should be so much disappointment, but on top of that was

TAYLOR A. BORRADAILE

TAYLOR ALBERT BORRADAILE was born on May 15, 1885, just northeast of Oxford, in tiny Camden, Ohio, and his family moved to nearby Eaton in January 1897. He became interested in science at a young age and chose to attend Miami University in the fall of 1904 because of the local reputation of its science faculty.

With his roommate, Dwight Douglass, Borradaile helped to arrange an alliance between the Delta Rho, Phi Delta Theta, and the unorganized nonfraternity men in 1904–05; and he viewed the founding of the Non-Fraternity Association primarily as a political move.

He was elected president at the Non-Fraternity Association's first meeting, and under his leadership, the political objectives of the association were thoroughly accomplished. He earned the nickname "Boss" for his prowess in campus political organizing.

He was also elected president of the Erodelphian Literary Society and president of the junior class. He earned enough credits to graduate by the middle of his senior year, so he was asked to teach chemistry at Tippecanoe City, Ohio, and returned to graduate with the class of 1908.

The majority of his career was spent in chemistry and chemical sales, serving as chief chemist of the city of Charleston, West Virginia, and he became an authority on toxicology. He retired from the Veterans Administration in Washington, D.C., where he served as chief chemist. Without ever attending law school, Borradaile passed the bar exam and was admitted to the Florida bar, but he never practiced.

Borradaile was not actively involved with the fraternity in the early years after he left Miami but did not miss a convention between 1951 and 1975. He had one son, Joseph R. Borradaile, with his first wife, Laura Reeve. His second wife was Letha Lively whom he married in 1937.

Borradaile and Letha retired to Beckley, West Virginia. He was ninety-two when he died in 1977. Because he had lived twenty years longer than any other of the Founders, Borradaile was the only link to the Founders that many younger members had.

Borradaile kept his dry wit until the very end. Indicative of his fun-loving attitude toward the fraternity were the last public words he spoke to its members in 1975: "There is more to college than book learning…there are, in addition, friendship, fellowship, and plain old fun, and organizations which supply these healthy leavenings will never be long from our campuses."

acute bitterness and much resentment at the way it had happened. With the lapse of a half century the whole affair seems trivial, but at the time it was a deadly serious matter.

"Inwardly boiling at the injustice of the whole affair, so typical of what had been going on for years, when returning from the Faries boarding house at the far corner of Oxford, Boyd and Shideler encountered Jim Coulter, a senior Deke. Again, after a lapse of half a century, and in the light of what Jim Coulter became in later years as vice president of the Colgate Palmolive Co., we can see now what we couldn't see at the time, which was that Coulter was sincerely though possibly somewhat clumsily trying to

compliment us on the effort we had made, and was encouraging us to continue our activities. But we took it that he was sarcastically rubbing in our defeat and in the language of the day, giving us a royal razzing. We returned to the old Phi Delta Theta [Founder's] room in the North Dorm in silence. Once there we looked at each other a moment, then automatically reached across the table and clasped hands, each saying the substance if not the exact words of 'God damn the sons of bitches! From now on we'll do them every bit of dirt that we can!'

"Phi Kappa Tau was not founded on that day of defeat. Actually, it was only a partial defeat at that. For though we failed to win the meet, we did find

Miami University's 1906 track team; Clinton D. Boyd holds the banner with his right hand, and William H. Shideler sits in the middle of the three men on the right.

CLINTON D. BOYD

FOUNDER CLINTON DEWITT BOYD came to Oxford in September 1903 as a third-year preparatory student in the Miami Academy and began his college work the next year. He was born and reared in Mount Orab, a tiny Brown County town east of Cincinnati.

At Miami, Boyd was both an athlete and one of the most silver-tongued of Miami's orators. He was a distance runner, representing the varsity track team in the mile and 880-yard events. He captained the team in his senior year and acquired the nickname "Teeny" because of his slight runner's build, and he was active on the intramural track and basketball teams.

Boyd was a four-year member of the Miami Union Literary Society and was elected vice president. His speech, "Emancipation of a Backward Race," won him the gold medal in the university's oratorical contest in 1907.

After Miami, Founder Boyd enrolled in the University of Cincinnati's law school, then transferred to the University of Michigan, where he earned his law degree in 1910. He opened a law office in Middletown, Ohio, and was appointed to the common pleas bench of Butler County in 1929. A Republican, he was twice reelected to that position, retiring in 1937. He was an unsuccessful candidate for Ohio attorney general in 1928.

Founder Boyd remained actively interested in the fraternity. He was the first person elected to the position of national organizer at the Danville, Kentucky, convention of 1915; and until Miami's withdrawal from Phrenocon in March of the following year, he was working aggressively to extend Phrenocon to Northwestern, Wabash, Purdue, Wisconsin, Nevada, and Carnegie Tech. He was a frequent speaker at Founders' Day gatherings at Miami and around the country. In the final year of his life, he visited several chapters and alumni on the West Coast.

Founder Boyd helped to initiate his son, Clinton Dewitt, Jr., at Alpha Chapter in 1948; and the younger Boyd, too, has been active in fraternity affairs, serving as chairman of Alpha's Chapter House Association in the 1970s. Founder Boyd's grandson, Mark, is a 1971 initiate of Alpha Chapter.

Boyd's untimely death occurred in 1950, when a car he was driving skidded on slick pavement into the path of an oncoming truck. He was on his way from his home to Columbus, Ohio, for the Ohio Republican state convention.

Dr. Edgar Ewing Brandon in the 1920s

what organization and cooperation could do, and so won something far more valuable than a track meet trophy. The result was the founding of our fraternity almost a year later."

In the fall of 1905, two loose political alliances were organized to give nonfraternity students a voice in the fall elections. Shideler and Boyd organized one group and Douglass and Borradaile led the other. The two groups soon realized that it would be advantageous to work together. Founders Borradaile, who had acquired the nickname "Boss" for his political activities and Douglass arranged an alliance of the nonfraternity men; the local fraternity Delta Rho; and Phi Delta Theta, the only national fraternity not part of the "ring." The first test of the alliance came in the fall of 1905, when they elected Ernest B. Southwick (a Phi Delt) and Boyd president and vice president of the sophomore class.

Boyd and Shideler focused their energies on organizing athletic teams, and by the annual indoor meet on February 28, 1906, the nonfraternity men were ready for the second major test of the year. In a bitterly fought meet, Boyd won the gold medal and a

Phi Delt won the silver. The "ring" was beaten once again, and the victory was sweet revenge for the previous year's unjust defeat.

In Shideler's words written in 1918, "Then while enthusiasm was the highest, all of the reliable nonfraternity men assembled in the hall of the Miami Union Literary Society, and organized."

In his recollections, Founder Borradaile disagreed that the track-meet victory was the real impetus for the first meeting. He remembered that Miami's profraternity president, Guy Potter Benton, a member of Phi Delta Theta, had called a faculty-moderated meeting early in 1906 to work out differences between the "ring" and the nonfraternity men. Borradaile and Douglass attended as representatives of the nonfraternity students and were told bluntly that, without some sort of organization behind them, they really did not represent anyone. According to Borradaile in a 1975 conversation, the meeting became a "near riot" and was adjourned until after the spring vacation. He asserted in a 1964 Oxford interview with Jack Anson that the founding of the Non-Fraternity Association was precipitated by the need to establish standing for the nonfraternity leaders when the adjourned meeting resumed. Robert L. Meeks (Miami, 1906), the Association's first secretary, supported Borradaile's assertion in a 1981 letter.

NON-FRATERNITY ASSOCIATION FOUNDED

Regardless of the specific reason for it, on Saturday, March 17, 1906, twenty-one men climbed two flights of ancient, creaking wooden stairs to the old Miami Union Hall in Miami's Old Main Building. Under the watchful eye of the Miami Union Literary Society's mangy mascot owl, Dwight I. Douglass called the meeting to order at one o'clock in the afternoon from the historic rostrum, where Miami's first fraternity had been harshly denounced in 1836 and from where John Reily Knox had led the first meeting of Beta Theta Pi in 1839. Except for a few bare electric light bulbs hanging on long cords from the water-stained ceiling, the Union Hall looked much the same as it had for more than seventy-five years, albeit a little shabby from wear. After Douglass made his introductory remarks, Taylor Borradaile, and Clinton Boyd, two of Miami's finest orators, spoke persuasively to the assembly about the urgent need for a permanent nonfraternity organization built on the principles of democracy, square dealing, and equality.

Someone in the group proposed the "Non-Fraternity Association" as an appropriate name, and the others readily agreed. William Shideler, who had been keeping minutes of the meeting, and Dwight Douglass agreed to draft a constitution for the association over the coming spring vacation. Since Douglass was set to graduate in June, sophomore Borradaile was elected as president for the coming year.

With its business concluded and winter-term exams looming, the meeting was adjourned after less than an hour and members of the new association headed back to their books. The men who attended that March 17 meeting have come to be known as Foundation Members of Phi Kappa Tau. The roster of Miami's most capable nonfraternity leaders was carefully selected to represent each of Miami's four collegiate classes, and men as young as fifteen in their final year at the Miami Academy, a preparatory school.*

Dr. Edgar Ewing Brandon, a red-goateed, forty-year-old professor of romantic languages, was one of a small group of Miami's nonfraternity faculty members. He took an active interest in the work of the Founders and became the association's faculty advisor almost immediately. Although he was not present at the first meeting, he is considered a Foundation Member and the first faculty initiate. Dr. Brandon's

leadership in the formative stages of the fraternity earned him the title, "Architect of Phi Kappa Tau."

Shideler and Douglass completed the draft of a Non-Fraternity Association constitution on March 28, 1906, the first day of the spring term. That constitution was ratified without change at a second mass meeting in the Miami Union Hall on April 8.

Under the leadership of Borradaile and Shideler, the Non-Fraternity Association came to dominate campus politics in the 1906–07 school year, effectively breaking up the old "ring" and generally democratizing the campus atmosphere.

Seniors:
Dwight I. Douglass
Glenn B. Britton
R. Burton Reed

Juniors:
Roy C. Pierce
F. Atherton Riedel

Sophomores:
William H. Shideler
Taylor A. Borradaile
Clinton D. Boyd
Harvey C. Brill
Dwight M. Britton
John G. Snyder
Stanley J. Moore

Freshmen:
Herman H. Beneke
Henry H. Reighley
George E. Booth
Harry R. Crauder
Earl T. Leeds
Cary S. Miller

Academy Students:
Robert L. Meeks
Paul Teetor
Hazlett A. Moore

FIRST ANNUAL BANQUET

It was in this atmosphere of triumph that the Non-Fraternity Association gathered for dinner on the warm spring evening of May 7, 1907, to celebrate its successes and contemplate the future. Though the location of the banquet has been lost to history, it was probably held on campus in the dining room of the new women's dormitory, Hepburn Hall. At the invitation of Dr. Brandon, Miami President Dr. Guy Potter Benton was the guest of honor and zoology Professor Steven R. Williams served as the evening's toastmaster. Benton, a future national president of Phi Delta Theta, praised the association's "democratizing influence" on the student body and gladly accepted Dr. Brandon's pledge that the association would continue to "work for the betterment of the university."

Though it may have been presumptuous of the young group to call that banquet the "first annual," a springtime banquet did become an annual event and was soon being called the Founders' Day Banquet. Now celebrated at Phi Kappa Tau chapters from coast to coast, the Founders' Day Banquet is considered to be the fraternity's oldest tradition.

The fourth great national fraternity to be borne by Miami University, "Mother of Fraternities," was well under way.

Miami University in 1906; Old Main is the towered building in the center, and the two matching brick buildings to its left are the North and South dormitories.

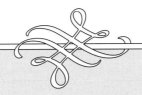

CHAPTER HISTORIES

ALPHA CHAPTER
Miami University
Oxford, Ohio

*Founded as Non-Fraternity
Association, March 17, 1906
Name changed to Phrenocon,
March 6, 1909
Adopted name Phi Kappa Tau,
March 9, 1916*

PHI KAPPA TAU'S first chapter has operated continuously since its founding in spite of two world wars and a major chapter reorganization in the early 1970s. The chapter has resided in its Memorial Chapter House since the fraternity's twenty-fifth anniversary in 1931. The house underwent a major restoration in 1988. The Alpha Chapter Foundation was formed in 1987 to support the educational aspects of the chapter's mission, and it has helped to enhance the individual and small-group study areas in the chapter house.

Alpha alumni have played significant roles in the national fraternity. Ten Alpha men have been elected national president, Richard J. Young was national secretary for more than thirty years, and four others have served on the National Council. Three men have received the Shideler Award, including William E. Cromer, the first man to win the award in 1938.

In service to Miami University, six Alpha men have served as university trustees, and Hugh C. Nichols, J. Oliver Amos, and William N. Liggett have chaired that body. The first recipient of Miami's highest alumni honor, the Bishop Medal, was Dr. Sam Clark and a long list of other Alpha men have won the award since then. Buildings on the Miami campus are named for Edgar Ewing Brandon, William H. Shideler, and Joseph M. Bachelor.

Phrenocon seniors at Miami University in July 1909; this is the first known group photo of Phrenocon members.
(left to right) top row: Duvall, Bowman, Lantis, Crauder*, Reighley*, Schilling;
bottom row: Beneke*, Cary Miller*, Stover, Guiler, V. Dredge, Teetor*.
* indicates Foundation Members.

CHAPTER TWO

BROTHER BARBARIANS

fter a session at Phi Kappa Tau's Thirty-fourth National Convention at Pasadena's Huntington Sheraton Hotel in 1958 the two living Founders, Taylor Borradaile and William Shideler, walked to their rooms. As they strolled, Shideler—who would die later that year, making this the last time any of the Founders would be together—asked his old friend, "Taylor, when we were organizing this thing in 1905 and '06, did you ever think that it would turn out the way it has today?" Known for his quick wit, Borradaile answered, "Bill, it's exactly the way I planned it."

The truth of the matter is that the Non-Fraternity Association's Founders never intended that their loose organization would become a fraternity, let alone a national organization with dozens of chapters and thousands of members. Rather, it was the vision of the younger members of the foundation group and the men they recruited in 1907 and 1908 that fueled the evolutionary process that transformed the Non-Fraternity Association into Phi Kappa Tau.

Having accomplished their political objectives during the first year, the members of the Non-Fraternity Association could have rested on their

laurels and rejoiced in all they had accomplished—or disbanded the organization altogether. But as early as 1907, the growing membership of the association began to talk of greater things.

The second president of the Non-Fraternity Association, Harvey C. Brill (Miami, 1906), took the first step to tighten the rather loosely organized association by convening a committee to revise Douglass and Shideler's constitution in the fall of 1907. The new constitution was adopted on January 20, 1908. Harvey Brill would probably be a footnote in the association's history were it not for two peculiar events. The identification of four primary Founders of the association was to some degree arbitrary, and Founder Shideler was clear that Harvey Brill was the fifth most influential of the Foundation Members. Brill's photo actually appears along with those of Douglass, Borradaile, Shideler, and Boyd in the *Nineteen Eighteen Year Book of the Phi Kappa Tau Fraternity* under the heading, "The Five Founders." The photos accompany the first detailed history of the fraternity prepared by Grand Historian Shideler, presumably a credible authority.

Since the 1920s Brill has not been listed on the Phi Kappa Tau membership rolls, because he joined Phi Sigma Kappa Fraternity as a doctoral student at the University of Michigan. When Phi Kappa Tau badge numbers were assigned, Brill was never included. Several early members of the associa-

tion joined fraternities at Miami and have long been forgotten, but Brill remains an anachronism because he was the second president. Founder Borradaile thought Brill got a "raw deal" in history. A credit to any fraternity, Brill had a long and distinguished career on the Miami faculty teaching chemistry, and he maintained a life-long friendship with Founder Shideler. Today, Miami's science library is named for Harvey C. Brill, Phi Kappa Tau's "fifth founder."

Wilmer Stover (Miami, 1907), who taught high school to earn money for college and was already a botany instructor in his senior year, was elected third president at the Non-Fraternity Association's Second Annual Banquet in February 1908. The Stover administration concentrated on the acquisition of club rooms and a change in name for the organization.

A Barbarian picnic at Ohio University in 1909

Herman H. Beneke (Miami, 1906), who had a long career as a finance professor in Miami's business school, was one of the first to advocate acquiring appropriate quarters. Miami's five fraternities occupied rented houses in the village, and the Phi Delts were even showing off blueprints for a luxurious brick house on a new "fraternity row." Beneke and others believed that a house would make the Non-Fraternity Association more visible and would give the men a place to hold the social events that were growing in importance to them.

FIRST
HOUSE

A house committee first asked the university if rooms could be rented in the North Dorm. Although these rooms were available, most committee members believed that finding a house to rent was a more favorable option. Early in February 1909, an Oxford landlord offered to rent the association a large, two-story family home at 14 North Campus Avenue. The new main campus gate being constructed to commemorate the university's centennial was clearly

visible from the house's wide and airy gingerbread porch. This became the official home of the association in March 1909 when ten seniors and two juniors moved into the house in time for the beginning of Miami's spring term. The house was immediately the most desirable address for Miami's non-fraternity men; and because the association's membership had grown to include nearly half of the male student body—over fifty men—a seniority system was developed to determine who would be the first to move in. Cary S. Miller (Miami, 1906), who would be the oldest living member of Phi Kappa Tau when he died in 1986, drew first choice of rooms and selected Walter S. Guiler (Miami, 1907) as his roommate.

To outfit the house, members of the association negotiated a two-hundred-dollar loan for equipment and furnishings. By the end of the second year in the house, the association was running a one-hundred-dollar deficit, and secretary Ralph Keffer (Miami, 1908) was instructed to prepare a fund-raising letter to be sent to alumni. Some things never change.

That first house served the chapter only until 1914 and is today directly across the street from the fraternity's National Headquarters. When the

property came on the market in the 1980s, Phi Kappa Tau Foundation Chairman Ewing T. Boles (Centre, 1914) came to Oxford to persuade Emeritus Mathematics Professor J. Paul Albert (Miami, 1920) to make a major contribution to help buy the house for use as offices for the national fraternity and foundation. As usual, Boles was successful securing a generous gift, and the building is now known as the J. Paul Albert Building. Perhaps it is appropriate that the fund-raising programs of the Phi Kappa Tau Foundation are today conducted in the same rooms where in 1911 Ralph Keffer wrote, "If every person who receives a copy of this paper would send just one dollar, that debt would not hang like a monster over us."

The prospect of a house of their own may have been motivation for the association to move on several organizational issues further tightening the still rather loose organization. Changing the name of the association was the first priority. Almost since the beginning of the Non-Fraternity Association, many of the members believed that the name was too negative. Members had been careful to say that they were "distinctly not antifraternity." They had formed political alliances with two fraternities, Phi Delta Theta and Delta Rho; and, according to Founder Shideler, "No particular objection was made to an association member joining either of these for it was 'all in the family anyway.'" Still, the consensus was that a more positive name was needed to better reflect the association's broad ambitions.

The Phrenocon Association members were photographed in front of their house at 14 North Campus Avenue, January 1911. Several of these men would play prominent roles in the development of Phi Kappa Tau. (left to right) seated ground: Ernest N. Littleton (1), Jesse Day (2); seated in chairs: Joseph Clokey (3), Edward E. Duncan (5), Anthony Poss (6), Roger C. Smith (7), Joseph Bachelor (10), Ralph Keffer (11), J. M. Robinson (16); third row: W. A. Hammond (5); fourth row: W. I. Easly (6).

NON-FRATERNITY ASSOCIATION BECOMES PHRENOCON

The name issue was addressed at a January 27, 1909, meeting during which the group's third president, Alexander Paxton (Miami, 1907), also was elected. A committee assigned to the task reported that "Miami Comrades" and "Student's Union," were both being considered, but wasn't until eleven days shy of the Non-Fraternity Association's third anniversary that thirty-six members met in the Miami Union Hall, to select a new name for the association. Sergeant at Arms Emery H. Petry (Miami, 1909) passed out the paper ballots on which members selected one of four alternative names: "Non-Fraternity," "Student's Union," "Miami Union," and "Phrenocom." They settled on the last and Petry moved that the spelling be changed to "Phrenocon."

The derivation of the name Phrenocon has been a subject of some discussion. In his 1957 *Golden Jubilee History of Phi Kappa Tau*, Jack L. Anson (Colgate, 1947) advanced the theory that Phrenocon was a combination of the proposed names, "Friends," "Non-Fraternity," and "Comrades." A 1953 letter from Ralph Keffer corroborates this theory. Two other 1953 letters from Wilford Sizelove (Miami, 1908) and George Oberfell (Miami, 1908), who was vice president of the association in 1909, contend that the words "Free" or "Freemen", "Non-Fraternity," and "Commons" or "Commoner" were combined to form "Fre-no-com." The "F" was changed to "Ph" simply because it looked more classical, and

Petry's motion to change the final "m" to "n" was probably just to make the name easier to pronounce. The fact that "phren" or "phreno" indicates something pertaining to the mind and "con" can mean learn or commit to memory seems to be an unintended but appropriate coincidence.

With a new house and name, the Phrenocon Association moved quickly to adopt symbols and other trappings similar to the fraternities. In April 1909 brown and white were adopted as official colors, and the red carnation that is still used as Phi Kappa Tau's official flower was adopted on May 12.

A third constitution in as many years was adopted on June 12, 1909, at the last meeting of the school year. Embodied in that constitution was a vague genesis of the first initiation Ritual. Apparently, members of Phrenocon wanted to establish some obligations of membership but were not interested in having an initiation ceremony like those of fraternities. Instead, they decided that all members would be asked to take an oath to uphold the new constitution.

On July 31, 1909, twelve senior members of the new Phrenocon Association, dressed in their best suits with

high, stiff shirt collars snug around their necks, posed for the association's first group photo in Frank Snyder's uptown Oxford studio; and Miami's 1909 annual, the *Recensio*, proclaimed that "this large organization is, without a doubt, at Miami to stay."

The membership of the Phrenocon Association included most of the non-fraternity men in those days, and the group was more than twice the size of the largest Miami fraternity. In fact, it was the largest student organization on the campus, with more than sixty members by January 1911. The association was so large that some believed it was becoming unwieldy, and there was still too little to bind members closely to the organization. Membership selection became considerably more restrictive in 1910–11, and an active "rushing campaign" was designed to compete with the fraternities in recruiting manpower.

THE STAR OF PHRENOCON

Another constellation has arisen in the sky;
It shines more bright than any other star;
It stands a beacon that will ever guide us
Over paths obscure and ways afar.

Chorus:
For other stars may fade away
And disappear at dawn,
But one is bright, both night and day—
The Star of the Phrenocon.

The light of Truth it spreads abroad that every one may know
Its place is in the zenith of the sky;
No time can dim the light that shines more constant,
Growing brighter as the years go by.

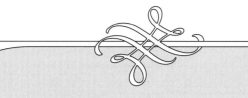

FIRST RITUAL & SONG

To more closely bind new members to the association, Anthony Poss (Miami, 1909) was appointed chairman of a Ritual committee on September 24, 1910. Joseph Bachelor (Miami, 1907), with some help from Ralph Keffer, wrote the Phrenocon Ritual that was adopted without revision on November 30, 1911. That brief Ritual, set out in Bachelor's bold hand, embodied the cardinal principles that are materially unchanged in the current Phi Kappa Tau Ritual. The twenty-one-year-old Bachelor—in the three cardinal principles—captured the essence of Phi Kappa Tau, which is as fresh and relevant today as it was then.

Phrenocon brought together two great budding talents in its new house. At the parlor piano, Joseph W. Clokey (Miami, 1908) whiled away the hours improvising original tunes to the delight of his Phrenocon brothers. When one of Clokey's tunes was ready for lyrics, he called for Bachelor to collaborate. One of the duo's earliest works, "The Star of Phrenocon," became the official song of the association. This song, later modified to reflect the association's name change to Phi Kappa Tau, articulated the vigor and enthusiasm of the Phrenocon men.

After leaving Miami, Bachelor worked on a graduate degree at Harvard and later joined the editorial staff of the Century Company in New York City. In 1927 Miami President Hughes finally persuaded Bachelor to join the Miami faculty, where he became so popular that students stood outside of his classroom to hear his renditions of Shakespeare. His memory remains alive at Miami in the four-hundred-acre Bachelor Wildlife Preserve he bequeathed upon his death in 1947 and in Bachelor Hall, built to house the Miami English department in 1979.

As for Bachelor's songwriting partner, Joseph Clokey became one of America's best known composers of sacred music, with more than three hundred works to his name, including six Phi Kappa Tau songs. He retired as dean of Miami's School of Fine Arts in 1947 to concentrate on composing, and his choral works of that period were some of the most frequently sung in church choirs of the 1950s. A Miami music-practice building was named Clokey Hall for several years, and after it was torn down, Alpha Chapter members placed a marker near its site.

To its new song, flower, colors, and Ritual, Phrenocon added a password, a grip, and a pin. The group also decided to publish a paper called *The Phrenocon*. Bachelor edited the first issue, which debuted on February 27, 1911, and was mailed to all of Miami's non fraternity alumni. It is not known how many more issues of *The Phrenocon* were published as only copies of the first issue have survived, and when the Ohio University Union became the second chapter of Phrenocon, its

publication, *Side Lights*, was adopted as the official organ of the association.

NONFRATERNITY MOVEMENT *at* OTHER COLLEGES

The struggle between fraternity and nonfraternity students was not unique to Miami University in the early years of this century. Fraternity domination of campus politics and social activities was typical in many small colleges and, in fact, continues today. But this was a period when many of the nation's small colleges, like Miami, Ohio University, Ohio State University, and Ohio Wesleyan University were experiencing tremendous growth.

Once-tiny colleges were just beginning to blossom into large universities, and the progressive politics of the era was also bringing great social change. College campuses were not immune

to the criticisms of the social reformers. There was a call for the abolition of the brutal brand of football in which twenty-six men were killed in the 1905 season. In the Ohio legislature, a law to ban hazing was passed in 1907, and a bill to ban fraternities entirely was building momentum.

Founder Dwight Douglass was certainly familiar with the strong nonfraternity movement during his freshman and sophomore years at Ohio Wesleyan University. At Ohio University in Appalachian Athens, non-Greek students formed a coed organization known as the Barbarians. ("Barbarian," or the shortened "Barb," was a common name for non-Greek students in that day.) The Miami men were aware of the Barbarians' struggles at Ohio University, and Dwight Douglass contributed articles to their magazine, *Side Lights*, as early as 1906. Both of these organizations were considerably more anti-Greek than the Phrenocon Association, but their objectives of democratizing their campuses were very similar.

OHIO UNIVERSITY BARBARIANS

Two hundred seventy people attended the Sixth Annual Banquet of the Ohio University Barbarians on the evening of February 19, 1910. Crowded in with the Barbarian men and women at long white-clothed tables were members of the Ohio faculty and board of trustees. The large guest list included Alexander Paxton, president of the Phrenocon Association at Miami, and Walter Guiler, principal of the high school at Covington, Kentucky, a Phrenocon alumnus.

A long program of singing and oratory followed a five-course dinner,

Program from the Sixth Annual Banquet of the Barbarians of Ohio University, February 19, 1910; Alexander Paxton's remarks were the first formal contact between Phrenocon and the Barbarians.

with the Phrenocons finding themselves on the program following two Irish melodies sung by Professor James P. McVey. The *Side Lights* account of the banquet describes Paxton's speech as "a short history of 'The Movement at Old Miami' in which he showed how the association has grown from an almost insignificant beginning to one of the strongest, worthiest, and most influential organizations in the college." He then presented the Barbarians with a brown pennant with "Phrenocon" handsomely lettered in white.

Walter Guiler then made an eloquent speech on the nonfraternity struggles in American colleges. This banquet was the first formal contact between Phrenocon and the Barbarians, who were so eager to hear about the Miami association that they paid Paxton's train fare and expenses to attend. Phrenocon reciprocated by paying the expenses of a Barbarian representative to attend the Fourth Annual Phrenocon Banquet a few weeks later.

The Barbarians had gotten their start at Ohio in early 1905 when a small group of nonfraternity men led by firebrand J. C. Timberman held a banquet and organized to establish the same political equality that the Miami men were seeking at the same time. This was a radical and unabashedly antifraternity group who, according to Barbarian L. M. Shupe (Ohio, 1911), "went to

battle like the Spartans of old, resolved to come out with their shields or upon them."

In 1906 the "Barbs" took steps to start a magazine to replace the college paper, *The Mirror*, which had been discontinued. Fred Shaw was the first editor, and the publication soon adopted *Side Lights* as its name.

As early as 1907, several of the more moderate "Barbs" thought that a closer organization should be perfected, and in 1910 a new constitution was adopted changing the group's name to the Ohio University Union for many of the same reasons that the Miami group had dropped its old name in favor of Phrenocon. The Ohio Union rented a house at 100 University Terrace that had a first-floor lounge and reading room and living quarters for some of the Union men upstairs.

As with the Miami group, the Union's political goals were achieved early, and the purposes of the organization broadened to stand "not only for democracy and equality of rights but also for the best interests of the non-fraternity students intellectually, socially, and morally."

PHRENOCON BEGINS EXPANSION

Phrenocon voted in early 1911 to actively pursue expansion to schools where similar groups of non-fraternity men were found, and when Roger C. Smith (Miami, 1908) represented Phrenocon at a second Ohio Union banquet in February, he "spoke very forcibly upon the nationalization of the non-fraternity movement in America pointing to the advantages of uniting all organizations of this type in a common brotherhood." This visit started an intense period of merger negotiations between the Union and Phrenocon, but an agreement could not be reached before the end of the school year.

Phrenocon President Ernest N. Littleton (Miami, 1909) finalized the merger in Athens during the weekend of October 21–22, 1911. In the merger agreement, the Union's constitution was modified to serve the new "National Phrenocon Association." *Side Lights*, which was being so successfully published, became the official national organ, while the Ritual, badge, grip, and password of the Miami group were retained by the National Phrenocon. It also was

Side Lights staff at Ohio University in 1908

agreed that female members of the Union would not be admitted to the National Phrenocon and that they would form their own organization. At first the women retained the name Ohio University Union but soon adopted "Aloquin." Their relationship with Phrenocon remained cordial, and Aloquin news and events continued to be covered in early issues of *Side Lights*.

Ewing T. Boles (seated, center) was president of the Centre College chapter of Phrenocon when this photograph was taken in 1914

FIRST NATIONAL CONVENTION

That momentous Athens meeting in 1911 is considered to be the First National Convention of Phi Kappa Tau. Graduate student Howard A. Pidgeon (Ohio, 1911) was elected national president and recent Miami graduate Roger C. Smith was chosen as the general secretary. When Littleton returned to the Phrenocon House in Oxford with news of the agreement, it was enthusiastically ratified on October 27; thus the National Phrenocon Association was born. After the ratification, minor changes to the Phrenocon badge were made, and a motion from the Ohio chapter to change the colors of the association to lavender and gold was adopted.

The development of the Booster Club at Ohio State University mirrored the formation of the Miami and Ohio chapters of Phrenocon. John J. Paine (Ohio State, 1912) led many successful efforts by Ohio State's independent men to band together and win campus elections; but until the fall of 1911, he was not able to form a lasting organization of nonfraternity men.

Finally on Sunday, October 15, 1911, Paine and three of his closest non-fraternity associates gathered at his home on West Sixth Avenue in Columbus to discuss forming a permanent organization. Paine and his compatriots, E. V. Mahaffey (Ohio State, 1912), Harold E. Cowser (Ohio State, 1912), and Walter G. Reitzel (Ohio State, 1912), kicked off an aggressive eight-week recruiting campaign among the campus independents. Thirty men came to the Board Room in the Ohio Union on December 12 to approve a constitution founding the Booster Club. Through the influence of Jesse Day (Miami, 1912), who joined the Ohio State faculty, Paine wrote to Oxford in October for information about the National Phrenocon.

SECOND NATIONAL CONVENTION

The Booster Club's application was the major item of business at the Second National Convention on February 24, 1912, at the Ohio Chapter house in Athens. The delegates developed a procedure for approving applications from potential chapters, after an affirmative vote of two-thirds of the chapters. In other business, a new grip, which has continued as the official grip of Phi Kappa Tau, was proposed and C. R. Ridenour (Ohio, 1911) was elected national president. General Secretary Smith, then living in Zanesville, Ohio, was reelected to a second term.

OHIO STATE INSTALLED

The Miami chapter proposed that new chapters be installed by the national officers, with the general secretary reading the Ritual and the president giving the oath of membership. That was the plan past President Pidgeon, substituting for C. R. Ridenour, and General Secretary Smith intended to follow in the installation of the Ohio State Chapter on May 9, 1912, except for one detail: Smith had never been given a copy of the Ritual, and Pidgeon forgot to bring his. So the first installation of a new Phrenocon chapter was accomplished with an improvised Ritual frantically reconstructed from memory. "I thought I could write some of it from memory, and [for] what I could not remember, we would try to supply

The Phrenocon coat of arms adopted in 1914

something just as good," Smith remembered fifteen years later. "We began a thirty minute brain scramble to fix up a Ritual." Pidgeon and Smith completed their work in time to join the Ohio State men and their guests at a banquet in the Music Room of the Ohio Union Building. The ladies and other guests moved to an adjoining room after dinner, and the improvised Ritual and oath of membership were recited by candlelight. No one knew that the official Ritual sheet was still in Athens, seventy-five miles away.

With its three chapters, the National Phrenocon was a national fraternity in all respects but its name. This situation seemed to please the Ohio and Ohio State chapters, but some members of the Miami group were leaving Phrenocon to join Greek-letter fraternities. In 1911 and 1912, small groups of Phrenocon men broke off to form Greek locals, which eventually became the Miami chapters of Sigma Alpha Epsilon and Delta Tau Delta. The Miami men believed strongly that Phrenocon should adopt a Greek-letter name immediately.

ZENOPHILIA at CENTRE

A fourth chapter was added to the Phrenocon roll when a local group known as Zenophilia was installed at Central University, now Centre College, at Danville, Kentucky. The story of Zenophilia is the familiar one of nonfraternity men seeking an organization to represent their welfare.

S. Frank Cox (Centre, 1914) was the driving force behind Zenophilia, which formally applied for admission to Phrenocon on November 22, 1913. The three existing chapters approved Zenophilia's petition in January, 1914, and the installation ceremony was scheduled for February 5, 1914. Founder Shideler, who had been elected national president in the spring of 1913, led the installation team wearing brand new initiation robes especially designed for chapter installations.

Delegates from the new Centre chapter joined representatives from Miami, Ohio and Ohio State at the Third National Convention at Athens, Ohio, on March 6 and 7, 1914. The pledge pin that had been used for several years at Miami was adopted for national use, and the coat of arms developed by the Ohio State chapter was modified slightly for use by all chapters. That coat of arms is similar to that of the modern Phi Kappa Tau, and it carries the Latin motto still used by the fraternity in a Greek translation.

The Miami delegation, led by Ernest H. Volwiler (Miami, 1911), a future chairman of pharmaceutical giant Abbott Laboratories, argued vigorously for the adoption of a Greek-letter name but to little avail. Although a motion to forever maintain the name Phrenocon was defeated, the name was retained and the convention would only go so far as to describe Phrenocon as "a democratic non-Greek fraternity."

AGORA INSTALLED at MOUNT UNION

When National Secretary Eckley G. Gossett (Ohio State, 1912) learned that a group of men at Mount Union College in Alliance, Ohio, was interested in forming a non-Greek fraternity, he traveled to the college to visit the group. On March 1, 1915, he described to about twenty eager men the procedure by which an interested group could apply for admission to Phrenocon. By the end of the meeting, the group had elected officers and adopted a constitution based on the National Phrenocon model. Adopting the name Agora, the Mount Union men intended to petition Phrenocon for admission as soon as possible. Six weeks later, on April 17, 1915, the Mount Union chapter became the fifth outpost of the growing Phrenocon Association in installation ceremonies at the Lexington Hotel in Alliance "at which the punch bowl held carnations and the cocktail glass was dry."

GREEK-LETTER NAME CONTROVERSY

Minutes of the Fourth National Convention at Ohio State reflect no discussion of the name issue, although the Miami chapter was still advocating change. The issue did come to a head in Danville, Kentucky, at the Fifth National Convention, held the weekend before Christmas 1915. The Miami men once again brought the motion to adopt a Greek-letter name to the floor only to have it rejected by the delegates a fourth time.

When the Miami Chapter men returned to Oxford after Christmas and learned from their convention delegate, Carl Bogart (Miami, 1912), that their proposal had again been rejected, they considered their options. Finally, on March 9, 1916, they voted to withdraw from the National Phrenocon. The proceedings recorded in the chapter's minutes leave no doubt about their intentions:

"Phrenocon House, Oxford, Ohio, March 9

Moved and seconded and carried to remove Phrenocon coat-of-arms from front door, March 9, 1916.
Moved and seconded and carried to drop name of Phrenocon and adopt Greek-letter name immediately.
Committee of three drew up name of Phi Kappa Tau.
Moved and seconded and carried that we drop from national organization altogether.
The meeting adjourned."

Founder Shideler led a three-man delegation to inform National President S. Frank Cox of the decision, and the Miami men set about organizing their new Greek-letter fraternity, Phi Kappa Tau.

CHAPTER HISTORIES

B

BETA CHAPTER
Ohio University
Athens, Ohio

Founded as Barbarians,
May 2, 1906
Name changed to Ohio University
Union, June 1910
Joined Phrenocon,
October 27, 1911
Chartered as Phi Kappa Tau,
February 1, 1917

WITH THE ADDITION of the Ohio University chapter, Phrenocon became "national" in 1911, and the Ohio men provided much of the early leadership to the national Phrenocon. Three of the four national presidents immediately following the merger were Beta men. The chapter's longtime influence in fraternity publications began when its magazine, *Side Lights*, was adopted as the official publication as a part of the merger negotiations. In later years, the *Laurel* and many other publications were printed at Lawhead Press, run for many years by P. F. Good and his son, John Good, the only father and son to serve on the National Council.

The Beta Chapter house was purchased from the Weihr sisters in 1920 and, except for a time of low membership in the 1970s and eighties, has been the chapter's home ever since. The building was substantially remodeled in 1937. Beta absorbed a seven-year-old local fraternity, Alpha Delta Beta, in 1934.

Among Beta Chapter's most notable alumni are actor Paul Newman and Ohio Governor George V. Voinovich.

Γ

GAMMA CHAPTER
Ohio State University
Columbus, Ohio

Founded as Booster Club,
October 15, 1911
Joined Phrenocon, May 9, 1912
Chartered as Phi Kappa Tau,
February 1, 1917

FOUNDED BY JOHN J. PAINE as the Booster Club in late 1911, Gamma became the third chapter of Phrenocon in May 1912. Except for a brief period of dormancy during World War II, the chapter has generally been one of the fraternity's strongest.

After moving between several rental houses, Gamma bought a home at 220 Fourteenth Street in 1922, which was sold in 1945. Columbus resident Ewing Boles was instrumental in helping the chapter buy a house at the highly visible corner of Fifteenth and Indianola in 1944. The current house was built during the 1953–54 school year on that site. It was extensively renovated after a major arson fire in 1995.

Above is a Phrenocon badge owned by Dr. Edgar Ewing Brandon used at Miami in about 1910.

The badge on the right is the one adopted by the Miami chapter when it operated as a local fraternity 1916-17.

Eckley G. Gossett (1915), Melvin Dettra, Jr. (1968–70), and Raymond A. Bichimer (1983–85) have served as national presidents of the fraternity. Bichimer, Dan Huffer, and Frederick E. Mills have kept the presidency of the Phi Kappa Tau Foundation in Gamma hands for the past twenty-five years, and a long list of Gamma men have served as foundation trustees.

Prominent alumni include late astronaut Charles Bassett and three-time Cincinnati Reds all-star John Edwards.

Longtime Chapter Advisor J. Phillip Robertson edited a history of the chapter in 1995.

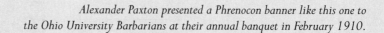

Alexander Paxton presented a Phrenocon banner like this one to the Ohio University Barbarians at their annual banquet in February 1910.

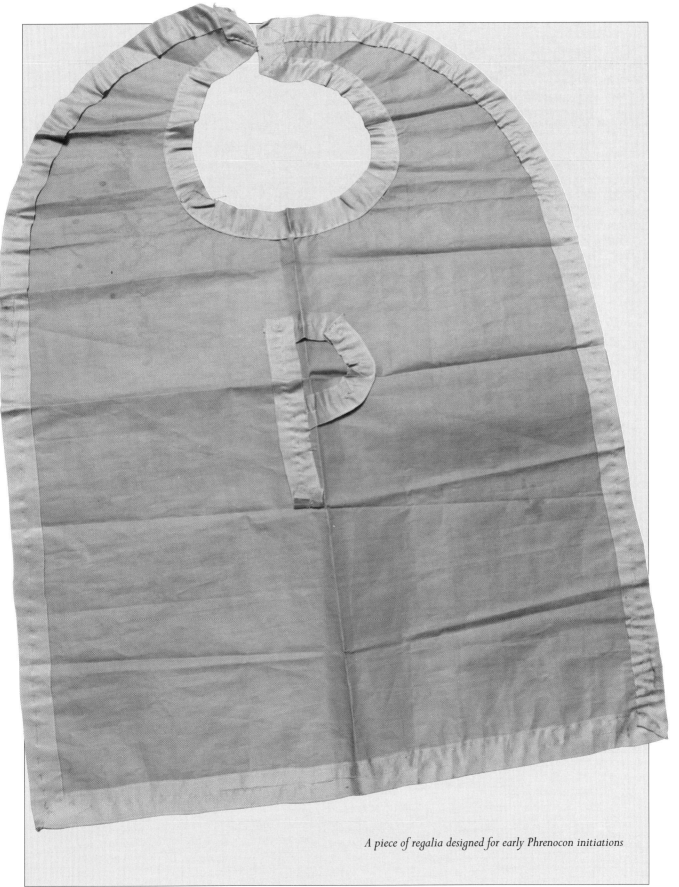

A piece of regalia designed for early Phrenocon initiations

Anticipating that a larger issue would later be published, Phi Kappa Tau's first songbook was published as a "Supplement" in 1920.

Δ

DELTA CHAPTER
Centre College
Danville, Kentucky

*Founded as Zenophilia, Fall 1913
Joined Phrenocon, February 6, 1914
Chartered as Phi Kappa Tau,
February 1, 1917*

S. FRANK COX organized a group of nonfraternity men who adopted the name Zenophilia in 1913. It was installed as the fourth chapter of Phrenocon in 1914. Three of the founders, or "immortals," as they are known at Delta, became national presidents: S. Frank Cox (1916), Ewing T. Boles (1917), and John V. Cotton (1923–1925).

*At the bottom is the diamond and opal badge
adopted by the National Phrenocon in 1911.*

*Opals were changed to pearls and the letters
Phi Kappa Tau added at the 1916 convention (center).*

*In 1926 the enamel center gained the same irregular octagonal shape
of the outer badge and the diamond was inset in a gold star (top).*

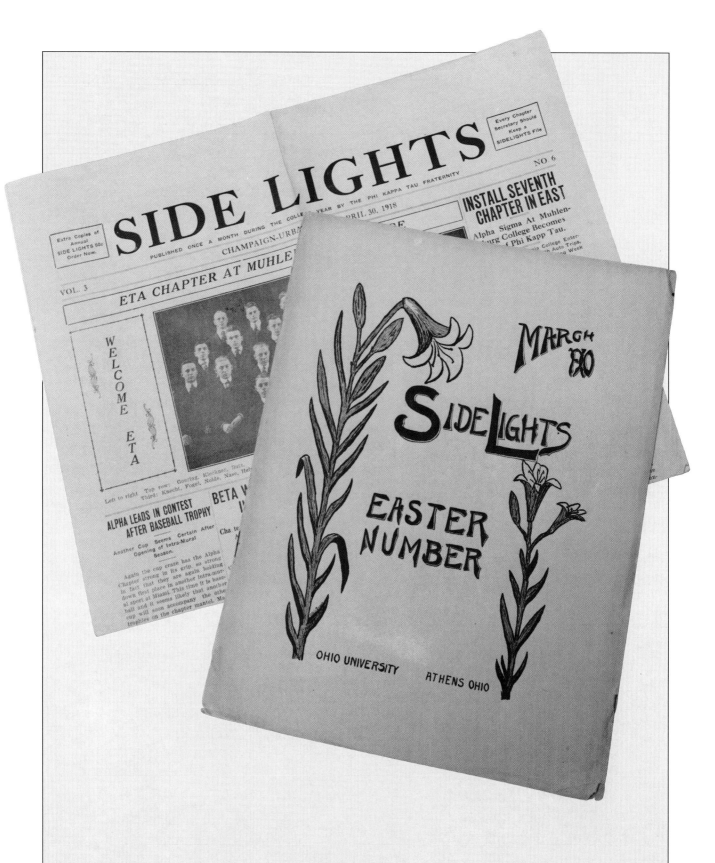

Two editions of Side Lights; *the March 1910 issue reported the first visit of Miami Phrenocons to Ohio University. The tabloid April 1918 issue reported the installation of Eta Chapter at Muhlenberg.*

Delta failed during the depression year of 1934 and was not restarted until 1948, with the assistance of Cotton and Boles.

Delta alumni built a new house on the Centre campus in 1950; and with the encouragement of Boles, as a trustee of the college, three identical duplex buildings were completed in 1961 to house the six Centre fraternities.

The chapter's best-known alumni have been Boles, who was named an honorary founder of Phi Kappa Tau for his lifetime contributions, and former Kentucky Congressman John Y. Brown, Sr., who was one of the state's best-known criminal defense lawyers.

The Grand Secretary's office as it appeared in 1931.

The Phi Kappa Tau National Headquarters was built as a memorial to the Founders in 1931.
It was named the Ewing T. Boles National Headquarters Building for Honorary founder Boles in 1983.

E

EPSILON CHAPTER
Mount Union College
Alliance, Ohio

Founded as Agora,
February 8, 1915
Joined Phrenocon, April 17, 1915
Chartered as Phi Kappa Tau,
February 1, 1917

UNDER THE LEADERSHIP of Clarence H. Bowers a group of nonfraternity men, several of whom were ministerial students, came to believe that the campus had room for a fourth fraternity. After a visit from Phrenocon's National Secretary Eckley G. Gossett, the group adopted the name Agora and immediately petitioned Phrenocon for membership.

The installation and banquet were held at the Hotel Lexington on April 17, 1915. W. D. Brenneman was the first president. In the fall of 1915, the chapter rented a house at 57 East College Street.

Two of Epsilon's most prominent early members were Ralph K. Bowers, national secretary from 1917 until 1929, who as the first full-time paid secretary ran the national office from his Alliance home; and Paul F. Opp, who was instrumental in developing a number of chapters.

In 1928 the chapter dedicated its newly constructed home at 136 Hartshorn Street. In 1940 the chapter sold their house to the college and purchased the spectacular Ramsey mansion on Union Avenue, complete with ballroom and bowling alley. After falling into disrepair, the house was sold to the college in the mid-1980s, and the chapter purchased a Tudor-style home across Union from the old house.

Dwight I. Douglass served in France during World War I.

CHAPTER THREE

EXPANDING INFLUENCE

By the early evening of Wednesday, December 20, 1916, all of the delegates but one had arrived at Phrenocon's Mount Union chapter house for the Sixth National Phrenocon Convention. Representing their chapters were: Howard E. Hendershott (Ohio, 1916); Willard Kirk (Ohio State, 1916); Arthur Dundon (Mount Union, 1915); and James M. Knappenberger (Illinois, 1916). A large contingent of Mount Union brothers crowded with the delegates onto an Alliance streetcar to meet the last delegate, William Wesley (Centre, 1916), from Danville, Kentucky, at the Pennsylvania railroad station.

Walking back to the streetcar for the return trip, Knappenberger asked where the nearest telegraph office was, and R. K. Bowers (Mount Union, 1915), from the local chapter, told him it was a block away—but why? Knappenberger explained that the deadline for the University of Illinois yearbook was the next day, and if the name was to be changed from Phrenocon to Phi Kappa Tau, he needed to know right away so that he could wire the answer back to Champaign. So there on the sidewalk in the dark December night, Knappenberger polled the delegates, and all said that they would vote to adopt the new name. All promised that their chapters would ratify the change. When

Knappenberger made the official motion to adopt the name Phi Kappa Tau the next afternoon, there was apparently unanimous approval and no discussion (but that would have been perfunctory anyway, as the decision had been made the night before).

Knappenberger's chapter at Illinois had been installed earlier that year, and the name change had not been an issue for Loyante, an Illinois local founded as a social club by men of modest means and very similar aims to the other Phrenocon chapters.

With the name changed, Willard Kirk moved that an invitation be extended to the Miami group, which had been functioning under the name Phi Kappa Tau for nine months, to

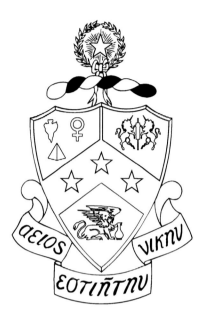

*Coat of arms adopted at the
1917 national convention*

return to the new national of the same name.

Ewing T. Boles, who did not attend the convention, was elected national president. It was the first of a long list of national positions Boles would hold over the next seventy years, but he would never play a more challenging role than his first—that of negotiating the return of Miami as Phi Kappa Tau's Alpha Chapter. Early indications were not positive. The Miami group was aggressively pursuing associations with established national fraternities, though Dean Brandon was advising against it.

Boles' great future career in the securities business was built on salesmanship, and that skill got an early test when he decided to make a personal visit to the Miami men. Dr. Shideler later remembered that Boles was allowed to come as a courtesy, but the Miami men had already decided to reject Boles' proposal. At the age of ninety, Boles clearly remembered practicing the speech that changed their minds in the woods of the lower campus before the meeting. He considered Miami critical to Phi Kappa Tau's future. "Anybody that knows anything about fraternities knows that if we were not able to return Alpha Chapter…that our existence and our

growth would come to an end, and so it was therefore necessary to persuade Alpha Chapter that it was in their best interest to come back into the organization with the other three chapters and adopt the name which they had adopted…Phi Kappa Tau," Boles said in 1986.

In addition to his efforts to get Miami to return to the fold, Boles started a local fraternity at the <$iUniversity of Kentucky, Theta Rho, which petitioned Phi Kappa Tau and was granted a charter to become Eta Chapter. But at the last moment (National Secretary A. C. Kerr [Ohio, 1914] was on his way to the train when the telegram arrived), the college administration rejected the plan because of the looming world war, and it was scuttled.

Boles called a special convention in Oxford in May 1917 to welcome Miami back. The convention decided to name chapters in Greek-alphabet order, with Miami as Alpha, Ohio as Beta, Ohio State as Gamma, Centre as Delta, Mount Union as Epsilon, and Illinois as Zeta. President Woodrow Wilson had been calling for America's entry into the war in Europe, and it was clear that many young men would be going overseas. The convention, anticipating the future, decided that Dr. Shideler would take over the presidency in case Boles went into the service before the next convention in December. Boles did enter the service in August 1917, and Shideler assumed the presidency.

HISTORIC CHAMPAIGN CONVENTION

The 1917 national convention, which was held in December at the University of Illinois at Champaign, is arguably the most important convention in Phi Kappa Tau's history. Delegates to that convention made a number of decisions that have had a lasting impact on the fraternity.

Members of host Zeta Chapter at Illinois had definite ideas about the direction in which Phi Kappa Tau should be heading and had expressed disappointment with the fraternity's slow progress in expansion and alumni involvement.

Phi Kappa Tau was becoming recognized as a national fraternity. In fact, the fraternity's entry in the National Interfraternity Conference (NIC) had been accomplished only days earlier at the ninth annual meeting of the conference. C. B. Richeson (Mount Union, 1916), along with Joseph Bachelor, who was then living in New York, represented Phi Kappa Tau at the meeting. The nonfraternity origins of Phi Kappa Tau haunted it in its request to join the conference. Old reputations are sometimes difficult to overcome. But to Phi Kappa Tau's great fortune, the Reverend Albert H. Wilson, an interfraternity leader and national officer of Sigma Nu from Mount Union

College, was well acquainted with the success of Epsilon Chapter. Based upon that experience, he took up Phi Kappa Tau's cause and saw to it that the fraternity was accepted as a full member of the conference. Wilson, who would actively continue to assist Phi Kappa Tau for years to come, was recognized by the convention for his efforts on Phi Kappa Tau's behalf.

If NIC membership confirmed that Phi Kappa Tau was a full-fledged national fraternity, it was the Champaign convention that took steps to establish that fact from an organizational standpoint.

Acting President Shideler appointed convention committees dominated by Zeta men to deal with insignia, Ritual, and nominations.

The Ritual Committee, chaired by William C. Troutman (Illinois, 1916), who was also elected grand ritualist, made significant additions to the existing initiation Ritual. The committee reversed the order in which the cardinal

Delegates to the 1917 national convention at Champaign, Illinois;
front row: Bowers, Henry, Murphy, Beekley, Schactsman, Ander, Yeager;
back row: Ogden, Knappenberger, Shideler, Fletemeyer, Sandler, Troutman, Shonkwiler

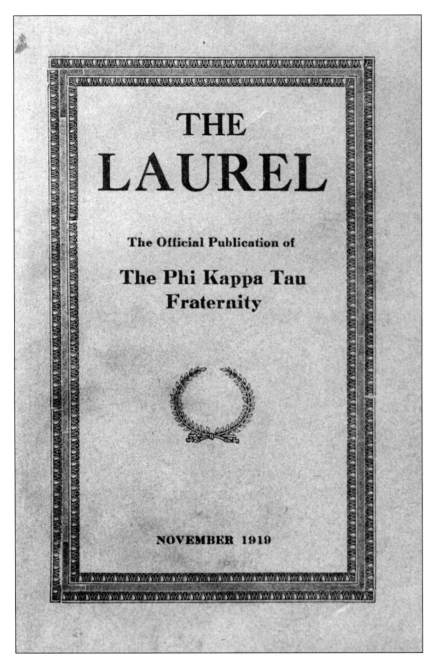

The first issue of The Laurel, *November 1919*

principles were introduced and added much drama to the simple ceremony, which had been written by Joseph Bachelor.

The committee on insignia, headed by James M. Knappenberger, Ralph K. Bowers, and John Beekley (Miami, 1911), proposed that the jeweled Phi Kappa Tau badge with a diamond star become the official badge but also approved a plain badge, suggesting that the star be changed from gold to white enamel. These were the last significant changes made to the badges. The committee then proposed major changes to the coat of arms, incorporating much symbolism about the fraternity and a Greek translation of the motto, which had appeared in the original Phrenocon coat of arms in Latin. A half-size sister badge, which could be presented to wives and girlfriends of members, was approved as was the pledge pin and grand seal, both unchanged to this day. Old gold and Harvard red were established as the fraternity colors, and the red carnation was retained as the official fraternity flower. Bowers, as an old man, was upset at the fraternity for using maroon as a color in sportswear advertised in the *Laurel* rather than the crimson Harvard red. He sent samples of a Winston cigarette carton to the editor to describe the correct color. The committee on songs awarded a silver loving cup to Gamma at Ohio State for submitting the best song and recommended that a songbook be published by the new secretary. Alumni dues were set at two dollars per year, to be collected by the alumni secretaries of the chapters.

Past the tenth anniversary of the fraternity's founding, a new sense of history led to the establishment of the office of grand historian, to which Founder Shideler was elected, and Alpha Chapter was authorized to have a tablet made and installed in Old Main on Miami's campus to commemorate the founding. *Side Lights* declared that "the Seventh Annual Convention has been the making of the fraternity."

F. L. Shonkwiler (Illinois, 1917) was put in charge of publishing the *Guide to Ritualistic Work*, including direction on pledge instruction and examination, installation of chapters, and opening and closing of chapter meetings, to replace the three-page *Phrenocon Ritual*, which had been in use up to that time. Grand Ritualist Troutman was directed to devise an officer-installation ceremony and to determine appropriate robes and regalia for the Ritual.

A committee on grip and password made a report that was not published and has since been handed down by word of mouth. The origin of the password was almost entirely forgotten until R. K. Bowers described the committee's work to members assembled at the 1981 and 1983 conventions.

Old stationery and Rituals bearing the name Phrenocon and the now-outdated coat of arms were to be sent in to the secretary and destroyed. Fortunately, several examples have survived and are retained in the fraternity archives.

A committee of the whole considered a complete revision (once again) of the constitution, and the newly elected secretary was instructed to investigate incorporation. To promote expansion, the office of grand field secretary was established, with James

M. Knappenberger being the first elected to the position. He was given a budget of four hundred dollars minimum and five hundred maximum.

Newly-elected Grand Secretary R. K. Bowers was authorized to secure a steel strongbox in which to keep important records. The box, which is still in the possession of the national fraternity, is emblazoned with the Greek letters Phi, Kappa, and Tau and Bowers' initials, R.K.B., in gold.

A new governing structure was established creating a Grand Executive Council proposed by Ewing Boles and several new national offices.

But even with all the work done, it is likely that the most memorable part of the convention for the delegates was the late night "pow wow" that was reported to have kept lights burning in the Zeta Chapter house until 4:40 a.m.

Edgar Ewing Brandon in his YMCA uniform, 1919

WORLD WAR I

Just as Phi Kappa Tau got up and running, World War I knocked the wind out of the fledgling national organization and its chapters. College campuses were nearly all becoming military training grounds under the auspices of the Student Army Training

Corps (SATC). Initially, the SATC prohibited its members from joining or participating in fraternities, and countless chapter houses were commandeered as SATC barracks. The NIC lobbied the secretary of war (who was a fraternity man) and SATC students were allowed to participate in fraternity activities. However, chapter sizes were much reduced, and meetings had to be held wherever they could. The Miami men, for example, rented a room above an Oxford movie theater.

More than 250 Phi Taus saw service in Europe. Darrell M. Stratton (Ohio, 1916) was the first member to be killed in action, while serving with the Canadian Expeditionary Forces. Major Samuel M. Johnson (Ohio, 1911) commanded a battalion of black troops in France, earning the Distinguished Service Cross at Bussey farm and France's Croix de Guerre for gallantry at the Argonne Forest.

Two letters from Founder Douglass, who was serving with the 27th Engineers in France, described the gruesomeness of war, saying that Sherman's famous quote should be

revised to read "War is smell—the smell of rotting flesh." Douglass, who was gassed in the final days of the war, would never completely recover from his war injuries.

Even Dr. Brandon at age fifty-three answered the call, serving in France as secretary in the *Foyer du Soldat*. Happily, the armistice was declared at the eleventh hour of the eleventh day of the eleventh month in 1918 after only several months of American involvement, and all was back to normal on the college campuses.

Grand Secretary Bowers was drafted and turned grand secretary responsibilities over to his brother Clarence (Mount Union, 1915) in Evanston, Illinois. But he had supervised Phi Kappa Tau's incorporation before he left for camp.

The earliest photo of Kappa Chapter (Kentucky), 1920; left to right: Mathis, Lemon, Luker, Anderson, Long, Pottinger, McWhorter, Cooper, Casner, Elder.

RECOVERY AND GROWTH

A hastily called convention was held at the Mount Union chapter house on February 8–9, 1919. Less than ninety days after the end of the war, many undergraduates still had not returned, and at least three of the delegates attended on leave and still in military uniform.

But the delegates were enthusiastic about getting on with the work of Phi Kappa Tau. Bruce K. Brown (Illinois, 1917) assumed the duties of editing *Side Lights*, which had not been published since June 1918. Henry Moehling (Muhlenberg, 1918) was elected grand alumni secretary, and the convention adopted an idea put in place at the new Eta Chapter. The graduate council concept has lasted until today, and Phi Kappa Tau has clung to the idea that there are no Phi Tau alumni—only resident members and graduate members, all having equal status. In addition, provisions were made to establish city alumni associations, a vote was given to graduate councils in the convention, and boards of governors were established.

One of the other most lasting actions of the 1919 convention was the establishment of geographical groupings of chapters, called domains, with a volunteer domain chief to handle chapter inspections.

It was decided to move future conventions nearer to the beginning of the school year rather than meeting during the holidays as had been the practice for several years. Delegates who had to travel a long distance had never liked having to attend a convention in the few days before Christmas.

So it was just seven months later that the convention met again in Alliance, Ohio, in September—just after the chartering of Theta Chapter at Transylvania University in Lexington, Kentucky.

At the Ninth National Convention, delegates decided to change the name of Phi Kappa Tau's magazine to the *Laurel*, retaining *Side Lights* as a secret "members-only" publication. Interestingly, from the few extant copies of the post-1919 *Side Lights*, the secrecy seems to have been unnecessary. Though its contents would hardly be interesting to outsiders; there is very little that could be considered "secret."

The *Laurel's* first issue appeared in November 1919 under the editorship of Leonard Utz (Muhlenberg, 1918). Originally published bimonthly, it soon became (and has remained ever since) a quarterly magazine.

The *Laurel's* second issue announced Beta Chapter's purchase of a new home from the Weihr sisters at 50 East State Street in Athens. Excepting a brief absence in the 1970s and early 1980s, this house, now considerably modified, has served Beta Chapter since that time.

Delta Chapter reported that several Centre College Phi Taus played on the famous "Praying Colonels" football team that beat Harvard in one of America's most famous college football games.

The chartering of the local fraternity Delta Gamma Rho at Coe College in Cedar Rapids, Iowa, increased the

Henry E. Hoagland and Edgar Ewing Brandon en route to the Nu Chapter installation at Berkeley, California, in 1919.

chapter roll to nine when the charter was presented during installation ceremonies at the Hotel Montrole in January 1920.

Eta Chapter at Muhlenberg College boasted the purchase of a $15,000 house at Poplar and Linden in Allentown, Pennsylvania. The brick-and-stone, Victorian-towered house was fitted with luxurious quarter-sawn oak trim throughout the interior.

FULL-TIME GRAND SECRETARY

Fifty Phi Taus attended the tenth convention in October 1920 at the Claypool Hotel in downtown Indianapolis, the first convention to be held outside of a chapter house. The convention was the culmination of years of discussion about the need to have a paid secretary to handle the fraternity's administration.

The fraternity voted to merge the positions of grand secretary, grand field secretary, and grand alumni secretary into a single, salaried grand secretary's position. R. K. Bowers, who had been grand secretary as a volunteer since 1917, was hired to continue full-time. Grand President E. E. Brandon, Grand Ritualist Arthur Amerine (Ohio, 1915), Grand Treasurer C. L. Riley (Mount Union, 1916), and Grand Historian Shideler were all reelected. Elected to the Grand Council were: Henry Hoagland, newly appointed to the faculty of Ohio State; Knappenberger, who had been grand field secretary; C. S. Weber (Coe, 1920), charter member of Iota; and Melville J. Boyer (Muhlenberg, 1918), charter member of Eta.

Six Alpha undergraduates, including Hugh C. Nichols (Miami, 1920) and faculty member Joe Clokey, conducted the first model initiation, a traditional convention highlight ever since.

After a failed effort before the war, a chapter was finally installed at the University of Kentucky in November 1920. Two Delta men, John Casner (Centre, 1918) and Otto V. Elder (Centre, 1918), recruited two UK students to help them start the local fraternity, Kappa Zeta Rho. The installation team included Centre's John Y. Brown (Centre, 1917), later speaker of the Kentucky house of representatives, a U.S. congressman, and father of Governor John Y. Brown, Jr.

Two weeks later, Beta Xi Alpha, a local fraternity at Purdue University, was installed as Lambda Chapter. With the fraternity's first chapter in Indiana, the gap between Ohio and Illinois was bridged.

Beta Chapter reported the achievements of two of its alumni to the *Laurel*. Roy J. Gillen (Ohio, 1911), who had been blinded in a foundry accident at the age of fifteen, was elected prosecuting attorney of Jackson County, Ohio, and was the county's Republican committee chairman. And Elver Porter (Ohio, 1914) shot and killed a fleeing bank robber across the street from his Bedford, Ohio, garage.

Gamma Chapter members pledged $1,250 in a student drive toward the construction of the new Ohio Stadium.

W. I. Easly (Miami, 1910) organized a local fraternity, Tau Alpha Sigma, at Lawrence University in Appleton, Wisconsin. The group, led by graduate student Graeme O'Geran (Lawrence, 1920), was chartered in ceremonies concluded on December 5, 1920.

Nu Chapter on the West Coast

Ensign Paul F. Opp (Mount Union, 1915) cultivated a relationship with the respected Orond Club at the University of California, Berkeley, while he was in the navy on the West Coast. Because of the quality of the group and Opp's strong recommendation, the Orond Club was chartered in four days of ceremonies at Berkeley. Secretary Bowers recorded his long train trip to California with Hoagland and Brandon on film with an early home-movie camera. Alumni from the area assisted in the installation, and

Opp made the trip up from San Diego, via destroyer, for the chartering. Opp was recognized at a Friday banquet at the famous Bohemian Club of San Francisco and the festivities concluded with a chartering ball at the Palace Hotel.

The Eleventh National Convention was held in a hot and humid Columbus, Ohio, at the Gamma Chapter house in September 1921. Over one hundred attended this largest convention in the fraternity's history, including two brothers from Muhlenberg who hitchhiked for five days from Allentown, Pennsylvania, to serve as editor and business manager of the *Eleventh Convention Morning Call.* This mimeographed newsletter was a forerunner of the newsletter *Sidelights* published by John Sayers (Bethany, 1978) at recent conventions. A highlight of the convention was a tour of the D. L. Auld jewelry factory, where the conventioneers watched a badge being manufactured from start to finish.

Near the end of the convention, Grand Secretary Bowers and Grand Councilor Boyer presented an ebony gavel with engraved sterling mountings to Grand President Brandon, who stated at the time that he intended to use the gavel as long as he was president and then pass it along to his successor. That gavel has remained the official gavel of the fraternity through more than fifty conventions held since that Columbus meeting.

The first year under a full-time grand secretary had been a good one financially, as installation income had helped bolster fraternity coffers. And

expansion was aggressively under way, with the convention approving expansion in all but the "Old South." Secretary Bowers reported to the convention on his visits to Arizona, Utah, Stanford, Wisconsin, Southern California, and Tulane. The convention tabled a plan to allow chapters to be admitted by a four-fifths vote rather than the unanimity of chapters that had recently been required.

Tinkering with fraternity jewelry continued; the size of the official plain badge was reduced. And it might be interesting to know what prompted convention action to go "on the record as officially opposing the practice of gambling on the outcome of the student athletic contests."

Brandon was reelected to his second of three terms as grand president, Howard Stephenson (Transylvania, 1919) was elected grand ritualist, and Bruce K. Brown was elected grand editor.

"Hey Fellers, I'd rather ride in your car" was the caption for this cartoon which was a part of the Delta Tau Omega's petition to become Omicron Chapter at Penn State.

SMALL-SCHOOL CONTROVERSY

Members of Gamma Chapter at Ohio State resisted approval of a petition from the Marshall Club at Franklin and Marshall College in Lancaster, Pennsylvania. The Gamma men believed that Phi Kappa Tau was too heavily represented in small schools and that the fraternity's future success would be determined by its ability to compete in larger state schools like theirs. But others argued that Franklin and Marshall was an excellent school and the Marshall Club, which had been established for more than twenty years, was a respected group. Gamma finally relented, and Xi Chapter was installed during Thanksgiving week 1921. Sixty-nine men were initiated, including many of the club's alumni, twenty-three of whom held the title of professor in colleges throughout the East. The installation banquet was held on Thanksgiving day, with a menu of traditional Pennsylvania country fare.

Alumni clubs were reported to be functioning in Los Angeles, Ann Arbor, Chicago, Philadelphia, and Boston (where a unique club was developed entirely from Phi Taus earning graduate degrees at Harvard).

Unpleasant news about Epsilon Chapter at Mount Union was getting a good deal of press in various Greek publications across the country. In some sort of scavenger hunt, Epsilon pledges overturned headstones and entered a locked toolshed at an Alliance cemetery. In addition to the bad press, the incident cost the chapter $245 to settle the issue with the township trustees.

In the March 1922 *Laurel*, E. A. Sandler (Illinois, 1917) critiqued several of the chapter publications, including Miami's newsletter, *The Link*; Mount Union's *The Fasces*; Illinois' *Inner Circle*; Muhlenberg's *Pep*; Coe's *Iotan*; Purdue's *Lambdanite*; and Berkeley's *The Nu Ray*.

Bruce K. Brown resigned as grand editor in February 1922, and he was replaced by Paul Opp, who was now in graduate school at Columbia Teachers College in New York. Opp's first issue was a directory of the membership as collected and organized in the files of the grand secretary.

Delta Tau Omega at Pennsylvania State University became Omicron Chapter in May 1922, and a second California charter was granted to Alpha Phi Kappa at the University of Southern California. Phi Kappa Tau became the fourth national fraternity on the Southern California campus when the installation activities concluded on May 26, 1922.

In considerable contrast to the spartan 1921 national convention at Ohio

State, the Twelfth National Convention was held at the Chicago Beach Hotel in September 1922. Organized by the Chicago alumni association, with Morgan Fitch (Illinois, 1918) as chairman, the convention had especially good turnout from the closest chapters at Illinois, Coe, and Lawrence. Petitions were accepted from Kappa Omicron Sigma at Rensselaer Polytechnic Institute and Phi Sigma Psi at Syracuse University. Grand President Brandon was elected to his third term, Norman M. Lyon (California–Berkeley, 1921) joined the Grand Council, Paul Opp was elected to a full term as grand editor, and Alvin Zurcher was elected to replace W. H. Shideler as grand historian.

Only once has a Greek-letter name been assigned to a Phi Tau chapter out of order. In November 1922 Sigma was assigned to Syracuse just days ahead of Rho's chartering at Rensselaer Polytechnic Institute at Troy, New York. Travel arrangements made it more convenient to install the Syracuse group first; but for alliterative reasons, the chapters each wanted the Greek-letter name that represented the first letter of its school name. Grand President Brandon led the installation team in ceremonies at Syracuse, beginning on November 23 and concluding two days later. Most of the same team continued on to Rensselaer on November 26. Initiations took place on Monday and Tuesday, and the installation banquet was Tuesday evening at the Ten Eyck Hotel in Albany

Phi Kappa Tau's historian, Jack Anson, claimed that Tau Chapter at Michigan was the first "colonization" of a new chapter. A Michigan chapter had been a goal of the fraternity for several years, and a good bit of negotiation

1922 national convention at the Chicago Beach Hotel

INSTALLATION BANQUET OF RHO CHAPTER
PHI KAPPA TAU FRATERNITY
THE TEN EYCK - ALBANY, N.Y. - NOV. 28. 1922.

PHOTO BY THE FELLOWCRAFTS SHOP.

Installation banquet of Rho Chapter (Rensselaer Polytechnic Institute) at the Ten Eyck

took place with a local fraternity there. But the group seemed to have some objectionable characteristics, and a petition was not encouraged. So Frank Mickle (Ohio State, 1912) and Alfred Fischer (Miami, 1912), both members of the Ann Arbor alumni association, called together four Michigan undergraduates and began the Phi Tau Club on November 10, 1921, with the express intention of petitioning Phi Kappa Tau.

But this probably was not a true colonization. That concept had not yet been approved, and the procedure for starting the chapter was no different from that used in two attempts to establish a chapter at the University of Kentucky. R. K. Bowers claimed that Kentucky was the first coloniza-

tion. Regardless, the Phi Tau Club's petition was accepted and Tau Chapter installed on February 17, 1923. It was an especially gratifying moment for Grand President Brandon, who was a member of Michigan's class of 1888.

The May 1923 *Laurel* reported on the new Burr-Patterson jewelry plant, built by contractor F. R. Fletemeyer (Illinois, 1916) and designed by the famous modern industrial architect, Albert Kahn.

The anti-small school prejudice that had caused Xi Chapter problems was much more serious for Phi Beta Sigma at Nebraska Wesleyan University, a small Methodist-affiliated college in suburban Lincoln. Phi Beta Sigma was the oldest social organization at

Wesleyan, organized as the Orophilian Literary Society in 1888. The faculty had opposed national fraternities until 1921, when Phi Beta Sigma sought to petition Phi Kappa Tau. But the petition was not initially encouraged. Past Grand President Henry Hoagland, who was an alumnus of Illinois and a member of the Ohio State faculty, opposed the admission of small-school chapters. His interest lay in the acquisition of a chapter at the University of Nebraska, also in Lincoln, and he hoped that the Phi Beta Sigma alumni also could bring along a local there. Hoagland made a personal visit to Dr. Harry Taylor, a Lincoln physician who was a prominent Phi Beta Sigma alumnus. Taylor convinced Hoagland to relent, and the petition was accepted.

Hoagland could have had no idea that as a chapter of Phi Kappa Tau the group would give the fraternity five national presidents, starting with Dr. Taylor.

Thirty-six undergraduates and thirty-two alumni (including a state legislator, five doctors, three lawyers, ten teachers, and five ministers) were initiated in three days and nights at a Lincoln Masonic lodge in spite of torrential rainstorms that prevented many alumni from navigating the muddy Nebraska roads to Lincoln. The installation banquet at the Hotel Lincoln featured a menu of caribou meat from Baffin Bay north of the Arctic Circle, which was a gift of Dr. Taylor.

The three Kentucky chapters at the University of Kentucky, Centre, and Transylvania hosted the 1923 convention at the Phoenix Hotel in downtown Lexington. Dr. Brandon reviewed his three years as president, saying, "When the national convention assembled in 1920, nine chapters responded to the call; four were located in Ohio, two in Kentucky, one in Illinois, one in Iowa and one in Pennsylvania. Since that time eleven new chapters have been added and this convention is to act upon the petitions of five more. Should these be granted...Phi Kappa Tau will be represented in thirteen states and its twenty-five chapters will stretch from coast to coast and from the Lakes almost to the Gulf."

He then reaffirmed the philosophy that he had initially articulated at that first Founders' Day Banquet in 1907: "At the installation of new chapters where I have had the pleasure of assisting in recent years, it has been my policy to pay a visit of courtesy to the president, dean of men or dean of the institution, and in the course of the interview to say that Phi Kappa Tau enters the college as an aid to the administration and as a help in formulating and advancing the best influences in college life."

The financial position of the fraternity was so strong that a proposal advanced by Grand Treasurer Ray Wilson (Illinois, 1915), Grand Councilor J. M. Knappenberger, and past Grand President Henry Hoagland to create a permanent endowment for chapter-house financing with $5,000 savings was heartily endorsed.

With the growth of the fraternity and an increased need for administrative support, the domain plan of chapter visitation was revived to allow Grand Secretary Bowers to spend more time in the Central Office which had been moved from Bower's home to rented space in downtown Indianapolis.

As usual, the convention passed some less-than-earth-shattering legislation, establishing that the official fraternity informal name should be "Phi Tau." A peculiar spelling, "Fitaw," had been used in some of the recent *Laurel* issues edited by Bruce K. Brown, and apparently some delegates disapproved.

Several new officers were installed: Delta Chapter founder John V. Cotton (Centre, 1914), an Akron, Ohio, attorney, replaced Dr. Brandon as grand president; past Grand Councilor Charles S. Weber was elected grand historian; and Grayson L. Kirk (Miami, 1921), who was serving as principal of the high school at New Paris, Ohio (though still an undergraduate), was elected grand editor.

Dr. Brandon initially declined a nomination for a five-year term on the Grand Council, replacing Dr. Shideler—not wanting to set a precedent that the outgoing president be elected to the Council. He was persuaded to accept.

Dr. Harry Taylor (Nebraska Wesleyan, 1923) wrote about his experiences at his first convention for the *Laurel*, saying, "The loyalty, the democracy and the very high moral and intellectual fiber of the delegates and grand officers stand out most prominently in my mind." Grand Editor Kirk responded: "When men of broad experience among collegians are so impressed, Phi Kappa Tau has indeed something to be proud of."

Nu Chapter at Berkeley was the first chapter on the West Coast and in 1923 became the first chapter to build its own house. Built on a prime (but narrow) lot next to Pi Beta Phi Sorority on Piedmont Avenue, the house was designed in the Italian Renaissance style and featured a huge living room with fireplaces at each end and views of San Francisco and (later) the

Golden Gate Bridge from the third-floor chapter room. Construction was supervised by Carl Loorz (California, 1921), who in later years also would oversee the building of the Hearst Castle at San Simeon. The same firm totally rebuilt the Nu house thirty years later, when Loorz' two sons had joined Nu Chapter (and the family firm).

The 1923–24 school year was busy with five charterings. The twenty-three-year-old Rechabite Fraternity was chartered as Phi Chapter at Bethany College in Bethany, West Virginia, on October 27. Phi Psi Lambda Fraternity at North Carolina State became Chi Chapter in three days of ceremonies during the first week of December 1923.

Alpha Beta Fraternity at the University of Colorado was the first chartering of 1924, when forty-one men were initiated into Psi Chapter in February. It was an impressive group, including Ward Darley, a future president of the University of Colorado; Lou Gerding, a future national president of Phi Kappa Tau; future Domain Chiefs Ray Bushey and Lew Culver; and Ed Paullin, who became a trustee of the Phi Kappa Tau Foundation.

Jesse Day, who helped to start Gamma Chapter, and Mu Chapter founder Graeme O'Geran, were prominent among the members of the alumni association in Madison, Wisconsin, who organized a local fraternity at the University of Wisconsin, Alpha Theta Pi. This group was installed as Omega Chapter in April 1924 after acquiring a chapter house as required by the Lexington convention. Of the forty-four men initiated,

Alpha Beta (New York) degree team, 1924

two would play prominent roles in the fraternity. Paul A. Elfers later established the Elfers Omega Scholarships with the Phi Kappa Tau Foundation, which would see that his name lived on for years to come. Alvin Huth gave a lifetime of service to Lambda Chapter at Purdue.

The Dorian Literary Society of Michigan Agricultural College (now Michigan State) became Alpha Alpha Chapter on May 14, 1924.

Detroit alumni intended to outdo the Chicago and Lexington convention hosts by putting on the best convention ever in 1924. Headquarters for the convention was the Hotel Tuller; but delegates were transported to the Masonic Temple Country Club for the convention banquet, where Harry Taylor gave an inspiring speech about how Upsilon alumni actively encouraged scholarship in their chapter— with admirable results.

Carl M. Tausig (Franklin and Marshall, 1921), secretary-treasurer of the American Seed Company at Lancaster, Pennsylvania, was appointed grand treasurer, and Bruce K. Brown succeeded his Zeta Chapter brother J. M. Knappenberger on the Grand Council. Capt. Frank W. Bryant (Purdue, 1921) replaced Howard Stephenson as grand ritualist.

For the first time ever, the Council approved a budget to bring the domain chiefs to Indianapolis for a workshop.

The fraternity's official flag was proposed by Eta at Muhlenberg and adopted.

Domain Chief Conference in Indianapolis, 1924. Seated (l to r) R. K. Bowers, Mrs. E. E. Brandon, John V. Cotton, Harry A. Taylor, Melville J. Boyer. Standing (l to r) E. T. Leutz, E. E. Brandon, L. M. Utz, C. C. Goddard, Richard C. Lennox, F. C. Ruskaup

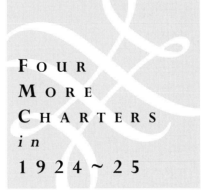

FOUR MORE CHARTERS *in* 1924 ~ 25

The Mount Union team of Paul F. Opp and Sigma Nu's A. H. Wilson worked to secure the Phi Lambda Beta Fraternity at New York University as Alpha Beta Chapter. Thirty-six men were initiated during Thanksgiving week 1924. Rev. Wilson spoke at the installation banquet at the Hotel Martinique on Wednesday evening, and the

*At the Psi Chapter (Colorado)
installation in 1924;
left to right: Harry A. Taylor, unknown,
unknown, R. K. Bowers,
H. Clay Burkholder, John V. Cotton*

festivities completed with a dance in the White and Gold Ballroom of the Plaza Hotel on Thanksgiving.

Opp and Wilson's work also resulted in a chapter at the University of Delaware, when Gamma Delta Rho Fraternity petitioned to become Alpha Gamma Chapter. Installation was completed during the first weekend in December 1924.

Tau Gamma Psi at the Case School of Applied Science (now Case Western Reserve) was chartered Alpha Delta Chapter after initiations conducted by the Cleveland alumni association on January 31, 1925.

The fourth charter of the 1924–25 school year, Alpha Epsilon, was granted to the local Phi Kappa Theta Fraternity on May 23, 1925. Dr. Roger C. Smith, the fraternity's first national secretary and member of the Kansas State University faculty, influenced the decision to choose Phi Kappa Tau.

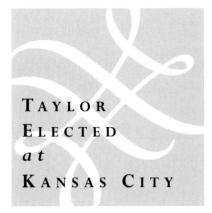

TAYLOR ELECTED *at* KANSAS CITY

Harry A. Taylor, the Lincoln, Nebraska, physician who had until 1923 been an alumnus of a local fraternity, so impressed his new brothers that he was elected grand president at his third convention at Kansas City in 1925.

Taylor had not traveled a great deal, but as grand president he visited every chapter he could to learn more about his fraternity. His first trip as president was to Oregon State University to install Lambda Phi Delta as Alpha Zeta Chapter, visiting Psi at Colorado, Pi at Southern California, and Nu at Berkeley on the way. Oregon State's Lambda Phi Delta accepted the Alpha Zeta charter on October 15, 1925.

On the way to the National Inter-fraternity Conference annual meeting in New York in December, Taylor visited Syracuse, Rensselaer, and New York University before the meeting, then visited Eta at Muhlenberg and locals at Pennsylvania and William and Mary on his return to Nebraska.

A third trip began with a visit to the petitioning local at Alabama Polytechnic (now Auburn) and continued with the chartering at the University of Florida, where professor Harley Chandler (Coe, 1920) influenced the members of Sigma Kappa Phi to petition Phi Kappa Tau.

The Alpha Eta charter banquet was held on March 9, 1926, ten years to the day after the Miami chapter of Phrenocon adopted the name Phi Kappa Tau. From Gainesville, Florida, Grand President Taylor and Grand Secretary Bowers headed north to Ohio to celebrate another anniversary.

CHAPTER HISTORIES

Z

ZETA CHAPTER
University of Illinois
Champaign, Illinois

Founded as Loyante, 1915
Joined Phrenocon, April 10, 1916
Chartered as Phi Kappa Tau,
February 1, 1917

A LOCAL ORGANIZATION called Loyante was formed as a junior-senior society by men of unusually high character who had come from families of modest means and could not afford to join fraternities. It affiliated with Phrenocon when it learned of the young organization's similar aims. Zeta members were prominent in the early years of Phi Kappa Tau.

While occupying several rented homes, the chapter was able to purchase a lot in an undeveloped area that was slated to be developed by the university. This astute purchase allowed the chapter to build its home in the midst of the fraternity district after holding the lot for several years. The attractive stone house on Gregory Drive was completed in 1928. During the Great Depression, the house was lost in a foreclosure and repurchased "on the courthouse steps." A disreputable mortgage holder had improperly sold the house to a sorority, which was supposed to be paying the chapter's mortgage payments while occupying the house during World War II. With financial backing from the national fraternity, a legal battle

was waged all the way to the Illinois Supreme Court where clear title was finally regained in 1951. Zeta's house corporation purchased the house back from the national fraternity in 1980.

Two of Zeta's earliest members served consecutive terms as national president: Frederick R. Fletemeyer (1917–19) and Henry Hoagland (1919–20). Both men remained active in fraternity affairs their entire lives.

H

ETA CHAPTER
Muhlenberg College
Allentown, Pennsylvania

Founded as Alpha Sigma,
March 31, 1914
Chartered as Phi Kappa Tau,
March 22, 1918

HENRY MOEHLING, JR., later a prominent minister, and Herman W. Nenow founded a clandestine organization in 1914 and adopted the name Alpha Sigma Club on March 31, 1914. After being rejected twice and ordered to disband by the college administration, Alpha Sigma gained the college's recognition on September 17, 1914, as its third fraternity.

Alpha Sigma was chartered in three days of receptions and ceremonies March 20–23, 1918. Eta became the first new chapter after

the adoption of the name Phi Kappa Tau.

The chapter first rented a home in 1914 and occupied that until 1920, when its first home was purchased. A larger home was purchased near the Muhlenberg campus, which served Eta Chapter until its current home was constructed on a lot leased by the college to the fraternity on the campus. Eta's Home Association dedicated its new $85,000 home in 1958. It was designed by Eta alumnus Robert Frey to house twenty-eight men, with large living and dining areas on the first floor and recreation space on the lower level.

Several Eta men have played prominent roles in the national fraternity's early history. Dr. Isaac Miles Wright was national president (1928–30); Leonard Utz and Melville Boyer both played several significant roles. A Muhlenberg science building is named for Dr. John V. Shankweiler, longtime Muhlenberg professor.

Θ THETA CHAPTER
Transylvania University
Lexington, Kentucky

Founded as Phi Beta Nu,
March 9, 1917
Chartered as Phi Kappa Tau,
September 16, 1919

EIGHT TRANSYLVANIA STUDENTS founded Phi Beta Nu on March 9, 1917, to "facilitate the expressing of our social natures, to furnish a channel through which our highest college loyalty could be expressed, and to uphold the ideals of fair play." It was installed as Theta Chapter of Phi Kappa Tau on September 17, 1919.

Transylvania is affiliated with the Christian Church (Disciples of Christ), and many distinguished Disciples clergymen have been Theta men.

Theta has been a campus leader consistently from its earliest days. Prior to World War II, the chapter maintained a house, but since 1953 it has had an attractively furnished chapter room in the Clay-Davis residence hall, where most members live.

Theta has one of the fraternity's most commendable records in scholarship, often leading and rarely out of the top three chapters. Dr. Monroe Moosnick, faculty adviser to Theta for more than thirty years, also served as the national educational director in the 1980s. Theta's Monroe Moosnick scholarship fund was begun at a roast held in his honor in 1983.

Ι IOTA CHAPTER
Coe College
Cedar Rapids, Iowa

Founded as Delta Gamma Rho, 1919
Chartered as Phi Kappa Tau,
January 15, 1920

DELTA GAMMA RHO, founded in 1917, was chartered as Iota Chapter on January 15, 1920. The local was organized by Charles S. Weber, who became prominent in Phi Kappa Tau affairs after the installation.

Iota fell victim to the Great Depression and closed its doors in 1934.

In 1951 Coe College Trustee John W. Miller and Cedar Rapids businessman Hamilton H. Morse, both early members of Iota Chapter, made contact with Chi Beta Phi, a prominent Coe local fraternity. Twenty-nine members of Chi Beta Phi signed the new charter of Iota Chapter on May 27, 1951. Chi Beta Phi was formed on May 11, 1930, by the merger of two older Coe locals. Beta Phi Omega was founded in 1909 and Chi Alpha Epsilon was founded at the same time that the original Iota was forming in 1917.

Fraternities at Coe are housed in dormitories and have chapter rooms there. In addition, Iota has maintained its own home from time to time. It currently has a house at 1502 C Avenue NE, which it purchased in 1990. A magnificent turnout of alumni attended Iota's seventy-fifth anniversary celebration in 1995.

Κ KAPPA CHAPTER
University of Kentucky
Lexington, Kentucky

Founded as Theta Rho,
March 31, 1917
Founded as Kappa Zeta Rho,
October 12, 1919
Chartered as Phi Kappa Tau,
November 6, 1920

A LOCAL CALLED THETA RHO, which was organized by National President Ewing Boles in 1917, was scheduled to become Eta Chapter; but installation plans were canceled at the last minute, when the onset of World War I caused the Kentucky faculty to withdraw its approval.

In 1920 transfer students John F. Casner and Otto V. Elder from Delta at Centre and Ray Vice from Theta at Transylvania organized Kappa Zeta Rho. Its petition to Phi Kappa Tau was accepted, and the installation of Kappa Chapter took place on November 6, 1920.

Kappa occupied a series of rented houses and rooms until 1948, when a house corporation was organized to purchase a home at 340 South Broadway. This was renovated and enlarged.

Through arrangement with the university, Kappa finally built a home of its own, a striking modern building on land leased from the university. The chapter was temporarily closed for disciplinary reasons in 1990, and the house was demolished by the university. Plans are underway to construct a new house on a different university plot.

Edward A. "Ted" Marye is the only Kappa man to serve as national president (1975–77).

Λ

LAMBDA CHAPTER
Purdue University
West Lafayette, Indiana

Founded as Beta Xi Alpha,
fall 1919
Chartered as Phi Kappa Tau,
November 20, 1920

BETA XI ALPHA was founded by a group of sophomore agricultural students at Purdue in the autumn of 1919. Through Lyle Willey, who was acquainted with several members of Beta Chapter, the group learned about Phi Kappa Tau and made a formal petition to become a chapter. The petition was accepted during the 1920 Indianapolis convention, and the installation was conducted on November 19–20, 1920.

A building association was incorporated in 1926 to purchase a prime lot across Northwestern Avenue from the developing engineering quadrangle. The following year, the chapter built a distinctive Tudor-style house, designed by architect Richard C. Lennox. Lennox served the fraternity as domain chief and member of the National Council and was the architect of the National Headquarters building in Oxford. In more recent years, the chapter acquired an adjoining lot for future expansion. The chapter has occupied the house

except for a period during World War II, when it was leased to the navy and then to Delta Gamma Fraternty.

Alvin Huth (Wisconsin, 1925), a local accountant, directed the business of the building association for nearly sixty years. Longtime Advisor Col. Frank W. Bryant served the national fraternity as grand Ritualist and was designer of the current badge.

Lambda hosted the fraternity's 1934 national convention at the Purdue Memorial Union.

The chapter's newsletter, *The Lambdanite,* has been published continuously since March 1921.

M

MU CHAPTER
Lawrence University
Appleton, Wisconsin

Founded as Tau Alpha Sigma,
October 24, 1919
Chartered as Phi Kappa Tau,
December 4, 1920

GRADUATE STUDENT Graeme O'Geran saw the need for an additional fraternity with the influx of World War I veterans and founded Tau Alpha Sigma in October 1919. Through Lawrence faculty member W. I. Easly (Miami, 1910), the group learned about Phi Kappa Tau and submitted a formal petition for charter in 1920. The installation ceremonies took place in the Knights of Pythias lodge rooms on December 4, 1920.

The chapter's first home was a house rented from the college at 549 Alton Street in the fall of 1919.

A series of homes were rented by the chapter until 1941, when the chapter moved into a home built by the college on the campus in a new fraternity quadrangle, which has served the chapter since that time. The house is located less than twenty feet from the location of the chapter's first house.

Probably the oldest theme party in Phi Kappa Tau is Mu's "Le Brawl," which has been transforming the Mu chapter house into the Paris of the 1920s for nearly seventy years.

Mu has been known over the years as a musical chapter. Alumnus Russell Danburg wrote a number of fraternity songs and edited several editions of the *Phi Tau Songbook.* Danburg's piano concerts were an important part of Phi Tau conventions between 1947 and the last performance before his death in 1993.

N

NU CHAPTER
University of California, Berkeley
Berkeley, California

Founded as the Orond Club,
October 16, 1916
Chartered as Phi Kappa Tau,
March 19, 1921

THE OROND CLUB was founded on the University of California's distinguished Berkeley campus in 1916. Norman M. Lyon was the first president. The club's activity was suspended when all the members entered the service during World War I but quickly restarted after the armistice.

Through Ens. Paul F. Opp

(Mount Union, 1915), the club learned about Phi Kappa Tau and was impressed with its concept of resident and graduate membership having equal standing. The Orond petition was approved and the club was installed as Nu Chapter on March 19, 1921, as the fraternity's westernmost chapter–by a thousand miles.

In 1923 Nu was the first Phi Kappa Tau Chapter to build a new home. Carl Loorz supervised the construction as an undergraduate, and his firm, later joined by Phi Tau sons Don and George, also would manage the major reconstruction of the house in 1953–54.

Nu Chapter's interesting history is chronicled in the 153-page book, *Phi Kappa Tau at Berkeley*, written by alumnus James Gilbert Paltridge, published in 1993.

Nu Chapter boasts a long list of outstanding alumni, and many have given service to the national fraternity. In 1995 Stephen Brothers became the first Nu member to be elected national president.

Xi Chapter
Franklin and Marshall College
Lancaster, Pennsylvania

Founded as the College Ralston Club, 1900
Became the Marshall Club, March 1909
Chartered as Phi Kappa Tau, November 24, 1921

THE COLLEGE RALSTON CLUB was an eating club, founded in 1900 with the motto "Home-Health-Wealth-Happiness." Members of the club joined with several other students to form the Marshall Club in March 1909. They chose a motto, "Esse Quam Videri," and maroon and white as official colors.

The Marshall Club's petition to Phi Kappa Tau was accepted, and the installation took place on Thanksgiving Day 1921, with Grand President Edgar Ewing Brandon presiding. Rev. Charles D. Spotts, a charter member, later served the national fraternity as scholarship commissioner, member of the National Council, and national chaplain.

The chapter's headquarters was a home at 365 College Avenue until 1931, when a house at 605 College Avenue was purchased. That house suffered major damage in a 1992 fire but has since been restored to its original appearance.

In recent years, the college decided to withdraw recognition of the campus fraternities. With the support of the national fraternity, Xi Chapter has continued to operate without the assistance of its host institution.

Omicron Chapter
Pennsylvania State University
State College, Pennsylvania

Founded as Delta Tau Omega,
March 7, 1921
Chartered as Phi Kappa Tau,
May 6, 1922

FIFTEEN STUDENTS at Pennsylvania State University formed the Delta Tau Omega Fraternity on March 7, 1921, and it was recognized by the university on May 6. Its petition to Phi Kappa Tau was approved, and the installation as Omicron Chapter was conducted on May 6, 1922.

Omicron's "dad's association" conceived the idea of building a new house for the chapter, and it made a down payment on the corner lot at Fairmont and Garner. A handsome red-brick house with stone trim was completed and occupied in the fall of 1930. The house was leased to the university during the final two years of World War II, when the chapter could no longer keep the house full. It remains the home of Omicron to this day.

Π

PI CHAPTER
University of Southern California
Los Angeles, California

Founded as Alpha Phi Kappa,
May 28, 1921
Chartered as Phi Kappa Tau,
May 26, 1922

PAUL F. OPP, who had helped to establish Phi Kappa Tau at Berkeley, approached University of Southern California student Archie Matson with the idea of establishing a Phi Tau chapter at USC. Richard Bird and Roy Johnson joined with Matson to help start a local fraternity. After an unsuccessful initial effort, Norman M. Lyon, a charter member at Berkeley, gave assistance to the group, and a more stable organization was perfected in November 1921, adopting the name Alpha Phi Kappa. Installation as Pi Chapter took place the following May.

Pi Chapter absorbed Alpha Nu Delta, a local fraternity, in 1933.

Four houses were rented between 1921 and 1936, when the chapter purchased a home on the fraternity row at 904 West 28th, which it had been renting. That house was substantially remodeled in 1939. The chapter continued to operate during World War II, although the house was rented to Chi Omega Sorority. In the 1960s, the chapter occupied a new home built by the university on the West 28th Street lot, which boasted a large open courtyard. Beginning with the construction of the new house, the chapter began to run up a nagging debt with the university, which was further complicated by low membership in the 1970s and early 1980s. Pi Chapter finally closed in 1988.

Pi Chapter produced a large number of outstanding alumni, including former Kansas Governor Fred Hall; John Berardino, pro baseball player and longtime star of "General Hospital"; and Roland Maxwell, the Pasadena attorney who was national president of the fraternity for twenty-five years.

P

RHO CHAPTER
Rensselaer Polytechnic Institute
Troy, New York

Founded as Knights of the Sphinx,
March 2, 1920
Changed to Kappa Omicron Sigma,
May 26, 1920
Chartered as Phi Kappa Tau,
November 28, 1922

J. DONALD MACKNIGHT organized a group of close friends as Knights of the Sphinx with a badge, charter, and initiation ceremony. Within weeks, the group decided to change its name to Kappa Omicron Sigma Fraternity to compete with other fraternities in recruitment.

As a local fraternity, the group was excluded from the Interfraternity Council; and when some members learned about Phi Kappa Tau through Paul F. Opp, then living in New York City, they petitioned to become a chapter in May 1922. The chapter was installed as Rho Chapter over Thanksgiving weekend 1922. The ceremonies were capped with a banquet at the Ten Eyck Hotel in Albany.

After renting a small gaslit house at 3 Walnut Grove and much larger ones near the Troy Hospital and at Peoples and Eleventh streets, the chapter leased an under-construction apartment building at 207 Hoosick Street; this was subsequently purchased along with some adjoining land in 1951.

The current Rho chapter house on Sherry Road was constructed in 1961. The building project was initiated when members of the resident council petitioned the house corporation and pledged $9,000 toward the building fund. This kicked off a major campaign among the alumni to construct the house. Since that time, every undergraduate has made a pledge to the building fund before he graduates, which has secured the future of the chapter without additional alumni drives.

Σ

SIGMA CHAPTER
Syracuse University
Syracuse, New York

Founded as Phi Sigma Psi,
February 20, 1920
Chartered as Phi Kappa Tau,
November 25, 1922

TEN SYRACUSE MEN founded Phi Sigma Psi on February 20, 1920. In the summer of 1922, the group submitted a petition, which was accepted at Phi Kappa Tau's 1922 convention.

Sigma is the only chapter to be chartered out of Greek-alphabetical order. By request, Rho was assigned to the Rensselaer chapter and Sigma reserved for Syracuse so that the Greek names would correspond to the first letter of each school's name. Sigma was chartered three days before Rho in November 1922.

The chapter maintained a home at 222 Euclid Avenue until World War II, when the property was sold to the university, which agreed to lease the house back to the fraternity when it returned to campus. Sigma did rebuild the chapter after World War II, but a steady decline in membership began during the Korean War, and it eventually became inactive in January 1957.

A colony existed at Syracuse for a short time in the mid-1980s but failed before it was able to earn the return of the Sigma charter.

T

TAU CHAPTER
University of Michigan
Ann Arbor, Michigan

Founded as Phi Tau Club,
January 11, 1922
Chartered as Phi Kappa Tau,
February 16, 1923

THE PHI TAU CLUB was organized with the help of Frank A. Mickle (Ohio State, 1912) and Alfred Fischer (Miami, 1913), who were living in Ann Arbor. The club petitioned Phi Kappa Tau for a charter on May 10, 1922, with twenty-four members.

When the petition was approved, the installation date was set for February 17, 1923. Dr. Edgar Ewing Brandon, a member of Michigan's class of 1888, led the delegation of installing officers, which included Founder Shideler and past National Presidents Henry E. Hoagland and Frederick R. Fletemeyer.

The chapter, which had weakened during the depression, became inactive during World War II but was rebuilt during the 1946–47 school year in a house at 808 Tappan Street.

The chapter enjoyed success until the unrest of the late 1960s took its toll, forcing the closure of Tau Chapter in 1971, when its house at 1910 Hill Street was sold.

John Bogema, brother-in-law of Domain Director James V. Lahman (Central Michigan, 1965), led the effort that resulted in the rechartering of Tau on December 1, 1984. That group, housed at the corner of Hill and Washtenaw, eventually closed because of low membership in the early 1990s.

Y

UPSILON CHAPTER
Nebraska Wesleyan University
Lincoln, Nebraska

*Founded as Orophilian Literary
Society, 1888
Changed to Oro Men, 1907
Changed to Phi Beta Sigma, 1909
Chartered as Phi Kappa Tau,
April 21, 1923*

NEBRASKA WESLEYAN's first social
organization was the Orophilian
Literary Society, founded in 1888.
Its name was changed to Phi Beta
Sigma in 1907, when its first chapter house was established. Phi Beta
Sigma remained a local organization until the university trustees
rescinded a ban on national fraternities in 1921, and the group began
to look for a national with which to
affiliate.

Initial inquiries to Phi Kappa Tau
in 1922 were positive but when the
National Council voted on whether
to encourage a petition, it opposed
the plan because of the small size of
the school. After a personal visit
from Dr. Henry Hoagland to Phi
Beta Sigma's alumni president, Dr.
Harry A. Taylor, the petition was
accepted and approved.

In three days of initiations, thirty-six undergraduates and thirty-two
alumni became members of Phi
Kappa Tau. The charter was presented on April 21, 1923, at the
Hotel Lincoln.

A forty-six-man house was completed on a double lot at 5305
Huntington Avenue in 1928, and an
addition that expanded the capacity
to sixty was built in 1970.

Upsilon has an outstanding record

of scholarship. It is a frequent winner of the national fraternity's
scholarship trophy and has won the
campus McKibbon trophy for scholarship almost every year.

An exceptionally large number
of Phi Kappa Tau leaders have come
from Upsilon. Five men have served
as national president: Dr. Harry A.
Taylor (1925–28), Warren Parker
(1966–68), Thomas C. Cunningham (1979–81), John M. Green
(1981– 83), and Dr. Rodney E.
Wilmoth (1993–95). John Green
has been executive director since
1987, and a long list of other men
have served in various staff and volunteer positions.

Φ

PHI CHAPTER
Bethany College
Bethany, West Virginia

*Founded as Rechabite Club,
September 20, 1910
Chartered as Phi Kappa Tau,
October 29, 1923*

BETHANY'S RECHABITE CLUB was
founded September 20, 1910, with
the motto "Manhood Demands
Purity" and the Book of Jeremiah as
its creed. Later, after adopting a
Ritual and amending the constitution, the club became the Rechabite
Fraternity and began to consider
affiliation with a national organization. Its petition to Phi Kappa Tau
was approved at the 1923 national
convention, and the installation was
held October 27–29, 1923, thus
formally creating Phi Chapter.

Phi Chapter has operated continuously since 1910 except for the

difficult period during the last two
years of World War II, when so
many chapters became inactive.

Until the college built the chapter's current house on the campus,
Phi had maintained rented off-campus quarters.

Alumni of the chapter have
formed the Harvard Red and Old
Gold Club as a fund-raising vehicle
for its members. A large number of
alumni have pledged $1,000 each
to join the club and they make
annual payments toward their
pledges.

The college is affiliated with the
Christian Church (Disciples of
Christ), and many alumni have gone
on to successful ministries. W.
Arthur Rush, a well-known Hollywood talent agent, served as a
college trustee and member of the
fraternity's National Council. Joel S.
Rudy, dean of students at Ohio University, is the fraternity's current
educational director.

X

CHI CHAPTER
North Carolina State University
Raleigh, North Carolina

*Founded fall, 1915
Affiliated with Phi Psi, spring 1916
Changed to Phi Psi Lambda, 1920
Chartered as Phi Kappa Tau,
December 7, 1923*

EIGHT MEN FOUNDED a local organization in W. A. Kennedy's Watauga
dormitory room in the fall of 1915.
The group was chartered as a chapter of Phi Psi professional textile
fraternity in 1916. Phi Psi allowed
the group to operate as a social fra-

ternity until 1920 when the group returned to local status under the name Phi Psi Lambda.

Phi Psi Lambda became the Phi Kappa Tau's first southern chapter with the granting of the Chi charter on December 7, 1923. Along with Grand President John V. Cotton and Grand Secretary R. K. Bowers, eighteen men signed the charter.

Chi Chapter moved from rented house to rented house, sometimes on-campus and sometimes in the town of Raleigh some distance from the campus. After a brief hiatus during World War II, the chapter was rebuilt and moved into a new university-built home in 1947 at Brooks and Clark avenues, then moved to 308 Horne Avenue in 1954, where it remained until the university began to develop new on-campus fraternity housing. Chi Chapter's current house, built in 1964, sleeps forty and can accom-modate up to sixty in the dining room. The house is leased from the university and furnished completely by the chapter.

John A. Edwards served as the fraternity's first national vice president in 1968–70, and two notable Chi members in higher education have been Dean E. L. Cloyd, former dean of students at North Carolina State, and William N. Aycock, onetime chancellor of the University of North Carolina at Chapel Hill.

PSI CHAPTER
University of Colorado
Boulder, Colorado

Founded as Alpha Beta,
November 2, 1922
Chartered as Phi Kappa Tau,
February 23, 1924

A GROUP OF SERIOUS-minded students, many of whom were World War I veterans, founded Alpha Beta Fraternity in 1922. The primary organizers were James R. Hoffman and Psi Chapter alumnus H. Clay Burkholder (Franklin and Marshall, 1921). From the outset, Alpha Beta's intention was to petition to become a chapter of Phi Kappa Tau. Alpha Beta signed a three-year lease on a house at 1229 University, which formerly had been the Kappa Sigma house and was large enough to sleep thirty-five men.

Alpha Beta's petition was approved, and installation ceremonies were held at the chapter house over a three-day period, concluding with a banquet on February 24, 1924, when the group officially became Psi Chapter.

Charter member Ray Bushey, later a member of the National Council and winner of the Palm Award, oversaw the construction of Psi's handsome chapter house at 1150 College Avenue during 1929. It cost more than $65,000. The chapter first occupied the house in the spring of 1930. During World War II, the university took over the house and rented it to the navy, although the chapter retained use of the chapter room.

After the mortgage was burned in 1954, a $75,000 addition, expanding the kitchen, dining room, and basement was constructed.

Psi hosted the 1964 national convention on the Boulder campus. Convention General Chairman Ray Bushey was elected to the National Council, and Lou Gerding was elected national president.

During a 1970s financial crisis, the national fraternity assumed ownership of the chapter house. Only recently have the Psi alumni repurchased the house.

Ω

OMEGA CHAPTER
University of Wisconsin
Madison, Wisconsin

*Founded as Alpha Theta Pi,
April 1922
Chartered as Phi Kappa Tau,
April 26, 1924*

ALPHA THETA PI was founded as a local fraternity in 1922, and in the 1922–23 school year, they leased a house where fifteen members were living. Jesse Day (Miami, 1912) and Mu Chapter founder Graeme O'Geran assisted in the organization of the chapter. Alpha Theta Pi petitioned Phi Kappa Tau for a charter in June 1923. Installation ceremonies took place April 24–27, 1924. Forty-four men signed the charter.

Omega bought a house at 615 North Henry Street, which the chapter occupied in the fall of 1926. A number of fraternities at Wisconsin slumped during the Great Depression, and declining membership forced the chapter to surrender its house and cease operations in June 1939.

In the fall of 1984, transfer students James Heinritz from Lawrence and Daniel Schleck from Coe worked with Douglas C. Adams (Miami, 1981), a member of the National Headquarters staff, to recruit a core group to restart Omega. The group grew steadily, and in the fall of 1985, it rented a five-bedroom apartment with a large room for social and chapter events. The following year, a house was rented at 151 West Gilman Street, and a new Omega charter was signed on November 15, 1986.

An original charter member, Paul A. Elfers, a trustee of the Phi Kappa Tau Foundation, made a $5,000 contribution to Omega's housing fund at the time of the chartering.

AA

ALPHA ALPHA CHAPTER
Michigan State University
East Lansing, Michigan

*Founded as Dorian Literary Society,
February 4, 1915
Chartered as Phi Kappa Tau,
May 16, 1924*

PROFESSOR JOHNSTON of the Michigan Agricultural College (now Michigan State) organized a group of upperclassmen into the Dorian Literary Society in 1915. The society met in old College Hall until 1920, when they occupied a house holding twenty-four members. The college had banned national fraternities until 1922, when the Dorians began to search for a national affiliation. The Dorians, with forty-three undergraduate members and 103 alumni, petitioned Phi Kappa Tau for a charter in 1923. After a thorough investigation of the Dorians, the fraternity granted the group its twenty-fifth charter, Alpha Alpha.

Alpha Alpha continued in the old Dorian house for several years and completed a major renovation in 1927. The chapter prospered through the depression but closed temporarily during World War II, when the university took over the house as a dormitory. The Dorian house was sold in 1956, but it took until 1959 to dedicate a new $145,000 home designed to house forty-four men in apartmentlike suites. During a low ebb in fraternity life, the chapter closed, and the house was sold in 1972. Proceeds from the sale were invested for a future return.

In November 1984, Director of Expansion K. Steven Lilly (Evansville, 1980) arrived on campus and recruited an initial interest group of thirty-two men. Twenty were eventually initiated. The colony was guided by transfer student Barth Wilson (Central Michigan, 1983), Dennis Rosenbrook (Michigan State, 1954), Tom Fassbender (Michigan State, 1961), and Ed Soergel (Michigan State, 1948). The alumni quickly found, leased, and furnished a house, and the group progressed rapidly toward the installation ceremonies on April 5, 1986. Since that time, the house corporation has purchased the much larger, former Evans Scholars house and renovated it for Alpha Alpha's use.

ALPHA BETA CHAPTER
New York University
New York, New York

Founded as C.L.B. Club,
June 1921
Changed to Phi Lambda Beta,
November 1921
Chartered as Phi Kappa Tau,
November 26, 1924

SEVERAL NONRESIDENT students at New York University formed the C.L.B. Club in June 1921, and meetings were held in the members' homes until a room at the school was acquired. These club members formed the Phi Lambda Beta Fraternity in November and were officially recognized by the university the following year. After outgrowing smaller houses, the fraternity established a headquarters at 70 Riverside Drive in November 1923.

Phi Lambda Beta learned about Phi Kappa Tau from Rev. A. H. Wilson, a national officer of Sigma Nu, and the local fraternity petitioned Phi Kappa Tau to become a chapter. The petition was approved, and the installation ceremonies took place over the Thanksgiving holiday in November 1924.

In 1925 Alpha Beta Chapter absorbed another local fraternity, Sigma Pi Epsilon, located in the University Heights division of NYU. That local, which was founded in 1918, brought a large membership to the merger.

Alpha Beta operated successfully through the 1930s but closed during World War II.

ALPHA GAMMA CHAPTER
University of Delaware
Newark, Delaware

Founded as Gamma Delta Rho,
October 4, 1920
Chartered as Phi Kappa Tau,
December 4, 1924

SEVEN STUDENTS formed the Gamma Delta Rho Fraternity in the Harter Hall dormitory on October 4, 1920. Later that month, the new fraternity adopted a constitution, an oath, and the colors navy blue and crimson. The Gamma Delta Rho badge was composed of the three Greek letters crowned by seven pearls, which represented the founders.

Upon approval of its petition, Phi Kappa Tau installed the members of Gamma Delta Rho as the Alpha Gamma Chapter on December 6, 1924. The depression of the 1930s took its toll on the chapter, and it closed its doors on December 8, 1936.

The chapter was revived in 1947 and moved into a house in the fall of 1948. In 1954 Alpha Gamma moved to another house "up campus." Its current house was formed by joining two identical homes on adjoining lots with an impressive pedimented connector, forming one large house in 1964.

In 1981 the chapter started its 5-K "Run for Bruce" as a philanthropy to provide assistance to a local man injured in a high school football accident. It is the largest race of its kind in Delaware.

ALPHA DELTA CHAPTER
Case Western Reserve University
Cleveland, Ohio

Founded as Iroquois Club, 1919
Changed to Tau Gamma Psi,
fall 1922
Chartered as Phi Kappa Tau,
January 30, 1925

FOUNDED AT THE CASE INSTITUTE of Technology just after the close of World War I, the Iroquois Club was a completely secret organization. In the fall of 1922, the group occupied its first home, changed its name to Tau Gamma Psi, and began to operate publicly. At the same time, it began to petition Phi Kappa Tau for membership, but the petition was initially rejected because of the fraternity's desire to expand outside of the state of Ohio. After intense lobbying from the Cleveland alumni association, the petition was approved at the 1924 national convention.

Alpha Delta became the fraternity's twenty-eighth chapter and the fifth in Ohio when it was installed in January 1925.

As Alpha Delta grew through the 1920s and 1930s, it moved frequently from one rented home to another. In 1941 a luxurious private residence on the Abington Road fraternity row became available; and through the efforts of Irven B. Prettyman, the Alpha Delta Alumni Corporation bought Alpha Delta's first home. That home was sold to the university in 1952, and the chapter purchased another fine home at 11318 Bellflower Road, where the chapter remained until moving into a modern four-story house built on the campus of the newly merged Case Western Reserve University in 1968. The Chapter ceased operations in 1992.

AE

ALPHA EPSILON CHAPTER
Kansas State University
Manhattan, Kansas

Founded as Phi Kappa Theta, spring 1922
Chartered as Phi Kappa Tau, May 23, 1925

WHEN MEMBERS of the Phi Kappa Theta local at Kansas State decided that it was desirable to affiliate with a national fraternity, a close investigation of all those not already represented on the campus found only one that was closely aligned with its own ideals, Phi Kappa Tau. They prepared a petition to Phi Kappa Tau, which granted the Alpha Epsilon charter to the group on May 23, 1925.

George Bond coined the name of the chapter's newsletter, *PaKeT*, combining the a and e from the chapter's name with P, K, and T.

The Alumni Building Association was formed in 1931 to purchase a new house for the chapter at the peak of its prosperity. The chapter closed during World War II, and the house was sold. In 1947 a movement began to reestablish the chapter, with the charter being returned on November 9, 1949. The national fraternity helped Alpha Epsilon buy a house at 1623 Fairchild in 1955.

In recent years, the national fraternity has maintained, owned and managed the chapter house.

AZ

ALPHA ZETA CHAPTER
Oregon State University
Corvallis, Oregon

Founded as Rainier Club, November 21, 1921
Changed to Lambda Phi Delta, October 1923
Chartered as Phi Kappa Tau, October 15, 1925

UNDER THE LEADERSHIP of Dr. Roy R. Hewitt, a business school professor, a small group of Oregon State campus leaders formed the Rainier Club in 1922. They soon adopted the Greek name Lambda Phi Delta and petitioned Phi Kappa Tau for a charter, which was granted on October 15, 1925, with National President Harry A. Taylor presiding at the installation. The chapter prospered until the depression, when membership began to lag and the chapter was forced to take boarders into its house at 242 N.W. 15th Street.

The national fraternity helped reorganize the chapter, and in 1938 it moved into new quarters at 27 Park Terrace, which served as home until the chapter closed in 1942 during World War II.

In 1947 the chapter was reestablished in a new house, purchased at 26th and Harrison, which was home until 1957, when the present house was purchased. Alpha Zeta closed its doors in 1982 and was briefly revived in the middle 1980s, only to fail once again. The house corporation has continued to maintain the house as a rental property in the absence of a chapter.

AE

ALPHA ETA CHAPTER
University of Florida
Gainesville, Florida

Founded as Sigma Kappa Phi, fall 1923
Chartered as Phi Kappa Tau, March 9, 1926

SIGMA KAPPA PHI was formed by a group of students who had become friends living in a boarding house at the University of Florida. Early in their history, they asked Harley W. Chandler, a charter member of Iota Chapter and mathematics professor, to serve as the faculty advisor to the fraternity. Chandler influenced the group's decision to petition Phi Kappa Tau for a charter, and in the process they gave a formal dinner with Phi Kappa Tau Founder William H. Shideler as guest of honor in April 1925.

The local's petition was approved, and the Alpha Eta charter was granted on March 9, 1926. Grand President Harry A. Taylor presided at the installation on his way to Oxford, Ohio, to celebrate the fraternity's twentieth anniversary.

In 1940, the Alpha Eta alumni completed the chapter's attractive forty-man house built of natural Florida stone in the Colonial style. Alpha Eta alumni have long been known for their success in government and politics. Among the long list of outstanding alumni have been Congressman William C. Lantaff, Marine Corps Commandant Leonard Chapman and Florida Attorney General Richard Ervin. John F. Cosgrove, a Miami attorney and member of the state house of representatives served Phi Kappa Tau as national president (1987–89).

CHAPTER FOUR

CELEBRATIONS & CRISES

J ust as they had done on another chilly March day twenty years earlier, Dr. William H. Shideler, now chairman of the geology department at Miami University; Judge Clinton D. Boyd of the Butler County Court of Common Pleas; and H. H. Beneke, professor of finance at Miami, climbed the creaking stairs to the old Miami Union Hall on the top floor of Miami's Old Main Building.

This day, March 13, 1926, the three old friends were not joined by their college contemporaries but by the national officers and representatives of six chapters of the mature Phi

Kappa Tau that had grown from the Non-Fraternity Association they had founded twenty years earlier. The task at hand now was to celebrate the accomplishments of those twenty years. In an afternoon ceremony in the Miami Union Hall, a bronze tablet was unveiled to reveal the simple inscription:

> IN THIS ROOM
> ON MARCH 17, 1906
> THE PHI KAPPA TAU FRATERNITY
> WAS FOUNDED BY
> DWIGHT I. DOUGLASS
> WILLIAM H. SHIDELER
> CLINTON D. BOYD
> TAYLOR A. BORRADAILE

Though a new building stands on the site of Old Main today, the tablet, periodically polished by Alpha Chapter undergraduates, is mounted just inside the east entrance of the new Harrison Hall, within sight of the Founders' old North Dorm rooms.

The second twenty years of Phi Kappa Tau continued the maturation of the fraternity and presented some of its greatest trials. Phi Kappa Tau was well established in the East to Delaware and New York, in the North to Michigan and Wisconsin, in the West to Oregon and California, and, with the chartering of Alpha Eta, in the South to Florida.

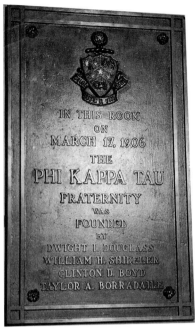

Memorial tablet in Old Main, 1926

FIRST RESORT CONVENTION

In splendor befitting a mature fraternity in the "roaring twenties," the luxurious West Baden Springs Hotel, famed southern Indiana resort, was the site of the Sixteenth National Convention in late August 1926. Near the end of the hotel's summer season, the convention nearly had the place to itself, allowing delegates to take the sulfur-spring baths, play golf, watch movies under the hotel's vast atrium dome, or even gamble in some of the illegal but well-known local establishments.

In convention business, statutes were passed requiring that a chapter get permission from the grand secretary prior to initiations, prohibiting intoxicants from being brought onto chapter property (even though prohibition had been the law of the land since 1920), and bonding chapter treasurers.

Phi Kappa Tau's first scholarship commissioner, Dean E. E. Brandon, recommended a statute that would automatically suspend any member placed on academic probation by his college or university. The statute was passed.

Grand Ritualist Frank W. Bryant was authorized along with patent attorney Bruce K. Brown to secure patents on the designs for Phi Kappa Tau jewelry. Bryant and a committee of Lambda men also were appointed to publish a coded edition of the *Ritual*, which could be kept by members without their having to hide it. After considerable effort by Bryant's committee, a coded *Ritual* was published but never widely used.

Two new Grand Council officers were elected at West Baden: L. W. Morris (Lawrence, 1920) became grand historian and Leonard M. Utz replaced fellow Eta charter member Melville Boyer on the Grand Council. Boyer was appointed by the Council to a new position of grand comptroller. Lest modern Phi Taus think that their predecessors had no sense of humor, copies of a postconvention newsletter, *The Stool Pidgeon,* full of "news that ain't fit to print," survive among the personal papers of Ernest Littleton and Melville Boyer to prove otherwise.

CHARTERS *in* VIRGINIA, PENNSYLVANIA, *and* WASHINGTON

Three new chapters were installed during the 1926–27 school year. Pi Epsilon Beta became Alpha Theta of Phi Kappa Tau at the College of William and Mary. Williamsburg minister Horace E. Cromer (Ohio, 1911) advised the seven-year-old local and encouraged its members to petition Phi Kappa Tau.

Sigma Alpha Fraternity at the University of Pennsylvania was founded in 1923, when members of the Philadelphia alumni association recruited two Penn undergraduates to form the nucleus of a new fraternity. Forty-five men signed the Alpha Iota charter on November 19, 1926.

At Washington State University, the local Omega Phi (whose name was derived from Greek symbols used in electrical calculations) petitioned to become Alpha Kappa Chapter. They already owned their own house when the thirty-six members signed the charter in June 1927.

MOTHERS FORM PHI ETA SORORITY

Mothers' clubs, or what today are more often known as parents' clubs, have been an important part of many Phi Tau chapters for years. But a concept unique to Phi Kappa Tau is Phi Eta Sorority, a national organization of Phi Kappa Tau mothers begun in 1927. The concept of a national organization was developed by Pi Chapter at the University of Southern California. Lyman Hazzard (Southern California, 1925) designed the Phi Eta monogram badge, and Raymond Harvey (Southern California, 1928) designed the attractive coat of arms containing much Phi Eta symbolism. A constitution and an elaborate Ritual were printed and bound.

Libby Rohr Cutting, mother of Henry Rohr (Southern California, 1925) was the first grand president of Phi Eta. The relationship with Phi Kappa Tau is described in an introduction to its constitution: "Politically and socially, the policy of Phi Eta towards Phi Kappa Tau chapters is 'hands off.' The policy of non-interference with the fraternity should be constantly guarded. It is ours to furnish the 'mother touch.' Any gossip regarding fraternity affairs is forever taboo."

Seven Phi Eta chapters were in operation by the end of 1928, and twenty-one chapters were listed in the *Laurel Wreath*, a magazine published in

Founders Boyd and Shideler with alumni and undergraduates in front of the Alpha Chapter house following the dedication of the memorial tablet at Old Main, 1926

January 1935. But the success of Phi Eta was not long-lived, and in 1947 the fraternity withdrew recognition of Phi Eta and encouraged the remaining few chapters to continue operating as local mothers' clubs.

Records of Delta Chapter of Phi Eta at Colorado and the correspondence of Josie Klotzbach, mother of Willis O. Klotzbach (Lafayette, 1934) and president of Phi Eta's Sigma Chapter at Lafayette, have been preserved in the fraternity archives and provide interesting insight into this unique organization, which has been out of existence for nearly fifty years.

CANADIAN CONVENTION STARTS 1927~28 YEAR

The Phi Eta concept was first presented to the 1927 convention, which was the first and only Phi Tau convention held outside of the United States. Capitalizing on the success of the resort convention at West Baden in 1926, delegates made their way to the Bigwin Inn on Bigwin Island in the Lake of Bays, Ontario.

The newly instituted Domain Chief Trophy, a forerunner of the Roland Maxwell Award, was presented to Alpha Beta Chapter at New York University as the outstanding chapter in the fraternity. Dr. Shideler was appointed grand comptroller, and Roland W. Maxwell (Southern Califor-

nia, 1922) was elected to the Grand Council, beginning his remarkable thirty-two-year tenure as a national officer.

Leo Raskowski (Ohio State, 1927) became the first Phi Tau football player to earn All-American honors when the Buckeye tackle made his way onto nearly every sportswriter's 1927 roster.

At Alabama Polytechnic (now Auburn), Sigma Theta Fraternity became Alpha Lambda Chapter on December 3, 1927. Prof. Jesse M. Robinson (Miami, 1909), chairman of Auburn's faculty fraternity committee, was instrumental in Sigma Theta's decision to petition Phi Kappa Tau.

Fifth anniversary dinner of the Rho Chapter (New York) of Phi Eta Sorority, November 11, 1930

A "who's who" in Phi Kappa Tau installed Phi Alpha Pi at Ohio Wesleyan University on March 16, 1928. The degree team included Founders Shideler and Boyd, Grand President Taylor, past Grand President Brandon, Grand Secretary Bowers, Grand Historian L. W. Morris, and Grand Councilor Leonard M. Utz.

PHI TAU HOUSING BOOM

A building boom responsible for some of the fraternity's most attractive chapter houses began at Purdue in 1927, when Lambda Chapter moved into the fifty-man, Tudor-style home designed by Richard C. Lennox (Purdue, 1921), still in use today. Epsilon Chapter dedicated a thirty-five-man house, which would serve the chapter for twelve years, on the Mount Union campus on March 19, 1928. Zeta dedicated its English Colonial-style house, sited at an angle on a prime lot in the Illinois fraternity district, later that spring. Upsilon built a red-brick colonial-style immediately adjacent to the Nebraska Wesleyan campus and took possession in the fall of 1928. The Upsilon and Zeta houses, though expanded, are also still in use

today. Psi, Omicron, and Alpha Chapters also would build substantial new homes before the end of the fraternity's first quarter century.

On May 19, 1928, Alpha Kappa Delta Fraternity became Alpha Nu Chapter at Iowa State University.

The fraternity returned to West Baden, Indiana, for its Eighteenth National Convention in August 1928. F. C. Ruskaup (Purdue, 1922) and brothers-in-law Richard C. Lennox and Joseph C. Matthews (Purdue, 1921) staffed the local organizing committee.

The 1928 convention adopted a new constitution and statutes, cleaning up the hodgepodge of additions and amendments made over the years. The major changes included the elimination of the offices of grand ritualist and grand historian and the combination of the offices of grand secretary and grand treasurer making it unnecessary. The addition of a grand comptroller in 1926 provided the appropriate checks and balances in the financial system but duplicated much of the role of the grand treasurer. Bookkeeping and check writing could be more efficiently handled in the Central Office. The Domain Chief Trophy went to Alpha Gamma at Delaware.

Dr. Isaac Miles Wright (Muhlenberg, 1918) was elected grand president, succeeding Dr. Taylor. Wright, like past Presidents Taylor and Brandon, was initiated into Phi Kappa Tau as an older man and was almost fifty when he became grand president. A highly regarded educator, he was chairman of the philosophy and pedagogy (education) departments at Muhlenberg. The age and

experience of these men certainly added a great deal of stability and wisdom to Phi Kappa Tau in its early years.

Outgoing Grand Treasurer Carl Tausig replaced Shideler as grand comptroller. Grayson Kirk, who was heading to Paris for a year of study at the Sorbonne, retired from the grand editorship and turned the job over to Jack Jareo (Wisconsin, 1926). Kirk was beginning a great academic career, which would lead to the presidency of Columbia University. A farm boy from Jeffersonville, Ohio, Kirk earned part of his way through graduate school with the few hundred dollars he earned in the five years he edited the *Laurel*.

CHARTERS for WEST VIRGINIA, LAFAYETTE, WASHINGTON, and GEORGIA TECH

Four more chapters accepted charters in the 1928–29 school year. Tau Theta Rho at West Virginia University became Alpha Xi Chapter. It was the fifth chartering in which Paul Opp, now a professor at Fairmont State College in West Virginia, played a major role. Opp and Founder Taylor Borradaile, living in Charleston, West Virginia, helped to install

Richard J. Young, 1928

the chapter. It was Borradaile's first opportunity to participate in such an event and possibly the first time he ever saw the Ritual performed. Morgantown's Mayor Barrickman declared a general holiday in the city on the afternoon of the installation banquet.

Delta Sigma Fraternity at Lafayette College in Easton, Pennsylvania, became Alpha Omicron Chapter on December 8, 1929. The Alpha Pi charter was granted to Sigma Tau Epsilon Fraternity at the University of Washington on April 6, 1929, and three weeks later Pi Lambda Delta at the Georgia Institute of Technology became Alpha Rho Chapter.

GRAND SECRETARY RESIGNS

Being the only paid staff member in an all-volunteer organization is often frustrating and never easy. For Grand Secretary Bowers, that frustration came to a head during the presidency of Dr. Wright. Though he had been the grand secretary since

1917, Bowers was just thirty-one years old in 1929, and fraternity work was practically the only work he had ever known. His youthful gregariousness and strong opinions rubbed some the wrong way and were criticized as "chronic infantilism." While he had many loyal supporters, others thought it was time for him to move on; and under increasing pressure, Bowers made his intentions to resign known to the Grand Council.

In June 1929 Dr. Shideler wrote to Richard J. Young (Miami, 1925): "Now as far as the secretaryship since it is officially and publicly known that Bowers will not be with us another year, the field is wide open for candidates." Shideler went on to explain to Young, who was just a year out of Miami and working as a newspaperman in Portsmouth, Ohio, that there were three official candidates for the secretary position and that the leading candidates were Domain Chiefs Ernest Littleton, a teacher in the Columbus, Ohio, public schools, and Harley Chandler, who was registrar at the University of Florida. Shideler confided that "neither is as 'flashy' as I would like…[though] either would make a good Secretary." Conceptually, the Council seemed to want a "more mature man of experience," but Shideler (who was chairman of the search committee) did encourage the twenty-two-year-old Young to become "an out and out candidate" by sending a biographical sketch to be circulated to the rest of the committee.

Members of Psi Chapter at Colorado in front of their new house

RICHARD YOUNG APPOINTED GRAND SECRETARY *at* LEXINGTON

The committee must have seen something it liked in the boyish Dick Young, and he was invited to a personal interview just prior to the Nineteenth National Convention at the Lexington, Kentucky, Phoenix Hotel in August 1929.

Young's appointment and Bowers' resignation were announced to the convention delegates at the same time. Young would begin as assistant to Secretary Bowers, whose resignation would become effective December 1, 1929. Harley Chandler was elected to the Grand Council, succeeding Bruce K. Brown. Past Grand Presidents Henry Hoagland and Ewing Boles were appointed to a committee to investigate a plan to establish a life-membership fee. Shideler replaced Tausig as grand comptroller, a position he would retain for the next thirty years.

The convention also accepted the petition of Alpha Kappa Fraternity at Colorado Agricultural and Mechanical College (now Colorado State), guided in its early years by Carrol O. Simmonds(Nebraska Wesleyan, 1929), whose undergraduate fraternity, Phi Beta Sigma, had become Upsilon Chapter. Installation ceremonies at Fort Collins were completed on November 16, 1929.

CENTRAL OFFICE MOVES *to* OXFORD

As grand comptroller, Dr. Shideler served as a mentor to Secretary Young as he assumed full responsibility for the Central Office of the fraternity. Shideler proposed moving the office from Indianapolis to Oxford, the birthplace of the fraternity and his home. Phi Delta Theta had recently moved its office from Indianapolis to Oxford, and Shideler believed that having Young close to the experienced Phi Delt secretary Arthur Priest would also be helpful. Shideler's persuasiveness was effective, and the Central

Delegates to the Eighteenth National Convention, West Baden Springs Hotel, West Baden, Indiana, August 1928

Office opened its doors in rented space at 121 East High Street in July 1930.

At the famed Grove Park Inn, nestled in North Carolina's Blue Ridge Mountains, Phi Kappa Tau's 1930 convention approved a plan to erect a headquarters building for the fraternity as a memorial to the Founders in Oxford. It was to be completed one year later in time for dedication ceremonies at the Silver Jubilee convention. The Founders' Memorial Fund, established ten years earlier, had grown large enough that a building costing $25,000 to $30,000 could be paid for completely in cash.

The Twentieth National Convention also went on record abolishing "Hell Week" as a pre-initiation practice. Hazing was repugnant to the Founders, but undesirable activities had crept into the traditions of some of the chapters; and the convention took a formal stand against hazing with this action.

Cornell's oldest local fraternity, Phi Delta Sigma, gained the convention's unanimous consent to become Alpha Tau Chapter. The local was the result of a 1918 merger of two earlier groups at Cornell: Bandhu, founded in 1901; and Skull, founded in 1902. Phi Delta Sigma occupied a beautiful home on the Knoll in Ithaca, New York, which had housed Bandhu since 1910. Still owned by Alpha Tau's Phi

Delta Sigma corporation, Cornell's chapter house is the fraternity's longest-held chapter property.

SILVER JUBILEE

In the depression year of 1931, Phi Kappa Tau celebrated its Silver Jubilee during the four-day August convention. Organizers hoped for four hundred to attend; but considering that the nation was nearly two full years into its greatest economic depression, the attendance of over two hundred was all the more impressive and still twice the attendance of any other recent convention. The convention was highlighted by the dedication of two beautiful new buildings, the Memorial Headquarters Building and the new Alpha Memorial Chapter House.

The red-brick colonial chapter house was dedicated first, with young attorney Hugh C. Nichols presiding over the short ceremony. William T. Amos (Miami, 1928) gave the dedication address as a "pinch hitter" for Anthony Poss, who was unable to attend. Dr. Shideler, as president of Alpha's house corporation, accepted the house, making glowing comments

about Alpha Chapter, which he believed to be at a particular high point in its history. But Shideler's greatest honor came about an hour later, when the delegates walked the dozen or so blocks from the Alpha house to the dedication ceremonies of the memorial headquarters.

Ewing Boles, who had tagged along with building committee chairman Henry Hoagland on trips from Columbus to Oxford to inspect progress on the headquarters, presided at the dedication ceremony on the Campus Avenue lawn in front of the building, the front porch making a stage.

Genuinely moved by the honor of such an impressive memorial to the Founders, Professor Shideler, his prematurely white hair blowing in the breeze, said, "I feel proud of the achievements that have been carried

out by this organization which is regarded as one of my children, so to speak. At probably no time in my career will I receive the honor that I am receiving right now."

With similar sentiment, Judge Clinton D. Boyd responded, "I have had a great many undeserved honors in my lifetime, but this is probably the greatest that I have ever had bestowed upon me, that is, being credited as one of the Founders of this great national fraternity."

The fraternity's new Central Office building was built on a lot at 15 North Campus Avenue, originally purchased by Alpha's house corporation for a chapter house. It is directly across the street from Phrenocon's original house, in the middle of a block between Beta Theta Pi's Alpha Chapter house and a large home built by Dr. Brandon some years earlier.

National Council meeting in Oxford, Ohio, in the 1930s; left to right: A. C. Eichberg, Harley Chandler, Richard J. Young, Roland Maxwell, Ernest V. Price, Richard C. Lennox

Dr. Hoagland chaired the building committee, composed of Herman H. Beneke, Hugh C. Nichols, and Richard C. Lennox, the project architect who also was elected to the Grand Council during the convention. Lennox designed a handsome, solid edifice of concrete and steel construction faced with red brick and Indiana limestone. Built with room to grow, the first floor contained an oak-wainscoted office for the grand secretary, a large clerical office, and a mail room. The second floor was designed with two spacious offices for future growth and a conference room large enough to hold meetings of the Grand Council.

Dedicated just weeks after Sigma Alpha Epsilon's Levere Temple in Evanston, Illinois, Phi Kappa Tau's headquarters was the second building built specifically for use as a fraternity headquarters.

The Silver Jubilee closed with a banquet at which Dr. Shideler recounted his familiar version of how the fraternity was founded. He read parts of a letter from Founder Borradaile, who was testifying in a trial and at the last moment unable to attend the convention. The closing paragraph is vintage Borradaile: "Well, Bill, have a great time and express my congratulations to the fraternity and my regards to my old personal friends—and Bill, if they begin to tell what a hell of a great bunch of guys we were, sneeze, cough, faint or anything else, but don't laugh. We'll do that when I see you later."

DEPRESSION TAKES TOLL

The Great Depression had a profound impact on Phi Kappa Tau in the 1930s. Expansion was curtailed after the Alpha Tau installation in 1930, and only six chapters were chartered between 1930 and the end of World War II.

A Pasadena convention originally planned to follow the Los Angeles Olympics in 1932 was twice postponed, and the plan was finally given up. In 1932 and 1933, the Grand Council, with the approval of a majority

Alpha Tau installation banquet at Cornell, 1930

Founder Shideler is the guest of honor at the Twenty-fifth Anniversary Founders' Day Banquet of New York and Pennsylvania chapters in Philadelphia, 1931.

of chapters, called the Twenty-second and Twenty-third National Conventions to order and immediately adjourned them for lack of a quorum. The Grand Council handled the routine business of the fraternity from the conference room of the Central Office.

Though several chapters struggled financially, the conservative management of secretary Young and Grand Comptroller Shideler kept the national fraternity on solid financial footing. In 1933–34 they were able to reduce the budget by about 25 percent.

Even in tough financial conditions, chapters persevered, and some prospered. At Pi Chapter, John Baker (Southern California, 1929) kicked the winning field goal in the 1931 Southern California defeat of Notre

Dame, the first Irish loss since 1928, earning Baker All-American honors. But for the first time in the fraternity's history, some chapters came perilously close to failing.

By 1933 the chapters at Centre, West Virginia, and Lafayette were in serious financial trouble, and the Grand Council appointed alumni to help resolve the difficulties. But in the spring of 1934, Delta at Centre and Iota at Coe fell victims to the depression and became the first two chapters to fail in Phi Kappa Tau's twenty-eight years.

PURDUE CONVENTION, MAXWELL ELECTED PRESIDENT

With the plan for a California convention totally abandoned, a more economical convention at the Purdue Memorial Union took place in August 1934. The general chairman was Lambda stalwart Col. Frank W. Bryant, a member of the Purdue staff and former grand ritualist.

Prompted by depression-era financial concerns, the convention adopted the policy that a resident council member whose account with a chapter became thirty days in arrears was automatically suspended, and a committee was appointed to consider holding conventions every two years. Rev. Horace Cromer was elected to succeed Roland Maxwell on the Grand Council. Maxwell, who had served seven years on the Council, became the fraternity's first president from the far West. He had hoped to be elected at his hometown of Pasadena but waited instead to attend his final convention as national president in Pasadena—twenty-five years later!

Maxwell was an impressive figure. Tall, handsome and a natty dresser, he "looked and acted the part of a president," remembered Ewing Boles, a man who was not easily impressed by such things. And not only did Maxwell look the part, but as a successful young attorney, he was a skilled writer and orator. Three objectives announced in 1935 would guide his twenty-five-year term:

First, a continued effort toward the elevation of the scholastic standards of the chapters. The college fraternity which does not promote scholarship has failed.

Second, a recognition of the serious nature of the responsibilities of fraternity leadership. The activities of each chapter should be of such a constructive nature as to provide the strongest possible answer for...criticisms.

Third, a general strengthening of our individual chapters. Without adequate personnel, no chapter can do more than preserve a precarious existence.

Again in 1935, the Grand Council dispensed with the work of the convention following its August meeting. The Twenty-fifth National Convention was convened long enough to accept a new proposed constitution submitted by Comptroller Shideler and Hugh C. Nichols, and then was promptly adjourned.

Delegates and guests at the 1934 national convention at the Purdue Memorial Union

MODERN GOVERNANCE STRUCTURE ESTABLISHED

At the 1936 national convention held at the Nittany Lion Inn in State College, Pennsylvania, Phi Kappa Tau's governance structure was given its present form and its current constitution adopted. The new constitution changed the officer titles from "grand" to "national." The size of the renamed "National" Council was increased from five to six members, with terms being lengthened by a year to six years. Conventions would only be held every other year, and two councilors would be elected at each convention.

An inefficient system of collecting annual *Laurel* subscription fees came to an end when the convention approved the long-standing procedure by which resident council members would pay a lump sum at the time of initiation to include a lifetime subscription to the *Laurel*. The portion earmarked for a lifetime *Laurel* subscription was to be set aside in the *Laurel* Endowment Fund, which could be invested in chapter-housing loans, with interest helping to defray the magazine's publication expenses.

EXPANSION MORATORIUM ENDS

Ending the seven-year expansion moratorium, the Alpha Upsilon charter was granted to a highly respected local Delta Pi Sigma at Colgate University in Hamilton, New York. Dr. Everett F. Cox (Miami, 1927), a Colgate physics professor, introduced the members of Delta Pi Sigma to Phi Kappa Tau, and the installation took place in May 1937.

In another modern innovation approved by the 1936 convention, Jerry D. Page (Southern California, 1936) became the fraternity's first field secretary in the fall of 1937. Page, who went on to a great military career, was the first of more than a hundred young alumni who would spend a year or two traveling the country to visit and encourage the fraternity work of undergraduates and alumni.

Using a newly revised Ritual prepared by Paul T. Gantt and Rev. Horace Cromer, a record one hundred eight undergraduates and alumni

of Sigma Beta Nu Fraternity at the University of Akron were chartered as Alpha Phi Chapter on February 20, 1938.

Mississippi State University's Phi Tau Club was organized by Professor Paul H. Dunn (Mississippi State, 1938), who was a graduate of Miami University, protégé of William H. Shideler, and chairman of the Mississippi State geology department.

At the Twenty-seventh National Convention at Troutdale-in-the-Pines, Colorado, Ewing Boles announced the organization of a trust fund to meet the growing need for financial support by chapters and members. Three membership levels offered were: Sustaining, at ten dollars; Life, at fifty dollars; and Memorial, at one hundred dollars. The establishment of this trust fund by Boles may be identified as the first direct antecedent of today's Phi Kappa Tau Foundation, though it would be another seven years before an Educational Endowment Fund would be officially incorporated.

The tradition of presenting a wide-ranging array of chapter and alumni awards was first implemented at the 1938 convention. Purdue was recognized for outstanding chapter publications, and Penn State earned the Central Office Cooperation Award. The first Shideler Award was presented to William Cromer (Miami, 1936), recognizing him as the fraternity's outstanding graduating senior based on fraternity activity, scholarship, campus activity, and personality.

The Palm Award for meritorious alumni service was inaugurated by presentations to five of Phi Kappa Tau's greatest past leaders: William H. Shideler, Edgar E. Brandon, Ewing T. Boles, Henry E. Hoagland, and Harry A. Taylor, all past national presidents of the fraternity.

When the Twenty-eighth National Convention met at the peaceful French Lick Springs Hotel in the rolling hills of southern Indiana in August 1940, no one could have imagined that conventions would be called off until 1947 because of a world war.

Two innovations at the 1940 meeting have continued in some form at many conventions since. A chapter officers' workshop, featuring a series of panel discussions, was an early effort in educational programming, so much a part of fraternity meetings today. And for alumni, an "oldtimers' roundtable" for past officers and others who had previously attended a convention was a welcome innovation.

Two Shideler Awards were presented to equally qualified contenders— Herman Taylor (Southern California, 1937) and Harold Short (Colorado State, 1936), who forty-five years later would become national president.

The thirty-fifth anniversary of the fraternity was celebrated by hundreds of alumni and undergraduates at Founders' Day Banquets at chapters and in major cities across the country. Ten chapters celebrated together in Philadelphia in one of the largest events. Founders Shideler and Boyd and past National Presidents Boles and Hoagland attended the Columbus, Ohio, event.

In May 1941, Rho Sigma Phi Fraternity was chartered Alpha Psi Chapter at Texas College of Mines (now Texas–El Paso).

By the time the Japanese bombed Pearl Harbor in December 1941, Phi Taus were already involved in the escalating world war. Richard Massock (Illinois, 1917), chief of the Associated Press Rome bureau, had predicted war since 1935. Watson Bidwell (Colorado, 1926) was the last American to leave the British ship *Athenia*, torpedoed in the Atlantic eight and a half hours after war was declared between England and Germany in September 1939.

James L. S. Dunlop (Bethany, 1939), who volunteered with the Royal Canadian Air Force in 1939, was the first Phi Tau killed in World War II as he flew over the English Channel three months before the Pearl Harbor bombing. Six Phi Taus were at Pearl Harbor during the bombing, and it is estimated that as many as eight thousand Phi Taus served in the military between 1941 and 1945.

In Jack Anson's *Golden Jubilee History of Phi Kappa Tau*, the immediate effort to maintain the fraternity through war is explained:

"Recalling two periods in the past when the fraternity was threatened — during World War I and again during the depression — the national officers immediately prepared to meet the consequences of war, to place full Phi Kappa Tau strength at work to gain victory for the cause of democracy and to weather the consequences of enrollment decreases and diminished income. Within a month after the first appeal for the War Emergency Fund was sent to alumni, more than 200 alumni responded and contributed approximately five dollars each to the fraternity's war chest. By January 1942, more than 500 members had answered the call for service in the nation's armed forces."

The most poignant story of Phi Tau heroism and sacrifice is that of Robert J. Meder (Miami, 1936). Meder was one of eighty volunteer "Doolittle Raiders" who flew from the aircraft carrier *Hornet* to bomb the Japanese mainland in April 1942. Meder, a B-25 pilot, ran out of fuel and was forced to crash-land in mainland China. His fate was unknown until the end of the war, when it was learned that he had been captured along with several other Doolittle Raiders and died of dysentery in Nanking, China, on December 1, 1943.

The February 1946 *Laurel* recounted the story of Meder's last days in the words of Robert Hite and Jacob DeShazer, who had been imprisoned with him:

"The rest of us figured he couldn't get well, but we did our best to cheer him up and Bob himself never lost hope. Sometimes the guards would permit one of us to clean up his cell. He was too weak to do it himself.

"The day he died, December 1, 1943, was a cold, clear day. Bob dragged himself out of his cell to join us at 10:30 in the morning for our exercise, though he was too weak to participate. One of the guards pushed him around a little,

Doolittle Raider Robert J. Meder died in a Japanese prison camp.

not so much in anger as in ignorance. Bob grinned at him.

"Mixing Japanese words with the English so the guard would understand, he said: 'Listen, sick as I am I can lick the whole damn bunch of you.'

"He staggered back to his cell at 11:00 and a couple of hours later he was dead."

Among Meder's few personal effects acquired after the war was his Phi Kappa Tau membership card.

Meder was just one of ten Alpha men and one hundred and fifty-one Phi Taus altogether to make the ultimate sacrifice during the war.

Members of Lambda Chapter at Purdue in 1943–44;
the chapter house in the background was leased to the navy.

WARTIME OPERATIONS

Even in the midst of war, two chapters were installed during the 1942–43 school year.

Zeta Kappa Fraternity at Baldwin-Wallace College in Berea, Ohio, had a heritage dating back to 1859, when it was founded as the German Verein Literary Society. When Zeta Kappa was chartered, Alpha Omega of Phi Kappa Tau became the Phi Kappa Tau chapter with the oldest tradition.

Phi Theta Tau at the University of Texas–Austin became Beta Alpha Chapter on February 6, 1943, the last chapter to be chartered before the end of the war.

Secretary Young was called to active duty in the naval reserve in October 1942. With Field Secretary Robert Decker (Syracuse, 1939) already entered in the service, the Central Office was left vacant. The National Council arranged for the business of the office to be handled by a committee of past Presidents Brandon, Hoagland, and Boles. Shideler, who lived within walking distance of the Central Office, chaired the committee and was named acting secretary. Past Editor William F. Smiley (Ohio, 1925) agreed to resume editorial responsibility for the *Laurel*.

Paul L. Newman (Ohio, 1943), arguably Phi Kappa Tau's most famous alumnus, was initiated into Beta Chapter during his short stay on the Ohio University campus in the military V-12 program. Phi Taus of that era remember the fun-loving Cleveland native entertaining at the chapter piano.

By the 1944–45 school year, a remarkable twenty-two chapters were still operating in a valiant effort to keep the fraternity alive. Most chapter houses were rented to schools or sororities or were being used as military barracks.

The surrender of Japan in August 1945 brought an end to a terrible chapter in the lives of America's young men. And with that came prospects for the greatest enrollment boom in the history of American colleges. Phi Kappa Tau was poised to capitalize on that opportunity.

CHAPTER HISTORIES

ALPHA THETA CHAPTER
College of William and Mary
Williamsburg, Virginia

Founded as Ewell Club,
October 1919
Changed to Pi Epsilon Beta,
fall 1922
Chartered as Phi Kappa Tau,
November 12, 1926

IN 1926 WILLIAMSBURG minister Horace E. Cromer (Ohio, 1911) learned of the existence of a local fraternity, Pi Epsilon Beta, at the College of William and Mary. Reverend Cromer assisted the group in submitting a petition to become a chapter of Phi Kappa Tau, and on November 12, 1926, twenty-four men signed the Alpha Theta charter.

Pledging some of the college's most outstanding men, the chapter prospered through the depression, overcoming a brief slump in membership in 1936. Like so many Phi Tau chapters, Alpha Theta was inactive during the latter part of World War II but was quickly restored in 1946. The college built a lodge for the chapter in 1948, and Alpha Theta operated successfully until 1981, when the chapter was closed by the university for disciplinary reasons.

In 1986 Gene Napierski (Rensselaer, 1985) transferred to the college and, with Joseph Walsh, began to organize an interest group. Alpha Theta alumni James Kelly, Thomas Athey, and William Miller all assisted in the effort.

Forty-eight undergraduates and ten of the colony's alumni signed the new Alpha Theta charter on April 8, 1989. Original charter member M. Carl Andrews spoke at the installation.

ALPHA IOTA CHAPTER
University of Pennsylvania
Philadelphia, Pennsylvania

Founded as Sigma Alpha,
January 11, 1924
Chartered as Phi Kappa Tau,
November 19, 1926

THIRTY-THREE MEMBERS of Sigma Alpha Fraternity petitioned Phi Kappa Tau for a charter in May 1926. Charles A. Seaman was president when the Alpha Iota charter was granted in November 1926.

The chapter's first home was at 232 South 39th Street. The Alpha Iota Association of Phi Kappa Tau, Inc., purchased a larger home at 2902 Locust Street in 1930. Growth was steady until 1935, when university officials suspended the chapter's recruiting privileges because of "illegal rushing." The suspension was later lifted, but that loss of potential members, coupled with the general financial difficulties of the 1930s, doomed the chapter. The Locust Street house was lost to foreclosure in 1938, and the chapter closed its doors on the eve of World War II in 1941.

ALPHA KAPPA CHAPTER
Washington State University
Pullman, Washington

Founded as Omega Phi,
January 1925
Chartered as Phi Kappa Tau,
June 4, 1927

THE IDEA FOR a new fraternity at Washington State was conceived by a group of students during the winter of 1923–24. Chester Calbick was the first president, and Homer J. Dana was the first faculty member and became the first advisor. The group chose the name Omega Phi because one of the engineering students knew that the two letters were used in electrical calculations. A ritual was designed from the pieces of other fraternities' rituals that friends were willing to reveal. A first house was rented at 1718 A Street in the summer of 1924, and two years later the fraternity obtained a mortgage to buy a former Delta Delta Delta Sorority house at 300 Colorado.

In 1927 the local petitioned Phi Kappa Tau, and upon approval, the installation took place in the parish house of the local Episcopal church.

In 1938 Alpha Kappa Chapter moved into its newly constructed home at 607 California Street. Advisor Homer J. Dana oversaw the construction and the financial affairs of the chapter. While the house was rented out during World War II and Professor Dana was in military service, Mrs. Dana ran the corporation.

Soon after the war, the thirty-two-man house was jammed with forty-five brothers, and in 1955 four lots adjacent to the chapter house were purchased for further expansion.

ΑΛ

ALPHA LAMBDA CHAPTER
Auburn University
Auburn, Alabama

Founded as Sigma Theta,
October 9, 1922
Chartered as Phi Kappa Tau,
December 3, 1927

THE SIGMA THETA Fraternity petitioned Phi Kappa Tau for a charter in 1927. Grand President Taylor had visited the local on his way to the Florida installation in March 1926 and encouraged the petition.

With approval of the existing chapters, the Alpha Lambda charter was presented to the new chapter on December 3, 1927.

The chapter grew steadily until the advent of World War II, when the chapter closed briefly. The local fraternity Kappa Phi petitioned to reopen Alpha Lambda in 1942; the charter returned on May 16, 1942, and the reorganized chapter managed to survive the war.

An alumni group called the Alpha Lambda Club formed on April 14, 1947, and incorporated as the chapter's house corporation. A new, modern house was completed in 1951.

Alpha Lambda has provided one national president, Walter G. (Sonny) Strange, Jr. (1989–93).

ΑΜ

ALPHA MU CHAPTER
Ohio Wesleyan University
Delaware, Ohio

Founded as Phi Alpha Pi,
May 1923
Chartered as Phi Kappa Tau,
March 16, 1928

PHI ALPHA PI was established at Ohio Wesleyan in May 1923. After working for over a year to obtain permission from Phi Kappa Tau, the members were finally encouraged

to petition in the fall of 1927. The charter was granted, and the installation took place in March 1928. The installation team included five national presidents: Harry A. Taylor, Edgar Ewing Brandon, Ewing T. Boles, John V. Cotton, and Ernest N. Littleton.

On February 22, 1930, Alpha Mu absorbed the ten-year-old Kappa Delta Alpha local fraternity in special initiation ceremonies. The depression took its toll on Alpha Mu, and the chapter folded in 1935.

With the help of the national fraternity, the house corporation purchased a house at 120 North Washington Street for a new group of men who were reviving Alpha Mu in 1949. The newly awakened chapter continued until 1957, when it failed once again. It has not been revived.

ΑΝ

ALPHA NU CHAPTER
Iowa State University
Ames, Iowa

Founded as Alpha Kappa Delta,
May 19, 1920
Chartered as Phi Kappa Tau,
May 19, 1928

A TIGHT-KNIT GROUP of friends decided to start their own fraternity rather than be split up by joining those that already existed in May 1920. They adopted the name Alpha Kappa Delta. After several years, they began to have difficulty competing with the national fraternities and petitioned Phi Kappa Tau for a charter. In May 1928 the Alpha Nu charter was delivered at a banquet held in the basement of a local Presbyterian church.

Gerald Lineweaver was the first president of Alpha Nu Chapter and remained an active supporter of the chapter for his entire life.

In the depression year of 1937, the chapter was down to five members, and the mortgage holder foreclosed on its house at 158 Hyland. The group was able to rent another house and hold the chapter together until the final two years of World War II, when the chapter was inactive.

By the fall of 1946, alumni and returning undergraduates revived the chapter, and a house was occupied beginning on September 1, 1947. Within a year, arrangements were made to purchase a house at 218 Welch.

A larger home purchased in the 1960s housed the chapter through the 1980s when it fell into disrepair and was condemned by the city of Ames. In September 1990 the empty house burned in an arson fire. Alumni rallied around the chapter and raised funds to build a new thirty-two-man house which was completed in January 1993 and its library was dedicated to the chapter's first president, Gerald Lineweaver.

ALPHA XI CHAPTER
West Virginia University
Morgantown, West Virginia

*Founded as Tau Theta Rho,
fall 1923
Chartered as Phi Kappa Tau,
November 10, 1928*

ONE OF PHI KAPPA TAU'S most prolific organizers, Paul F. Opp, helped to form the Tau Theta Rho local at West Virginia University in 1923. Opp was teaching at Fairmont State College nearby. The group quickly grew to become one of West Virginia's strongest fraternities. The local asked Phi Kappa Tau for permission to petition as early as 1924, but it took until 1928 for a petition to be accepted.

Installation ceremonies took place in November 1928, and the degree team included Grand President Isaac Miles Wright, past Grand President Edgar Ewing Brandon, Grand Secretary R. K. Bowers, Domain Chief Paul F. Opp, and Founder Taylor A. Borradaile, who was participating in his first chapter installation.

Alpha Xi Chapter occupied seven different houses between 1924 and 1943, when the chapter closed after all of the members entered military service. Alumni decided not to reopen the chapter immediately after the war, and it has remained inactive.

ALPHA OMICRON CHAPTER
Lafayette College
Easton, Pennsylvania

*Founded as Delta Sigma,
February 4, 1925
Chartered as Phi Kappa Tau,
December 8, 1928*

CLAYTON R. HORTON, a member of the Sigma Alpha local at the University of Pennsylvania that later became Alpha Iota Chapter, brought the idea of forming a fraternity to the Lafayette campus. A banquet on February 4, 1925, marked the beginning of Delta Sigma Fraternity at Lafayette. Three charter members worked with Horton and a faculty advisor to develop a constitution, a ritual, a badge, and a pledge pin.

With a membership of twenty-eight, the group petitioned Phi Kappa Tau for a charter in 1928. The installation took place on December 8, 1928. The charter members were initiated at the lodge rooms of Vanderveer Hall, and the new members gathered in the Gold Room of the Hotel Easton to receive the Alpha Omicron charter.

In 1933 the chapter was financially strapped and forced to give up its house. To survive, Alpha Omicron absorbed two local fraternities, the Arrows (founded in 1920) and Sphinx (founded in 1921). The merged organization survived until 1937, when the chapter finally failed.

Dr. L. Shimer Serfass, who had been president of the chapter in 1930, led the effort to revive the chapter after World War II. Field

Secretary Harold E. "Hap" Angelo helped in the effort, and Edward Blair, a transfer from Muhlenberg, got the old chapter back on its feet.

The chapter prospered until declining membership forced it to close its doors in February 1975.

ΑΠ

ALPHA PI CHAPTER
University of Washington
Seattle, Washington

Founded as Sigma Tau Epsilon, December 1926
Chartered as Phi Kappa Tau, April 6, 1929

WORTHINESS, trustfulness, and honor were the founding principles of Sigma Tau Epsilon, founded on the University of Washington campus in December 1926. Ray Miller was elected president in January, and purple and white were the fraternity colors. A diamond-shaped badge also was adopted, and by the end of January a simple ritual was written.

Upon the approval of Sigma Tau Epsilon's petition to Phi Kappa Tau, April 6, 1929, was the date set for the installation. The ceremonies concluded with an installation ball at the Olympic Hotel.

In 1940 the chapter purchased the former Pi Beta Phi Sorority house on Seventeenth Avenue and converted it into a fraternity home. The chapter operated during World War II through the 1942–43 school year, when an alumnus began to manage the house as a home for war workers in the area. Six men reopened the chapter in March 1946. After the war, the membership exploded, and the house proved to be too small. In 1954 the chapter was able to buy the former Alpha Gamma Delta Sorority house, which was in good condition and suited to the chapter's needs. The house has served Alpha Pi well since that time.

ΑΡ

ALPHA RHO CHAPTER
Georgia Institute of Technology
Atlanta, Georgia

Founded as Pi Lambda Rho, fall 1921
Chartered as Phi Kappa Tau, April 27, 1929

C. F. HALLBERG and several of his closest friends founded Pi Lambda Rho in 1921, and the group gained the recognition of the Pan-Hellenic Council in January 1922. By the start of the next school year, the fraternity was renting a house on Peachtree Street.

A petition committee formed in 1924 began to look at possible national organizations with which to affiliate, and soon Phi Kappa Tau was a target. Robert M. Ervin (Centre, 1920), a member of the faculty, helped with the petition process. Though contact was made with Phi Kappa Tau as early as 1924, a petition was not approved until March 1929.

Installation took place in April 1929, when the charter members were initiated at the Knights of Columbus hall. The installation banquet followed the initiations at the Atlanta Athletic Club. The chapter was successful until 1939, when a perilously small membership prevented the reopening of the chapter house in the fall.

Robert Ervin played a major role in reestablishing the chapter with the influx of veterans in 1946. The chapter rapidly grew from seven to thirty-two men in 125 days.

ΑΣ

ALPHA SIGMA CHAPTER
Colorado State University
Fort Collins, Colorado

Founded as Alpha Kappa, March 16, 1921
Chartered as Phi Kappa Tau, November 16, 1929

ALPHA KAPPA Fraternity was founded in 1921 by five men who wanted to promote scholarship and provide activities for the members. In 1925 the fraternity purchased a house at 729 Peterson Street, four blocks from the campus. C. O. Simmonds (Nebraska Wesleyan, 1929), secretary of the college YMCA, became closely associated with the local and suggested that it investigate Phi Kappa Tau. A petition was approved in 1929 after overcoming the objections of Psi Chapter at

Colorado, who had opposed Alpha Kappa's petition.

Alpha Sigma Chapter was installed in November 1929. Charter members were initiated in the American Legion Hall, the banquet was held at the Hotel Northern, and a dance followed at the Union Building on campus.

In 1930 the chapter moved to 425 South College Avenue; and in 1935 the chapter moved to 415 South Remington, staying until 1942, when a house was rented at 718 College Avenue. The chapter closed during the 1942–43 school year and was reestablished at 708 South Remington in 1947. The house corporation purchased that house in 1952, and the chapter remained in that property until its current house was purchased in 1963.

In 1976 the chapter was in severe financial difficulty and in risk of losing the house, when former Chapter President Harold H. Short bought the house and donated it to the Phi Kappa Tau Foundation. The foundation still owns the property. Short was elected to the National Council in 1981 and became national president in 1985.

ALPHA TAU CHAPTER
Cornell University
Ithaca, New York

Skull Fraternity, founded 1901
Bandhu Society, founded 1902
Merged to form Phi Delta Sigma, 1918
Chartered as Phi Kappa Tau,
October 24, 1930

PHI DELTA SIGMA, the local that petitioned to become Alpha Tau Chapter, was founded in 1918 as a merger of two societies that were both older than Phi Kappa Tau, Skull and Bandhu. Skull had been founded in 1901 and purchased a house at 96 Wait Avenue in 1908. In 1902 eight Cornell students founded an organization which they named Bandhu, a Sanskrit word denoting "good fellowship." In 1910 the members raised $3,000 to buy a house and were given the opportunity to purchase the home of a Prof. Tanner, who had come to respect the organization. This spacious home on The Knoll remains in Alpha Tau's hands to this day, though the chapter temporarily ceased operations in June, 1995.

With declining membership during World War I, Bandhu changed its name to Phi Delta Sigma, and Skull merged with that organization thereafter. The Skull house was sold to Cornell; the Bandhu house was retained. Phi Delta Sigma decided to petition Phi Kappa Tau for a charter in 1930, and the installation was conducted in October. The new Alpha Tau Chapter survived the

depression but was forced to close in June 1943 for the duration of World War II. The house was rented for an army training program, and it stood empty in 1944–45. It was rented to Sigma Alpha Epsilon during 1945–46 while Alpha Tau regrouped.

Bandhu, Skull, Phi Delta Sigma, and Alpha Tau Chapter alumni have all remained loyal to the organization, and many have had considerable success in business and the professions.

ALPHA UPSILON CHAPTER
Colgate University
Hamilton, New York

Founded as Delta Pi Sigma,
March 1927
Chartered as Phi Kappa Tau,
May 22, 1937

ALEXANDER J. SUNDBERG was the first president of the local Delta Pi Sigma, founded at Colgate in 1927, becoming the thirteenth fraternity at the school. The members of Delta Pi Sigma purchased a $14,000 home on the fraternity row in 1928. It was a close-knit organization, limiting its membership to thirty-five for many years.

From its beginning, Delta Pi Sigma had considered the eventual affiliation with a national fraternity. Through Dr. Everett Cox (Miami, 1927), who joined the physics faculty in 1933, it learned about Phi Kappa Tau, and a dialogue was opened with the fraternity in 1936. A personal visit from National Secretary Richard J. Young persuaded the local to petition for a charter. Upon approval, the installation was scheduled for May 21–22, 1937. Founder Shideler presided at the installation and gave the principal banquet address at the Colgate Inn.

Alpha Upsilon was immediately one of Phi Kappa Tau's strongest chapters, and its members maintained a high standard of scholarship and campus involvement. Friction with the national fraternity began in the 1950s, when Alpha Upsilon became a leader in the effort to break down the racial and religious barriers maintained in most chapters. In the early 1960s, the chapter wrote its own ritual because some of its members objected to the religious content of Phi Kappa Tau's Ritual. The National Council made two serious efforts to make changes to the Ritual that would be acceptable to Alpha Upsilon, but national convention delegates did not accept these changes and pressured the recalcitrant Colgate men to conform.

Rather than conform, the chapter chose to secede from the national fraternity and since 1972 has operated as a local fraternity, Phi Tau.

The chapter has many outstanding alumni and has the distinction of being the only chapter to provide the fraternity with two executive directors, Jack L. Anson and John W. Meyerhoff.

In 1988 the Delta Pi Sigma Alumni Corporation published a book, *Scholarship and Brotherhood: The Story of Delta Pi Sigma, Phi Kappa Tau and Phi Tau at Colgate University*, by Watson Fenimore.

ΑΦ

ALPHA PHI CHAPTER
University of Akron
Akron, Ohio

*Founded as Sigma Beta Nu,
February 19, 1923
Chartered as Phi Kappa Tau,
February 20, 1938*

SIGMA BETA NU was founded at the University of Akron in a period of tremendous growth in enrollment. On February 19, 1923, the first nine men officially pledged their loyalty to the new organization. Quickly the fraternity began to recruit new members and to get involved in campus and fraternity activities.

The Akron Fraternal Home Holding Company was incorporated in 1924, and a $15,000 home was purchased. Sigma Beta Nu petitioned Phi Kappa Tau for a charter in 1937; the installation ceremonies took place on February 20, 1938. Past National Presidents John V. Cotton (an Akron resident), Ewing T. Boles, and Ernest N. Littleton participated in the installation. One hundred eight members were initiated during the three days of ceremonies establishing Alpha Phi Chapter.

Alpha Phi continued to prosper after the installation and managed not to close during World War II, although as few as two undergraduates remained. Part of the house was rented to a sorority. Alpha Phi was well known in Akron for its luncheon program run by longtime Advisor Harmon O. DeGraff. A different prominent leader from business, government, or other organizations spoke to the chapter over lunch each week.

Alpha Phi alumni have had a remarkable influence in local and national politics. Ray Bliss was chairman of the Republican national committee and John Ballard, Roy Ray, and Tom Sawyer controlled the Akron mayor's office for twenty years (1966–86). Sawyer is now a member of the U.S. House of Representatives.

ΑΧ

ALPHA CHI CHAPTER
Mississippi State University
Starkville, Mississippi

*Founded as Phi Tau Club, fall 1937
Founded as Phi Kappa Tau,
April 30, 1938*

PROF. PAUL H. DUNN, a protégé and former student of Dr. William H. Shideler, brought together a group of sixteen men in the fall of 1937 to organize a Phi Tau Club. Professor Dunn provided a vacant room in the geology department as temporary headquarters.

The installation took place over the weekend of April 30, 1938. Dr. Brandon and Dr. Shideler both participated in the installation.

The chapter grew quickly until the advent of World War II, when Alpha Chi temporarily ceased operation. Six returning members reestablished the chapter in February 1946. The Korean War hit the chapter hard, with two entire pledge classes being drafted.

Thomas L. Stennis II, from a distinguished Mississippi family, won the Shideler Award in 1960 and later served the fraternity as domain director and national president. The award for the outstanding domain director is named in his memory.

In 1960 the first house was purchased at 304 South Jackson Street. It was condemned in 1987, and a house was rented at 19 Page Street in the Cotton District from 1988 to 1990. Mrs. Paul H. Dunn cut the ribbon on the new thirty-six-man Alpha Chi chapter house on September 7, 1991.

Jerry Clower, longtime member of the Grand Ole Opry and country comedian is Alpha Chi's most widely known member.

ΑΨ

ALPHA PSI CHAPTER
University of Texas–El Paso
El Paso, Texas

*Founded as Rho Sigma Phi,
December 20, 1939
Chartered as Phi Kappa Tau,
May 10, 1941*

J. D. LAMBETH and Robert C. Carlson worked during the fall of 1939 to build a new fraternity to compete with the two existing locals at Texas Western College (now UTEP). The school granted a charter to Rho Sigma Phi Fraternity in December. After having considerable success on the campus, Rho Sigma Phi petitioned Phi Kappa Tau for a charter in 1941.

Installation ceremonies took place May 8, 9, and 10, 1941, and Phi Kappa Tau's Alpha Psi Chapter became the first national fraternity chapter on the campus. National President Roland Maxwell presented the charter to Chapter President William Calderhead. Following the installation banquet at the Hotel Cortez, the new chapter entertained five hundred guests at a formal dance at the El Paso Country Club.

Chartered on the eve of World War II, the chapter survived that period with great difficulty but did remain open through the war. After several years of postwar growth, the chapter dedicated a newly built lodge on the campus in May 1955.

The chapter is now inactive.

ΑΩ

ALPHA OMEGA CHAPTER
Baldwin-Wallace College
Berea, Ohio

*Founded as German Verein
Literary Society, August 1859
Changed to Gordian Society,
January 1918
Changed to Zeta Kappa,
October 9, 1922
Chartered as Phi Kappa Tau,
May 10, 1943*

ONLY ONE OTHER Phi Kappa Tau chapter has historical roots as long as Alpha Omega's. The chapter traces its history back to the German Verein Literary Society, founded by seven members of the German department of Baldwin University in 1859. In 1864 the Baldwin German department became a part of the new Wallace College. The merger of Baldwin University and Wallace College in 1913 strengthened the German Verein Society, which soon dropped the German language from its programs. The group adopted the name Gordian Society because of the anti-German sentiments of World War I, and in 1922 the name was again changed to Zeta Kappa. A house was acquired in the 1930s.

Careful investigation by undergraduates and alumni recommended affiliation with Phi Kappa Tau, and the Alpha Omega charter was granted on May 16, 1942. For many years, the chapter lived in the Dunham Estate at 325 Front Street in Berea. In 1963 the college built on-campus housing for its fraternities, which included housing for fifty men, ample public areas for social and chapter events and a private chapter room.

BA

BETA ALPHA CHAPTER
University of Texas
Austin, Texas

Founded as Phi Theta Tau,
June 21, 1942
Chartered as Phi Kappa Tau,
February 6, 1943

PHI THETA TAU was founded by twenty students at the University of Texas in June 1942. The group soon became a Phi Kappa Tau colony and occupied a house at 2306 Sabine that could hold about eighteen men.

Installation ceremonies were conducted by National President Roland Maxwell and National Secretary Richard Young on February 6, 1943, as many Phi Tau chapters were closing under the stresses of war. Initiation teams from Mississippi State and Texas–El Paso handled the initiation of the twenty-nine charter members.

The chapter struggled through the duration of the war and began to rebuild in the fall of 1945. A new house was rented, and soon the chapter was operating on a peace-time basis.

A major fund-raising drive began in the middle 1950s for a long-awaited house, which was finally completed in 1964. The house slept twenty-four and had facilities for 120 at social functions. Founder and Mrs. Taylor A. Borradaile attended the dedication in November, 1964. After closing for a time, Beta Alpha was reorganized in 1979 and rechartered in 1982.

THE PHI TAU FIFTIES

Within weeks of the Japanese surrender in August 1945, Phi Kappa Tau's National Secretary Richard J. Young had traded his navy uniform for a business suit and was back in his Oxford office putting the pieces of a war-strained fraternity back together. "Prospects for Phi Kappa Tau are brighter than at any time in the Fraternity's 40-year history," Young declared in the February 1946 *Laurel*. "All chapters are not back in operation, but an excellent start has been made, and there is every reason to expect that many more will be restored by the fall of 1946. The

goal is to return to the 49 schools in which chapters are located. The Central Office is working with might and main to return to peacetime basis of operation." *Laurel* headlines were already proclaiming "Fall Initiations at All-Time High" and "Rushing Breaks All Records."

In addition to the efforts to rebuild existing chapters, expansion work began immediately. Prof. Morton Walker (Kentucky, 1930), a faculty member in the University of Louisville's engineering program, selected a core group of five undergraduates who, with the help of the Louisville alumni association, devel-

oped into Beta Beta Chapter, the fraternity's fiftieth, which was chartered on May 30, 1947.

Typical of the thousands of veterans returning home to attend college, taking advantage of the GI Bill of Rights, was a twenty-four-year-old infantry veteran of the European theater, Sgt. Jack L. Anson. Coming home in the fall of 1946 to Huntington, Indiana, where he had been a cub reporter for Huntington's newspaper, the *Herald-Press*, out of high school, Jack was planning to attend Indiana University. For Jack, like so many other veterans, a college education had been only a dream before the war. Now that he had the opportunity, he was impatient to start school but found out that it was too late in the fall to register at Indiana. However, he learned from a friend in the service that he could still enroll at prestigious Colgate University in Hamilton, New York. Once at Colgate, he fell in love with the school, enrolled, and soon chose English as a major. In March 1947, Anson was asked to join Colgate's Alpha Upsilon Chapter of Phi Kappa Tau, an offer that he readily accepted.

VICTORY CONVENTION

Just as the fraternity had done for the last convention before the war, it returned to an Indiana resort for the June 1947 "Victory Convention" at the Hotel Spink on Lake Wawasee. Jack Anson was elected to represent Alpha Upsilon's resident council at the convention, because he lived nearest the convention site. At the first of twenty-one Phi Tau conventions Anson was to attend over the next forty-two years, he met some of the true giants of the fraternity, including Roland Maxwell, Dr. Shideler, Dr. Brandon, and six other past national presidents.

It was a bittersweet convention.

While everyone was invigorated by the fraternity's rapid recovery and prospects for the future, many, like Anson, were veterans and keenly aware of the tremendous price that so many members of the fraternity had paid to achieve victory in the world war.

Past National President Harry A. Taylor conducted the moving memorial service for the 151 members of Phi Kappa Tau who had given their lives. After quoting Lincoln's Gettysburg Address, Dr. Taylor closed his remarks, saying, "It is for us who live to bear their torch, to resolutely advance their beloved fraternity, and to emulate their indomitable spirit." As Russell Danburg (Lawrence, 1928) played soft background music on the piano, secretary Young read the list of 151 Gold Star brothers into the official minutes of the convention.

The primary agenda for the convention was to discuss the business of Phi Kappa Tau that had been neglected during the war. Russell Danburg was chosen to edit his first of several

Delegates to the victory convention at Lake Wawasee, Indiana, June 1947

editions of the *Phi Tau Songbook*, and the thirty-year-old coat of arms underwent its last significant change, being simplified by deleting certain symbols that did not conform to heraldic strictures. Donald A. Pearce (California, 1921) and Ernest F. Nippes, Jr. (Rensselaer, 1935), were elected to the National Council, replacing A. C. Eichberg and Ernest V. Price, who had had no idea their six-year commitments would turn into eleven-year terms when they were elected back in 1936. Roland Maxwell entered his fourteenth year as national president.

POST-WAR EXPANSION

No time in the history of fraternities had presented such a fantastic opportunity for expansion. Secretary Young, Dr. Shideler, Roland Maxwell, and other Phi Kappa Tau leaders had been anticipating the opportunity for expansion ever since it had become apparent that victory was imminent. They were keenly aware of the success Phi Kappa Tau had had in expansion following World War I, and they were eager to capitalize

upon this unique opportunity. But most other national fraternities had the same idea, so aggressive action was important. In his address to the Wawasee convention, President Maxwell set a goal of establishing twenty-five additional chapters for a total of seventy-five by the fraternity's fiftieth anniversary in 1956. An enormous step toward that goal was taken in the 1947–48 school year, when twelve colonies were established.

Three field secretaries joined the Central Office staff to help Dick Young manage the aggressive expansion program, including future National President Harold E. "Hap" Angelo (Mississippi State, 1942), who became the first postwar field secretary in February 1947, just out of the Marine Corps. Young wanted a war veteran in the job who could exert some influence on the ex-servicemen who were swelling the ranks of the chapters. Young had confided to Shideler before the end of the war that the veterans would "exert a mighty influence—for good and bad—on the younger men."

Chapters were installed at nine new campuses in the two years between the 1947 and 1949 national conventions. Four Phi Taus on the campus of the University of Idaho established a colony which was chartered as Beta Gamma Chapter in December 1947. In Florida, Beta Delta Chapter at the University of Miami became the fraternity's southernmost chapter during installation ceremonies on February 28, 1948.

Past National President John V. Cotton, a charter member of Delta Chapter at Centre College, returned the original Delta charter on April 10, 1948 to eleven undergraduates

Coat of arms as revised at the 1947 convention

Founders Shideler and Boyd at Alpha Chapter's Founders' Day, 1948

who were working to restore Phi Kappa Tau to the Danville, Kentucky, campus. Delta had been dormant since the depression year of 1934.

By the 1948–49 school year, every prewar chapter had been restored except those at Coe, Wisconsin, New York University, Kansas State, Pennsylvania, and West Virginia. Jack L. Anson, who had graduated in just two years, Thomas W. Athey (William and Mary, 1942), and Birney A. Stokes (Pennsylvania State, 1947) assumed the three field secretary positions at the Central Office in the fall of 1948.

Phi Kappa Tau was the first national fraternity to enter Mississippi Southern College (now Southern Mississippi) when the local fraternity Beta Kappa Tau was installed as Beta Epsilon Chapter on October 15, 1948. The fraternity's first two chapters in New Mexico were chartered

on two successive days in November 1948. President Maxwell and Domain Chief Lou Gerding took part in ceremonies establishing Beta Zeta Chapter at New Mexico College of Agriculture and Mechanics (now New Mexico State) on November 15, 1948, and the next evening at Beta Eta Chapter at the University of New Mexico.

Just two days later, in Lawrence, Kansas, a colony at the University of Kansas became the Beta Theta Chapter. Chapter President Alan Pickering (Kansas, 1948) would serve as the fraternity's educational director some forty years later. For the first time in the fraternity's history, the national fraternity used its assets to purchase a house, which it leased to the new chapter at Kansas.

In unique ceremonies at Florida State University, Phi Kappa Tau, along with six other national fraternities, chartered the school's first seven fraternity chapters at once in an enormous installation banquet on the Tallahassee campus on March 5, 1949. The petitioning local Gamma Phi Fraternity was founded on December 1, 1947.

In four days in May 1949, new chapters were chartered in three states. Beta Kappa was installed at Oklahoma State on May 16, Beta Lambda was installed at Indiana University on May 18, and Beta Mu became Phi Kappa Tau's sixtieth chapter at Kent State University, the ninth chapter in Ohio. Don Ebright (Ohio State, 1921), treasurer of the state of Ohio, was toastmaster at the Kent installation banquet.

MEMBERSHIP RESTRICTIONS RECONSIDERED

At the Elms resort hotel in Excelsior Springs, Missouri, just outside Kansas City, delegates to the fraternity's Thirtieth National Convention began to grapple with the issue of racial and religious membership restrictions. Though the idea of restricting membership to white men was not a part of the founding principles of the fraternity, that racial restriction had found its way into the new National Constitution adopted in 1936. By 1949 many members of the fraternity were uncomfortable with these restrictions and believed that it was time for the racial barrier to come down, though Phi Kappa Tau's first African-American member was probably not initiated until 1954.

Lengthy discussions resulted in two actions—a compromise of sorts. First, restrictive language was removed from the constitution to simply state: "Any male student not a member of a national college fraternity other than an honor society or professional fraternity, who is pursuing undergraduate, post-graduate or professional study, or is a member of the faculty of the institution where a chapter of Phi Kappa Tau is located, may be pledged and initiated into Phi Kappa Tau Fraternity." But that noble move was tempered by the adoption of a "declaration of policy," which would continue to be debated and altered at many coming conventions. This policy, binding on all chapters but not a part of the National Constitution or statutes, stated that "Phi Kappa Tau as a national fraternity includes members from all sections of the country and of widely varying viewpoints. In selecting pledges and members, a chapter has the obligation to keep in mind the varying viewpoints and shall not select any man who for any reason would cause embarrassment to the other chapters or their members."

Dr. Shideler wrote at length about the issue. His views seem to reflect the action of the convention. He was against an overt policy of discrimination but was staunchly opposed to the infringement on the rights of a fraternity to freely associate. Further, he believed that it was important that no chapter initiate a member who would be objectionable to others. The inherent difficulty with this idea was that certain chapters, if they forced the issue, could object to any member pledged by a more progressive chapter.

Other important actions of the Thirtieth National Convention included the approval of the new Key Award to be given to an alumnus for outstanding contributions to a chapter. It was first given to Paul DeCora (Akron, 1938), a member of the University of Kansas faculty, who had been helpful in establishing Beta Theta Chapter. Domain Chief Lou Gerding, who had been active in the establishment of the two chapters in New Mexico, and Morton Walker, founder of the Beta Beta at Louisville, were elected to the National Council.

—THE FIELD SECRETARY ARRIVES!

—by Don Gibbons, ΛΤ

The aggressive expansion program continued into the 1949–50 school year, bearing new chapters in the Far West, the South, and in the East and establishing the first Phi Tau outpost in New England.

The nearly twenty-five-year-old local Kappa Phi Sigma became Beta Nu Chapter at San Diego State University on February 24, 1950. Thirty-two members of a colony at the University of Georgia became Beta Xi on March 10, and four days later President Maxwell and Secretary Richard Young installed Beta Omicron at the University of Maryland. Ned Brooks (Ohio State, 1922), moderator of "Meet the Press" on NBC radio, was toastmaster and Founder Borradaile came from his Washington, D.C., home as well. Beta Pi Chapter became the fraternity's first in New England, when a colony at Middlebury College in Vermont was installed on March 16, 1950, two days after the Maryland chartering.

President Maxwell had been personally involved in efforts to establish a chapter at the University of California, Los Angeles. Beta Rho was installed at UCLA on May 12. And a week later, at the University of Idaho in Pocatello, a colony started by transfer students Bernard "Gus" Bengal (Colorado, 1947) and Culbertson Martin (New Mexico, 1948) became Beta Sigma Chapter.

The Korean conflict in the early 1950s did not have a significant effect on the membership of existing chapters, but it curtailed the fraternity's rapid expansion program. Field Secretary Anson was recalled into the service and temporarily left Dick Young short-handed in the office.

FOUNDER BOYD DIES

Honored Founder Clinton D. Boyd, Sr., entered chapter eternal on September 29, 1950, when the car he was driving to the Ohio Republican convention skidded into the path of a truck four miles west of Lebanon, Ohio, on U.S. 42. His wife was seriously injured, and her sister also was killed in the accident. A large contingent of Phi Taus from southwestern Ohio attended the funeral. Boyd's son, Clinton D. Boyd, Jr. (Miami, 1948), whom Founder Boyd had helped to initiate, was an undergraduate at Miami when his father died.

When Delta Phi Beta Fraternity at Bowling Green State University in Ohio began to consider national affiliation early in 1950, it gave Phi Kappa Tau an opportunity to enter a school it had long had its eye on. Through the influence of past National President Ernest N. Littleton, a member of the National Council and well-known Bowling Green school principal, the local chose to become Beta Tau Chapter. Four national presidents attended the installation, including Littleton, Ewing T. Boles, Founder Shideler, and Roland Maxwell on November 17, 1950.

MAXWELL WRITES CREED

At a meeting of the National Council on November 19, 1950, immediately following the installation weekend at Bowling Green, President Roland Maxwell wrote the "Creed of Phi Kappa Tau." Details of just how he came to write the creed are not clear, but it seems that it was a pragmatic decision—a brainstorm. Maxwell, so the legend goes, simply wrote the creed out in longhand on a scrap of paper. Those words, now memorized by almost every new member of the fraternity and recited at conventions and chapter events across the country, state in succinct terms what it means to be a member of Phi Kappa Tau:

"Phi Kappa Tau, by admitting me to membership, has conferred upon me a mark of distinction in which I take just pride. I believe in the spirit of brotherhood for which it stands. I shall strive to attain its ideals, and by so doing to bring to it honor and credit. I shall be loyal to my college and my chapter and keep strong my ties to them that I may ever retain the spirit of youth. I shall be a good and loyal citizen. I shall try always to discharge the obligation to others which arises from the fact that I am a fraternity man."

The number of inactive chapters was reduced to four when twenty-nine members of Chi Beta Phi at Coe College reactivated Iota Chapter, closed since the depression year of 1934. Chi Beta Phi was founded in 1930 when two older societies founded in 1909 and 1917 merged.

BEDFORD SPRINGS CONVENTION

At the Bedford Springs Hotel in Pennsylvania, the fraternity assembled for its Thirty-first National Convention. It was not uncommon for two Founders to attend a convention. Shideler and Boyd had been together many times, and Douglass had joined Shideler for the 1917 convention. But 1951 was the first national convention for Taylor Borradaile, though he had participated in two chapter installations and activities of the Washington, D.C., alumni association. Shideler was widely known in the fraternity, but it was a special treat for delegates at Bedford Springs to get to know Founder and Mrs. Borradaile. They enjoyed the meeting so much that they attended every convention for the next twenty-five years.

Attorney Hugh C. Nichols and Prof. H. Adam Durham (Nebraska Wesleyan, 1923) were elected to six-year terms on the National Council, and retiring Councilor Littleton was named alumni commissioner. Dean Morton Walker from Louisville was appointed scholarship commissioner.

OLYMPIC SWIM COACHES

For the 1952 Olympics in Helsinki, Finland, Matt Mann (Michigan, 1926) coached the men's swimming team, and Richard Pappenguth (Michigan, 1923) coached the women's team. Mann headed the Michigan swimming program, and Pappenguth, Mann's former student and protégé, was coach at Big Ten rival Purdue.

The local society Phi Tau, organized by C. Brandon Chenault (Cornell and Hobart, 1948) at Hobart College in Geneva, New York, became Beta Upsilon Chapter on May 17, 1952. A three-year-old local, Delta Nu, was installed as Beta Phi Chapter at Westminster College in the Amish village of New Wilmington, Pennsylvania.

National President Roland Maxwell presents a Golden Jubilee medallion to Grayson L. Kirk, 1956.

THREE COLLEGE PRESIDENTS

"Kirk Named Columbia Head as Successor to Eisenhower" was the front-page headline of *The New York Times* on January 6, 1953. Grayson Kirk, vice president and provost of 199-year-old Columbia University, had been acting president since Dwight Eisenhower took leave from the university presidency to head NATO. The appointment was effective January 19, the day before Eisenhower was inaugurated president of the United States. *The New York Times* made much of the urbane Kirk's Ohio farm upbringing and public education—but no mention of his older brother, Willard, an early member of Gamma Chapter at Ohio State who stayed on the family farm near Jeffersonville, Ohio, and was named 1953 "Corn King" at the International Livestock Exhibition in Chicago for his outstanding hybrid-corn production.

In addition to the Columbia presidency, Phi Taus captured the presidencies of two of the nation's leading public universities in the 1950s. At the University of Colorado, Ward Darley, a charter member of Psi Chapter, was inaugurated as Colorado's seventh president in 1953. Darley had headed CU's medical center and been at CU for more than thirty years as student and faculty member. William Aycock (North Carolina State, 1934) became chancellor of the University of North Carolina at Chapel Hill, where he had been a leading member of the Law School faculty.

At Transylvania, Theta Chapter dedicated a tiny chapel, eleven feet wide and twelve feet long, designed for personal devotion, in Old Morrison, the historic main building on the Transylvania campus.

FRENCH LICK CONVENTION, 1953

Returning to the sulfur-spring resort area of southern Indiana for the fourth time, the fraternity's 1953 convention was held at the French Lick Springs Hotel. A highlight was the initiation of the 20,000th member of the fraternity, W. Lee Hidy (Miami, 1953), whose father, Frank Hidy (Miami, 1925), participated. At this convention, the issue of membership restriction was debated again, as a few chapters, primarily in the East, were anxious to break the racial barrier. The only progress was a resolution: "Resolved, that it is the opinion of the

convention that the best means of insuring the continuation of our democratic society is through education; and that it is the opinion of this convention that in the future it may be possible to break down the racial barrier, but that any breaking down must come through educational means."

One of the most lasting actions of the convention was the approval of a "development fund." Alumni would be solicited for funds to develop new chapters and alumni associations for the fraternity.

Franklin and Marshall charter member Rev. Charles Spotts (Franklin and Marshall, 1921) and former Field Secretary "Hap" Angelo, who was in his final year of law school at Michigan, were elected to six-year terms on the National Council. Roland Maxwell was unanimously reelected president to begin his twentieth year in that office.

Chi Delta Chi Fraternity, with a distinguished local history dating to 1932, became Beta Chi Chapter of Phi Kappa Tau on November 24, 1953. Beta Chi, at Southern Illinois University in Carbondale, increased the fraternity roster to seventy chapters.

BUILDING BOOM

A tremendous 1950s building boom began during the 1950–51 year, when new chapter houses were built at Centre College, Auburn, and Colgate. By the middle of the decade, new houses had been dedicated at Ohio State and at Southern Mississippi, where Phi Kappa Tau was the first chapter to build a house. The Illi-

For the first time, two members of Phi Kappa Tau were serving in the U. S. House of Representatives in 1953. William C. Lantaff (Florida, 1931) and William E. McVey (Ohio, 1915) were representing districts in Florida and Illinois, respectively.

It was an all-Theta event when at Transylvania's 1955 commencement, four prominent ministers in the Christian Church (Disciples of Christ) received honorary degrees. Charles Lynn Pyatt (Transylvania, 1921) was retired president of the College of the Bible; Earl Rhodes Thompson (Transylvania, 1921), a minister at Paris, Kentucky, had initiated the effort to preserve the denomination's founding site, the Cane Ridge meeting house; Hoke S. Dickinson (Transylvania, 1925) was leading the Wilshire Boulevard Christian Church in Los Angeles; and Joseph S. Faulconer (Transylvania, 1925) was a minister at the First Christian Church of Ashland, Kentucky. Faulconer's son Harold "Ted" (Transylvania, 1951) also was graduating that day.

nois house was expanded considerably, and in Berkeley, Nu Chapter almost entirely reconstructed its house, dramatically transforming the style into a modernist showpiece. Alumni at Texas–El Paso and New Mexico designed and built lodges for their chapters.

FRATERNITY CELEBRATES FIFTY YEARS

Fiftieth anniversary Founders' Day celebrations were held across the country in the spring of 1956. Founder Shideler attended celebrations at Miami and Muhlenberg, and Founder Borradaile helped celebrate at Maryland. But the largest celebration was combined with the installation of Phi Kappa Tau's seventy-first chapter at Long Beach State University. Members of the Southern California alumni association, the Pi resident council, and the Beta Rho resident council all attended the March 17, 1956, installation of the newest chapter.

Phi Kappa Tau entered her Golden Jubilee year in outstanding condition, with strong and stable leadership. Maxwell had been president for twenty-two years, and Young had been secretary for twenty-seven years.

The fraternity had assets of $328,936.85; the *Laurel* Endowment Fund had grown to $220,498.98 in twenty years, and the bulk was invested in chapter-house loans. Contributions of $20,054.02 had been made to the Educational Endowment Fund, precursor to the Phi Kappa Tau Foundation.

In all, 22,705 men had been initiated, with 96 percent still living. Seventy-one charters had been granted, and sixty-five of those chapters were operating.

John Heisey (Miami, 1948) directing the Phi Tau Warblers at the Golden Jubilee convention, 1956

The Golden Jubilee celebration held at Miami University in June 1956, showcased some of Phi Kappa Tau's great successes. Hugh C. Nichols, chairman of the Miami University board of trustees, was general chairman, and two featured speakers were Grayson Kirk, president of Columbia University, and Fred Hall, the recently elected governor of Kansas, the first Phi Tau to govern a state.

The Phi Tau Fifty Club was unveiled, and Shideler and Borradaile were there to accept their memberships along with Dean Brandon at age ninety, attending his last convention. To honor Brandon, a scholarship fund in his name was begun at Miami, with a gift of $2,500 raised mostly from Alpha alumni.

Governor Hall and Reid Morgan (Auburn and Washington, 1951), a Seattle architect, were elected to the National Council. Three hundred fifty attended the final banquet, including eight national presidents and eighty-one members of Alpha Chapter. Brothers Glenn and Dwight Britton were among the early members of Alpha who came to that dinner. Many years later, Borradaile's wife, Letha, told the story that Taylor and the Brittons began their celebration prior to the final banquet in an uptown Oxford watering hole and were having such a good time that they forgot about the banquet. The Brittons were able to slip into the back of the banquet hall, but Borradaile had to make his way to the head table, rather late and bow tie askew.

HISTORY PUBLISHED

The Golden Jubilee History of Phi Kappa Tau, a monumental work, documented the fraternity's first fifty years. A history committee was appointed at the 1953 convention, but the work fell primarily to Jack Anson, who collected material and worked closely with Shideler, the fraternity's informal historian, to write the book. The 409-page work included detailed histories of the first seventy-one chapters. It was published in 1957.

Founders Borradaile and Shideler at the Golden Jubilee banquet, 1956

Jack L. Anson (in suit) in the buffet line at the welcome luau of the 1958 Pasadena convention

BRANDON DIES *in* NINETY-SECOND YEAR

The grand old man of Phi Kappa Tau, Dr. Edgar Ewing Brandon, died at almost ninety-two on June 8, 1957. Just a week earlier, he had completed work on the manuscript of the fourth volume of his work, *Lafayette, Guest of the Nation*, which chronicled the Marquis de Lafayette's travels in the United States. His will included a $5,000 bequest to the Educational Endowment Fund, which he had been so active in establishing.

INSTALLATION *and* CONVENTION *in* CALIFORNIA

More than two years since the installation at Long Beach State, Phi Kappa Tau added another California chapter at Chico State. Beta Omega Chapter evolved from a thirty-six-year-old local fraternity, Iota Sigma, the oldest Greek-letter organization on the campus. The group had thirteen hundred alumni at the time of the installation.

Pasadena, California, was the scene for Phi Kappa Tau's 1958 convention. Roland Maxwell had originally hoped to welcome the convention to his hometown in 1932 but because of the depression, the 1932 and 1933 conventions were called off, and Purdue University was chosen as a less expensive alternative for the 1934 convention, where Maxwell was first elected president.

The meeting, held at the Huntington Sheraton Hotel, set an attendance record that still stands for a Phi Tau convention. Over five hundred delegates and guests, including many local alumni, each attended some part of the convention. W. Arthur Rush (Bethany, 1925), a Hollywood talent agent, arranged the entertainment for the convention, which ranged from a diving exhibition and the Hawaiian music of Johnny Ukulele's Polynesians at the opening luau to appearances from Doc and Kitty from television's "Gunsmoke." Rush and airline executive Carryl "Casey" Britt (Transylvania, 1935) were elected to the National Council.

Dr. William A. Hammond (Miami, 1910), president of the Phi Kappa Tau Foundation, reported to the convention that its name was changed from the Educational Endowment Fund on May 21, 1958, and that the assets of the foundation had grown substantially thanks to the Brandon bequest, an anonymous gift of $5,000 (from Dr. Shideler), and a small number of other substantial contributors. He closed his talk saying, "Let's build the Phi Kappa Tau Foundation to the point where every chapter that needs financing can have it and every able young prospect who needs help can receive it."

Founder Shideler watching the demolition of Old Main, 1958

FOUNDER SHIDELER ENTERS CHAPTER ETERNAL

As a college student, Dr. Shideler had jumped over some of the trees that now stood in the way of a hundred-foot crane that was demolishing Miami University's Old Main Building. Shielding his eyes from the sun, Shideler, now seventy-three, could see the niche in the third-story wall from where the Miami Union's mascot owl had watched over the first meeting of the Non-Fraternity Association fifty-two years before. By December 1958, the remains of Harrison Hall (as Old Main had come to be known in more recent years) would be cleared away and a new Harrison Hall would begin to rise.

Dr. Shideler never saw the new building. He died from a cerebral hemorrhage on December 18, 1958, after a very short illness. He had been in the Central Office conducting fraternity business the day he went into the hospital for the final time. Founder Shideler's pallbearers were five of his closest Phi Kappa Tau associates: Ewing Boles, Henry Hoagland, W. A. Hammond, Paul Dunn, and Richard J. Young. The sixth was Karl Limper who replaced Shideler as chairman of Miami's geology department.

The last Old Main tower comes down in 1958. The niche visible on the third floor is in the remaining wall of the Union Literary Society Hall.

The house of Gamma Alpha Chapter at Michigan Technological University, chartered in 1959

CHARTERS *to* MICHIGAN TECH *and* CINCINNATI

Even though Shideler had passed on, the ideals that he and the fraternity's Founders stood for were very much alive in a group of students at Michigan Technological University on the Upper Peninsula of Michigan. In 1957 they founded Mu Kappa Mu in opposition to the other campus fraternities and were chartered as Gamma Alpha Chapter of Phi Kappa Tau on April 24, 1959.

Gamma Beta Chapter was installed at the University of Cincinnati on November 9, 1959. It was the last charter signed by Roland Maxwell as national president and Richard J. Young as national secretary.

MAXWELL, YOUNG COMPLETE LONG TENURES

Roland Maxwell was the first Phi Tau to be elected president of the National Interfraternity Conference. He had been an NIC officer since 1958 and was serving as vice president when he was elected to the top office during the Thanksgiving weekend 1959. Because of the demands of that office, he resigned the Phi Kappa Tau presidency after more than twenty-five years, and Harold E. "Hap" Angelo was appointed by the National Council to fill the remainder of Maxwell's term.

Richard Young retired as national secretary on June 30, 1960. He had been in his position for thirty-two years and only the second man to hold the job in forty years. He had recently been involved with the formation of the Oxford Natural Gas Company and would spend his retirement working with that new firm and his real-estate interests.

It is not a cliché to say that the absence of two Phi Kappa Tau leaders of such long standing brought an end to a distinct era of Phi Kappa Tau's history. New leadership would guide Phi Kappa Tau into the 1960s, which would be a decade of revolutionary change for the fraternity and the world.

*Thomas L. Stennis II, receiving the
1961 Shideler Award from
Dr. Obed L. Snowden, chapter advisor
at Mississippi State*

Outgoing National President Harold "Hap" Angelo with incoming President W. A. Hammond in 1962

CHAPTER HISTORIES

BB

BETA BETA CHAPTER
University of Louisville
Louisville, Kentucky

Chartered as Phi Kappa Tau,
May 10, 1947

MORTON WALKER (Kentucky, 1930) founded the colony at Louisville by personally selecting prospective members from the student body and soliciting help from the Louisville alumni association.

Beta Beta became Phi Kappa Tau's fiftieth chapter in ceremonies at the Kentucky Hotel in Louisville on May 30, 1947. Morton Walker was the banquet toastmaster, and speakers included Founder Shideler, past National President E. E. Brandon, and National Secretary Richard J. Young.

During the summer of 1947, Beta Beta began negotiations to purchase a chapter house at 2020 South First Street. The house was occupied on November 7, 1947. The First Street house served the chapter for a number of years, until

the university constructed the fraternity quadrangle where Beta Beta acquired its present home.

In 1984 Beta Beta's Mitch McConnell became the second Phi Tau elected to the U.S. Senate. Shortly after his election, a dinner was given in his honor at the Kentucky Center for the Performing Arts. The dinner was attended by a large number of Beta Beta undergraduates and alumni as well as the chapter's founder, Morton Walker.

BΓ

BETA GAMMA CHAPTER
University of Idaho
Moscow, Idaho

Chartered as Phi Kappa Tau,
December 4, 1947

DOMAIN CHIEF Ernest Price called together four members of the fraternity living in Moscow, Idaho, who worked with members of nearby Alpha Kappa Chapter at the University of Washington to develop a colony at the University of Idaho. Price, who was an architect, arranged for the purchase and remodeling of a house at 730 Deakin Avenue, which was occupied by the colony in September 1947; and by October 1, the group had grown to twenty-eight.

National President Roland Maxwell presided at the installation on December 4, 1947, presenting the Beta Gamma charter to Harold Neill, the chapter's first president. In addition to Price, E. B. "Jim" Newsome (Mississippi State, 1940) was a key alumnus in the early years of the chapter, serving as house corporation treasurer and financial advisor.

When the chapter outgrew the Deakin Avenue house, a former sorority house on the Greek row became available and was purchased. This has remained the chapter's home through the present time.

BΔ

BETA DELTA CHAPTER
University of Miami
Miami, Florida

Chartered as Phi Kappa Tau,
February 29, 1948

A CORE GROUP of transfer students from the University of Florida formed the nucleus for Phi Kappa Tau at the University of Miami in 1947. Among the Alpha Eta transfers were William Kapp, John Council, H. Booth, T. Harris, T. Brumlik, and Forrest Bell.

The chapter was installed on February 29, 1948. Initiations were conducted at the Coral Gables Elks Club. The installation banquet was held at the Garden Restaurant in

Miami. Past President Edgar Ewing Brandon, who wintered in Miami, led the delegation from the Miami alumni association attending the banquet to watch National Secretary Richard Young present the Beta Delta charter to president William Kapp.

Beta Delta became inactive in 1963

BE

BETA EPSILON CHAPTER
University of Southern Mississippi
Hattiesburg, Mississippi

Founded as Beta Kappa Tau,
summer 1947
Chartered as Phi Kappa Tau,
October 15, 1948

BETA KAPPA TAU was founded on the ideals of "cooperation with other organizations for the betterment of the school, fraternal brotherhood in school and social activities and continued close coordination with the school after graduation." When Beta Kappa Tau chose to affiliate with Phi Kappa Tau, the fraternity became the first national to grant a charter at Southern Mississippi. Beta Epsilon was chartered on October 15, 1948, and the installation banquet was held at the Forrest Hotel in Hattiesburg, with Founder William H. Shideler as the principal speaker. Members of Alpha Chi Chapter at Mississippi State conducted the initiation of the thirty new members. Sam B. Tidwell, who would later serve as domain chief and national alumni commissioner, was initiated as a faculty sponsor.

On September 22, 1949, Beta Epsilon dedicated its first chapter house. The governor of Mississippi attended the housewarming. In September 1955, the chapter opened the first fraternity house to be constructed on the Southern Mississippi campus. The modern home was built to house forty men.

Plans for the current chapter house were unveiled at the 1983 national convention banquet held on USM's Gulf Park campus. The new chapter house was dedicated on November 2, 1985. The forty-eight-man house was completed at a cost of nearly $550,000.

BZ

BETA ZETA CHAPTER
New Mexico State University
Las Cruces, New Mexico

Chartered as Phi Kappa Tau,
November 15, 1948

ON NOVEMBER 15, 1948, Herbert Haas, Louis Snow, Joe Provencio, Joe Cooper, James Weiso, and twenty-one others signed the Beta Zeta charter, which was presented by National President Roland Maxwell.

By 1953 Beta Zeta had prospered and acquired a house. The chapter continued to be successful through the 1950s and 1960s. In 1968 the fraternity house was moved from the site of the future student union to the new Greek complex. In 1972 Phi Kappa Tau became the first Greek organization to initiate an African-American member. Mike Davis, who would go on to play professional football, was initiated into Beta Zeta Chapter that year.

Beta Zeta was among the strongest chapters at New Mexico State in the 1980s, until a 1989 disciplinary action caused the charter to be revoked. In 1991 Reyes Martinez, Jason Ralph, and Josh Walling, along with Advisor William Soules were instrumental in reviving the chapter.

The new charter was presented on Saturday, May 1, 1993, in ceremonies on the New Mexico State campus.

BH

BETA ETA CHAPTER
University of New Mexico
Albuquerque, New Mexico

Founded as Phi Tau Club,
April 16, 1948
Chartered as Phi Kappa Tau,
November 16, 1948

IN A CLASSROOM at the University of New Mexico, thirteen men founded the Phi Tau Club in 1948. H. Frank Sowers was the first president, having been initiated into Phi Kappa Tau at Alpha Chapter while a student at Miami University.

A first house was rented in the fall of 1948, and the group promptly recruited the largest pledge class on campus.

Seven months after the group's first meeting, it had grown to sixty members, and National President Roland Maxwell presented the Beta Eta charter to the new chapter. Domain chief Lou Gerding, who lived in Albuquerque, also participated in the installation ceremonies.

Beta Eta Chapter assumed a leadership role on the New Mexico campus until the Korean War, when its membership was severely depleted. The chapter closed in 1954.

BΘ

BETA THETA CHAPTER
University of Kansas
Lawrence, Kansas

Chartered as Phi Kappa Tau,
November 18, 1948

PHI KAPPA TAU came to Kansas at the invitation of the university in May 1948. Field Secretary George E. Wilson recruited twelve initial members, who were initiated at Nebraska Wesleyan on May 22, 1948.

The Beta Theta charter was granted on November 18, 1948.

Alumni formed a house corporation in the spring of 1953 to purchase the home at 1408 Tennessee Street that had been bought by the national fraternity at the time of the chartering. In 1955–56 the chapter acquired an additional house two and a half blocks away. The chapter prospered until the late 1960s, when membership began to decline. The charter was suspended in 1972.

In 1984 a recolonization effort was initiated by National Headquarters. The colony struggled to build its membership and had a membership of twenty-one by the end of its second year. A new house corporation acquired a permanent home for the chapter in 1987, after occupying four temporary houses.

The new Beta Theta Chapter was installed on January 14, 1989. The chapter's first president, Alan Pickering (Kansas, 1948), attended the installation ceremonies held in the Crystal Room of the Eldridge Hotel. Pickering was national educational director for six years (1989–1995).

BI

BETA IOTA CHAPTER
Florida State University
Tallahassee, Florida

Founded as Gamma Phi,
December 1, 1947
Chartered as Phi Kappa Tau,
March 5, 1949

BETA IOTA CHAPTER was started in a unique way. Until the close of World War II, Florida State had been a women's college. With the influx of veteran students, it became coed Florida State University. University President Doak Campbell had the idea to bring eight fraternities to the campus at once to develop a fraternity system. Phi Kappa Tau's colony was founded as Gamma Phi Fraternity on December 1, 1947, and was housed in a military-surplus building on the rapidly expanding campus.

All eight new chapters were installed in a single installation banquet on March 5, 1949, sponsored jointly by the national fraternities and the university.

The university also built modern-style chapter houses for the eight chapters, which were completed in early 1952. The chapter's only responsibility was to furnish the dining room and lounges. The concrete-block house designed for forty men remains the home of Beta Iota to this day.

BK

BETA KAPPA CHAPTER
Oklahoma State University
Stillwater, Oklahoma

Chartered as Phi Kappa Tau,
May 16, 1949

A MEETING OF MEN interested in forming a colony of Phi Kappa Tau took place on October 20, 1948, in Morrill Hall at Oklahoma State. Beta Kappa members who attended that first meeting were: Henry Beers, Ray Bergman, Gene Burns, Darrel Fahler, Gerbert Goodenough, Ivan Griffith, Walter Hamilton, Don Notary, Wayne Settles, Lawrence Sigler, Bob Stout, and Charles Wolfe. Field Secretary Jack L. Anson conducted the meeting, and the first

steps toward forming a new chapter were taken that night. Ivan Griffith was elected president. Soon a constitution was drafted and accepted.

The installation took place on May 16, 1949, officially making the group Beta Kappa Chapter of Phi Kappa Tau. National President Maxwell presided at the installation, and Jack L. Anson presented the charter to President Ivan Griffith. The day after the installation, the chapter finalized the details of a chapter-house lease for the coming year.

The chapter bought its first home in 1952, acquiring a house at 1203 West Third. Adjoining property was purchased in 1954.

When the chapter was ready to build a new house in the 1960s, a design competition was conducted among Beta Kappa architects. Elbert Wheeler won the competition to build the modern home, which featured a circular sunken-seating area with a large fireplace in the center. In the middle 1980s, this house was remodeled and expanded to hold up to seventy members. The house corporation became overextended financially, and the house was lost through foreclosure. The national fraternity stepped in, buying the house literally on the courthouse steps, and began a massive effort to rebuild the struggling chapter.

Beta Kappa's F. L. "Mac" McKinley was national president for two years (1977–79).

BΛ

BETA LAMBDA CHAPTER
Indiana University
Bloomington, Indiana

Founded as Garnet Club, 1947
Chartered as Phi Kappa Tau,
May 18, 1949

THE GARNET CLUB was built by a group of Indiana University students opposed to hazing and the silly antics of many fraternities but desiring to form bonds of brotherhood. Several national fraternities approached the Garnet Club to affiliate with them, and the members determined that the values of Phi Kappa Tau were most similar to their own. They became a Phi Kappa Tau colony in 1948. After a short time in a rented house, the chapter made arrangements to purchase the limestone Showers home at 520 North Walnut Street.

The colony was installed on May 18, 1949, and became the fifty-ninth chapter in Phi Kappa Tau. National President Roland Maxwell conducted the installation, and National Secretary Richard Young presented the Beta Lambda charter.

After Walnut Street, the chapter leased a house in an excellent location in the center of campus at Tenth and Jordan. As the chapter grew and prospered, it neared its goal of building its own home on the row, and ground was broken in the late 1960s. Unfortunately, the chapter membership declined. It ran up a debt with the university, losing the house in the early 1970s. After living in inadequate rented housing for several years, the chapter became inactive in 1993.

BM

BETA MU CHAPTER
Kent State University
Kent, Ohio

Founded as Phi Tau Club, 1948
Chartered as Phi Kappa Tau,
May 20, 1949

EARLY IN 1948, transfer students Harry Snyder (Akron, 1943), Richard Hyer (Akron), and Don Clough (Case Western, 1942) built a group of thirteen men and adopted the name Phi Tau Club.

The Phi Tau Club was chartered on May 20, 1949, as the fourth fraternity on the Kent State campus. Beta Mu prospered through the 1950s and early 1960s, but with the decreasing popularity of fraternities at Kent State, Beta Mu was forced to close in 1969.

In October 1986, a second generation of transfer students helped to restart Beta Mu. Craig Koszycki (Muskingum, 1985) and Richard Donmoyer (Rochester Tech, 1985) met in an English class and collaborated to form a colony. With the help of C. Todd Patton (East Carolina, 1982) from the National Headquarters staff, a group of twenty-five was recruited and established as a colony in January 1987.

After completing the chartering requirements, the new Beta Mu was installed on March 18, 1989. Two original charter members, James K. Heilmeier and G. E. Freezel signed the new charter. David Renniger chaired the board of governors, and Brian Breittholz (Ohio, 1983) advised the chapter. The charter president was Scott Malkus, and installation coordinator was Robert Reese, both of whom would later join the national fraternity's staff.

BN

BETA NU CHAPTER
San Diego State University
San Diego, California

Founded as Kappa Phi Sigma,
June 6, 1926
Chartered as Phi Kappa Tau,
February 24, 1950

KAPPA PHI SIGMA was founded in the days when San Diego State was the state normal school. It had been a successful organization with a large and active group of alumni. The local fraternity decided to petition Phi Kappa Tau for a charter in the fall of 1949 after a long investigation of potential nationals.

Members went to the Pi chapter house at the University of Southern California to be initiated in January 1950, and the installation ceremonies took place on February 24, 1950. A large contingent of Southern California Phi Taus turned out for the installation banquet at the Franciscan Room of the El Cortez Hotel in San Diego. In addition to the undergraduates, several Kappa Phi Sigma alumni were initiated and participated in the installation. National President Roland Maxwell gave the main address of the evening, and Richard J. Young presented the charter to Wallace T. Geathergill, the president of the new chapter.

Kappa Phi Sigma never had a house, and plans for a lodge were in consideration when the chapter failed in 1954. It had been severely affected by the Korean War.

BΞ

BETA XI CHAPTER
University of Georgia
Athens, Georgia

Chartered as Phi Kappa Tau,
March 10, 1950

PHI TAUS FROM three different schools, Carl Smith (Georgia Tech, 1947), John Carreker (Auburn, 1928), and Dean Donald J. Weddel (Michigan State, 1925) worked to form a colony at the University of Georgia. Field Secretary George Wilson facilitated an initial meeting, and his colleague Thomas W. Athey became involved throughout the colony period. Athey and local alumni helped the group to acquire its first home, a white-pillared house that had been the home of another fraternity.

The installation ceremonies took place on March 10, 1950, with thirty-two members signing the charter. Roland Maxwell spoke at the banquet in the Georgian Hotel in Athens. National Secretary Richard J. Young presented the charter to George Moore, the chapter president.

Young Beta Xi had a few difficult years as a result of the Korean War, but the chapter managed to survive in spite of low membership and a major fire in the chapter house in December 1953. No one was injured, but the chapter members did have to find temporary quarters.

In later years, Beta Xi moved to another historic white-pillared chapter house, which it proudly maintains today.

BO

BETA OMICRON CHAPTER
University of Maryland
College Park, Maryland

*Chartered as Phi Kappa Tau,
March 14, 1950*

A PHI KAPPA TAU colony was first formed at Maryland in 1949 and was granted a charter on March 14, 1950, in ceremonies attended by National President Roland Maxwell and Founder Taylor A. Borradaile.

A home that would last the chapter for many years was purchased in the late 1960s through the efforts of C. Ricardo Hamilton. The chapter closed in the early 1970s and restarted in 1974 under the leadership of Greg Hollen, who would join the fraternity staff and then be elected to the National Council and vice presidency.

The chapter closed once again in 1986, and in the fall of 1987, efforts to recolonize were begun. It took

until March 27, 1993, for the charter to be granted to the colony. The old house was reclaimed in 1993, and in the fall of 1995, the chapter moved to a much better home at 5 Fraternity Row on the College Park campus.

BΠ

BETA PI CHAPTER
Middlebury College
Middlebury, Vermont

*Chartered as Phi Kappa Tau,
March 16, 1950*

BENJAMIN F. WISSLER (Muhlenberg, 1923), head of the Middlebury physics department, suggested his own fraternity when the dean of men was considering expansion of the fraternity system in 1948. Field Secretary Thomas W. Athey visited a group of nonfraternity men interested in forming a colony in the fall of 1948.

Athey returned in the spring of 1949 to form a colony with the help of Professor Wissler and the dean of men, W. Storrs Lee. Jack Mulcahey became president of the colony, and with a loan from the national fraternity, a fraternity home was established in the Wright House. The colony was in full operation by the fall of 1949 and had met the requirements for installation by the following spring.

The colony officially became Beta Pi Chapter on March 16, 1950. The installation banquet was held at the Dog Team Tavern. The usual

installing officers, Roland Maxwell and Richard Young, were assisted by Field Secretary Thomas Athey and Professor Wissler.

Beta Pi became inactive in 1972, and all fraternities are now banned from the Middlebury campus.

BP

BETA RHO CHAPTER
University of California,
Los Angeles
Los Angeles, California

*Chartered as Phi Kappa Tau,
May 12, 1950*

VINCE ZIMMERER, Harry Hanbury, Al Hjerstedt, and Rod Mortenson founded the group that became Beta Rho Chapter in the fall of 1948. Five more men had joined by the time Field Secretary "Hap" Angelo organized the group into the UCLA colony. In February 1949, with the help of a national fraternity loan, the group bought the Clarence Darrow mansion in Santa Monica as its first home.

National President Roland Maxwell spoke at the installation ceremonies at the Mona Lisa Restaurant on May 12, 1950, as the Beta Rho was officially born.

Finding the Santa Monica location to be too far from campus, the dwindling membership regrouped in Westwood, acquiring an apartment building on Landfair Avenue in the spring of 1952. Struggles to maintain a membership adequate for the new house plagued the chapter off and on through the 1950s, and the chapter was forced to suspend operations at the close of the 1958–59 school year.

In October 1980, Chapter Consultant Mark Placenti (Ohio State, 1976) formed a new Beta Rho colony with fourteen men. In January 1982, the colony established 406 Kelton Avenue as a headquarters. When membership reached thirty-eight, the charter was returned to UCLA on June 3, 1984, and Beta Rho was a chapter once again. But inadequate housing never allowed the chapter to prosper. It closed for a second time in 1987.

ΒΣ

Beta Sigma Chapter
Idaho State University
Pocatello, Idaho

*Chartered as Phi Kappa Tau,
May 20, 1950*

On October 10, 1949, transfer students Culbertson E. Martin (New Mexico, 1948) and Bernard F. "Gus" Bengal (Colorado, 1947) met with a group of seven Idaho State students to form a Phi Kappa Tau colony. Parvin Witte (Nebraska Wesleyan, 1923) advised the group, starting with that first meeting. Bernard Bengal was the first president, and Culbertson Martin became vice president; the colony immediately became involved in campus activities.

The installation of Beta Sigma Chapter was conducted on May 20, 1950. In the Pioneer Room of the Hotel Bannock, Field Secretary Jack L. Anson was toastmaster, and National President Maxwell presided at the banquet. A formal dance in the Wedgewood Room of the hotel followed the installation.

Members of Beta Sigma Chapter lived in the residence halls until a house was located and acquired at 241 North Hayes in Pocatello for the 1954–55 school year.

In spite of the chapter's early success, the chapter became inactive in 1961.

ΒΤ

Beta Tau Chapter
Bowling Green State University
Bowling Green, Ohio

*Founded as Delta Phi Beta,
April 6, 1948
Chartered as Phi Kappa Tau,
November 17, 1950*

Beta Tau Chapter's roots are traced to the Delta Phi Beta social club, founded in April 1948, when some Bowling Green students saw the need for an additional fraternity on the campus. While waiting for official university recognition, the group located and rented meeting rooms above a local dairy bar at the southwest corner of campus for the 1948–49 school year. The following year, the group shared a house near the campus with its elderly owners. Acceptance by the Interfraternity Council was gained in the fall of 1949.

As the local fraternity began to investigate possible national affiliations, they were so impressed with the presentation of Phi Kappa Tau's past President Ernest N. Littleton, a Bowling Green school principal, that they immediately asked to hear more, and Jack L. Anson arrived from Oxford to continue the discussion. Anson and Littleton officially formed the colony in March 1950.

The colony was living in a university-owned house in the fall of 1950 when the installation took place. Beta Tau became the fraternity's sixty-seventh chapter at the presentation of the charter on November 17, 1950. The chapter president, Jack L. Myers, received the Shideler Award as the fraternity's outstanding senior in 1952.

Beta Tau has provided several excellent leaders to Phi Kappa Tau, including former Executive Director William D. Jenkins, who is currently executive vice president of the Phi Kappa Tau Foundation, and past National President Ray A. Clarke.

The chapter is currently housed in a large on-campus house provided by the university.

BETA UPSILON CHAPTER
Hobart College
Geneva, New York

Founded as Phi Tau Fraternity,
October 1949
Chartered as Phi Kappa Tau,
May 17, 1952

PHI KAPPA TAU was one of four new fraternities to enter Hobart in the years following World War II. C. Brandon Chenault (Cornell, 1948) transferred to Hobart and quickly formed a group of twelve men interested in starting a new fraternity. The first formal meeting was held in October 1949. Chenault was the first president. As soon as the Hobart bureaucracy recognized the new organization in 1950, it began to petition Phi Kappa Tau for a charter.

Early alumni support came from architect Thomas L. White (Pennsylvania State, 1922) and Robert M. Brandt (Colgate, 1940). In the fall of 1951, the group moved from its barracks housing to a campus dormitory, Medbery Hall.

Thirty men signed the Beta Upsilon charter on May 17, 1952, in ceremonies attended by National President Roland Maxwell, National Secretary Richard Young, and the president of Hobart College and several members of the faculty. Also that same spring, the chapter purchased a Victorian house on the fraternity row at 573 South Main Street, which had formerly been the home of Kappa Alpha Society. The house was substantially renovated by a private investor just before the chapter was closed for disciplinary reasons in 1985. It has been leased to the college since that time.

BETA PHI CHAPTER
Westminster College
New Wilmington, Pennsylvania

Founded as Delta Nu,
November 28, 1949
Chartered as Phi Kappa Tau,
May 19, 1952

WILLIAM STEDMAN, Henry Kautz, and Raymond Splitstone formed the nucleus of a new fraternity on the Westminster campus on September 19, 1949. Soon joined by five other men, the Delta Nu local was formed on November 28, 1949, with the Greek motto: "Equality in attitudes, superiority in deeds."

Phi Kappa Tau Field Secretary Thomas W. Athey visited the campus in September to ask the group to consider petitioning Phi Kappa Tau. The college later promised to recognize Delta Nu if it would seek affiliation with Phi Kappa Tau.

The fraternity's first permanent meeting place was a rented two-bedroom apartment taken in September 1950. A year later, Delta Nu moved into its present house at 134 Waugh Avenue.

Thirty-four men signed the Beta Phi charter on the afternoon of May 19, 1952, prior to an all-college open house at the chapter house.

The history of Beta Phi has been one of steady and consistent progress. At the present time, a fund-raising campaign is being conducted to build a new home for Beta Phi, as the years have taken a toll on 134 Waugh.

BETA CHI CHAPTER
Southern Illinois University
Carbondale, Illinois

Founded as Chi Delta Chi,
December 6, 1932
Chartered as Phi Kappa Tau,
November 24, 1953

CHI DELTA CHI, founded on December 6, 1932, was the first social fraternity at Southern Illinois to survive for any length of time. It represented the ideals of manhood, brotherhood, and scholarship. Its goal had been to obtain a national charter from the early days, but it would take twenty-one years for that goal to become a reality.

The local, which had been extremely active on the Southern Illinois campus, had produced a long list of student leaders.

In 1953 Chi Delta Chi petitioned Phi Kappa Tau for a charter, and the installation date was set for November 24, 1953. National President Roland Maxwell was the principal speaker at the installation banquet in the school cafeteria, and the national secretary presented the charter to Beta Chi President Harlan Seats.

In 1955 the chapter bought a new home at 510 West Walnut, which was financed by the national fraternity.

IMPACT 1970 came to the Southern Illinois campus in the days just prior to the Saint Louis convention. The chapter became inactive in 1979.

BΨ

BETA PSI CHAPTER
California State University–
Long Beach
Long Beach, California

*Chartered as Phi Kappa Tau,
March 17, 1956*

PAUL J. STANICK (Southern California, 1948) convinced some friends who were attending Long Beach State to form a Phi Kappa Tau colony to bring the fraternity to their campus. To the fraternity's good fortune, three well-placed administrators at Long Beach also were members of Pi Chapter at Southern California, and they immediately became helpful to the new group. Dr. David L. Bryant (Southern California, 1926) was executive dean of the college, Dr. Francis Flynn (Southern California, 1927) was the dean of students, and Clarence R. Bergland (Southern California) was an admissions officer.

William S. Maddio was the first president of the colony, and he oversaw an aggressive recruitment program that resulted in thirty-four members by the time the National Council approved the installation date of March 17, 1956, fifty years to the day after the fraternity had been founded at Miami University.

More than three hundred people attended the installation, which was held in conjunction with the Founders' Day celebration at the Southern California alumni association and the chapters of the University of Southern California and the University of California, Los Angeles. Judge Eugene Fay (Southern California, 1925) was the master of ceremonies, and National President Roland Maxwell gave the main address. Jack L. Anson presented the Beta Psi charter to the new chapter president, William S. Maddio.

BΩ

BETA OMEGA CHAPTER
California State University–Chico
Chico, California

*Founded as Iota Sigma,
winter 1922
Chartered as Phi Kappa Tau,
April 8, 1958*

IOTA SIGMA FRATERNITY was founded as an industrial arts club in 1922. Its principles were industry and community, and a plumb bob was the group's symbol. Iota Sigma began to operate as a social fraternity in the early 1930s. The local was regarded as the foremost student organization at Chico, and every other fraternity there was an offshoot of this distinguished society.

Iota Sigma began the search for a national affiliation in 1957. Field Secretary James Dutch (Long Beach State, 1956) visited the local, and following that contact, its members voted to petition Phi Kappa Tau. Iota Sigma brought an alumni membership of 1,300 to the merger. Many alumni were initiated into Phi Kappa Tau.

Phi Kappa Tau's seventy-second charter was granted on April 8, 1958, with Roland Maxwell presiding. Chapter President James E. Brown received the charter from Maxwell. Thirty-seven undergraduates, twelve alumni, two advisers, and ten members of an advisory council were initiated as charter members.

ΓΑ

GAMMA ALPHA CHAPTER
Michigan Technological University
Houghton, Michigan

Founded as Mu Kappa Mu,
May 7, 1957
Chartered as Phi Kappa Tau,
April 24, 1959

MU KAPPA MU was established in 1957 as a protest against existing fraternity practices. The founders included eleven freshmen and one junior. Twenty-seven additional men pledged the new fraternity almost immediately. Enough money was accumulated in those first weeks to make a down payment on an old hotel in Hancock, a town adjoining Houghton, where the school is located. The house has served the chapter well since that time.

In the fall of 1957, the search for a national affiliation began, and a visit from Field Secretary Roger J. Bell (California–Los Angeles, 1954) persuaded the group that Phi Kappa Tau was the right choice. Fifty-three undergraduates and advisers were initiated by men from Michigan State and Lawrence with help from Jack L. Anson.

The installation of Gamma Alpha Chapter was conducted on April 24, 1959, in the ballroom of Michigan Tech's Memorial Union. National Secretary Young presented the charter to Chapter President Joe Jenney, and National President Maxwell gave an impressive talk on fraternity conduct.

Gamma Alpha has had a history of consistency and excellence.

ΓΒ

GAMMA BETA CHAPTER
University of Cincinnati
Cincinnati, Ohio

Chartered as Phi Kappa Tau,
November 9, 1959

THE UNIVERSITY OF CINCINNATI invited Phi Kappa Tau to establish a chapter there in 1956, and an initial nine men joined the colony on November 13, 1956. In December 1958, the national fraternity purchased a house for the colony at 2645 Clifton Avenue across from the university, which was remodeled by colony members in time for the fall rush in 1959.

John C. Hardebeck served the first two years as colony president and was treasurer of the senior class. Harry Addison was vice president of the Interfraternity Council.

After three years of work, the colony received the Gamma Beta charter on November 9, 1959, in the Union's faculty dining room. Several university officials welcomed the new chapter, and Board of Governors Chairman Joseph K. Dunker (Miami, 1948) described the colony's progress toward chartering. National Secretary Young presented the charter to Gamma Beta President Jack Maisel. National President Maxwell's address concluded the ceremonies, which were followed by a reception at the chapter house.

ΓΓ
GAMMA GAMMA CHAPTER
Saint John's University
Jamaica, New York

Chartered as Phi Kappa Tau,
December 10, 1960

PROF. JOHN B. MARAN (New York, 1924) introduced a group of students to Phi Kappa Tau in October 1958. Frank Sacco became the first president of this interest group. It took three efforts to become recognized by the student council. By the third attempt, Howard Englehart had been elected to the council, and Jack L. Anson came to New York to make a personal appeal on behalf of the national fraternity. Recognition was finally achieved in 1959.

The colony became deeply involved in the activities of the university and was especially successful in philanthropic work. The Gamma Gamma charter was granted on December 10, 1960, in ceremonies at the Queens Terrace on Long Island. Jack L. Anson represented the national fraternity, along with Domain Chief Don Zeissett (Rensselaer, 1941). Professor Maran was master of ceremonies, and Jack Anson gave the primary address. Domain Chief Zeissett presented the charter to Gamma Gamma President Maurice McDermott.

The chapter became inactive for a period of years and was revived with the assistance of the New York City Area alumni association. The re-chartering ceremonies were held on March 28, 1987.

Gamma Gamma celebrated its twenty-fifth anniversary by donating a specially designed stained glass front door for the National Headquarters.

ΓΔ
GAMMA DELTA CHAPTER
Northern Michigan University
Marquette, Michigan

Founded as Sigma Rho Epsilon,
November 1956
Chartered as Phi Kappa Tau,
May 13, 1961

TEN MEN AT Northern Michigan University who were not satisfied with any of the existing fraternities formed Sigma Rho Epsilon, which was given formal recognition by the student council on April 1, 1957. By that time, the group had forty-one members and had established the objectives of academic prowess, fellowship, and service to the college community and self.

Following an inquiry from the local, Field Secretary William D. Jenkins spent four days with the group in December 1960. They voted to petition Phi Kappa Tau for a charter on January 9, 1961. The petition was approved, and the installation was set for May 13, 1961.

Installation ceremonies were held at the Marquette Armory following the charter signing in the Student Union Building. National President Harold E. Angelo gave the primary address.

For many years, Gamma Delta was housed in a large Victorian home. This was destroyed by fire in 1986. Another house was acquired, which housed the chapter until it was closed for disciplinary reasons in the early 1990s.

CHAPTER SIX

BOOM & BUST

Who would shape the new era for Phi Kappa Tau? Many assumed that Administrative Secretary Jack Anson, who had been Young's assistant since 1950, was the heir apparent for the national secretary position. But members of the National Council had other ideas—or more accurately, didn't have a clear idea whom they wanted in the job. Anson was clearly a Richard Young protégé, and those on the council who were interested in dramatic change thought Jack would simply be a continuation of the past. When Anson was not immediately appointed to the position, he

resigned and wrote in the *Laurel* that he was relocating on the West Coast. William D. Jenkins (Bowling Green, 1957), a relatively new field secretary who had joined the staff in early 1960, was appointed acting secretary late in July 1961 and coincidentally received a draft notice the same day. He was able to get a deferment until September, presenting a very short deadline to make a permanent appointment. Jenkins was assisted by Field Secretary Ross Roeder (Michigan Tech and Michigan State, 1957), who was destined for a successful business career and important leadership roles in the fraternity.

When the decision was made to make Anson an offer to accept the national secretaryship, President Angelo found Jack fishing in Colorado, and the two negotiated a deal for Anson to return as national secretary. In addition, Anson would retain the responsibility for editing the *Laurel* until a new editor could be appointed. Jack returned to Oxford and took over the national secretary duties, well rested from a six-week "vacation," on September 11, 1961.

One of Anson's first public responsibilities as national secretary was to participate in the installation of a distinguished local society, Archania at

University of the Pacific, as Gamma Epsilon Chapter on November 13, 1961. Archania was founded as a literary society in 1854 and at the time of the chartering was the oldest local fraternity in America. Dean Edward Betz (Pacific, 1961) and the university's academic vice president, Dr. Samuel Meyer (Pacific, 1961), were initiated as charter members.

Two weeks later, on the opposite coast, Phi Chi Alpha was installed as Gamma Zeta Chapter at the University of Connecticut. Phi Chi Alpha was an outgrowth of the pharmaceutical fraternity, Phi Delta Chi, which had been on the campus since 1949.

Gamma Eta Chapter was installed at East Carolina University on February 4, 1962. The East Carolina colony had been organized by Field Secretary Roger W. Vaughn (Illinois, 1954).

And on April 13, Gamma Zeta was chartered at Western Michigan University. The local Beta Theta Epsilon negotiated the purchase of a house that spring, which the new chapter renovated for occupancy in the fall of 1962.

Over the years, few chapters have consistently celebrated Founders' Day as well as Alpha Eta at Florida, and the 1962 celebration was an especially outstanding event. Two prominent Floridians, State Senator Verle Pope (Florida, 1962) and Dean Robert L.

Beatty (Florida, 1962), director of Florida's Alumni Loyalty Fund, were initiated in special ceremonies. Participating were a long list of Alpha Eta's political notables, including U.S. Congressman William Lantaff, Florida Attorney General Richard W. Ervin (Florida, 1926), and Clyde Atkins (Florida, 1935), past president of the Florida Bar Association and a future federal district judge. Pope's initiation brought the number of Alpha Eta members serving in the Florida legislature to four.

ASHEVILLE, 1962

In North Carolina's Blue Ridge mountains, the 1962 national convention was held at the Grove Park Inn. In 1930 the first national convention under Richard Young's direction also had been held at the Grove Park Inn. Both meetings were filled with the optimism and ambition of new leadership.

At the Thirty-sixth National Convention, Roland Maxwell was named president emeritus, and the handsome new Maxwell Award trophy purchased by the Chicago alumni association was presented to Upsilon Chapter at Nebraska Wesleyan, the outstanding chapter in the fraternity. Their success was not surprising considering that the chapter had two future national presi-

dents among its outstanding leaders, John M. Green (Nebraska Wesleyan, 1960) and Thomas C. Cunningham (Nebraska Wesleyan, 1960). For the first time, the traditional model initiation was conducted by domain chiefs using a newly updated set of recommended regalia.

Dayton CPA Donald E. Lease (Miami, 1950) and an outstanding domain chief, Melvin Dettra, Jr. (Ohio State, 1945), won election to six-year terms on the National Council, and the convention initiated the practice of making the past president of the fraternity an ex-officio member of the National Council.

But the election of a national president may have been the most important part of the convention. Many of the delegates wanted the dynamic "Hap" Angelo to run for a second full term; and while he could have been easily reelected, he thought running would be hypocritical since he had long argued that Roland Maxwell's extensive service had prevented capable men from serving in the fraternity's highest office. He believed it was important that he step down and set a new precedent for national presidents, serving only one term.

Well-respected National Councilor and Domain Chief Lou Gerding from Albuquerque had expressed an interest in running and seemed to some to be the likely candidate. However, another last-minute candidate presented himself. Seventy-three-year-old businessman Dr. W. A. "Arch" Hammond, president of the Phi Kappa Tau Foundation, seemed to be an excellent candidate for two reasons. First, he lived in Dayton and was close enough to the Central Office to provide some assistance and supervision to secretary Anson, who was still new on the job. Ewing Boles and some of the fraternity's other "old timers" believed that Maxwell had been too far removed from the headquarters to provide much oversight.

In addition to Hammond's proximity, some also believed that he was in a position to give substantial financial support to the fraternity or foundation. He had been a trustee of the foundation since its incorporation in 1945 and one of its largest contributors. Hammond had recently given a gift of $25,000 to Miami University to establish the W. A. Hammond lecture series.

Gerding agreed not to give opposition in 1962, and Dr. Hammond was elected, promising to visit every chapter in the fraternity at his own expense.

The Phi Kappa Tau that Arch Hammond found in 1962 was much different from the one he had known as an undergraduate fifty years earlier; but in general, the fraternity was still enjoying enormous strength and success. Two chapters were chartered during the Hammond presidency. Gamma Iota at Sacramento State was installed in California, and Gamma Kappa was chartered at C. W. Post College campus of Long Island University on Long Island, New York.

And the fraternity's housing boom continued. Beta Kappa dedicated a handsome new home at Oklahoma State, with such unique features as a sunken fireplace seating area. Elbert Wheeler (Oklahoma State, 1951) won a design competition held among several Beta Kappa architects. Baldwin

National Chaplain Charles D. Spotts, National President W. A. Hammond, and National Secretary Jack L. Anson at the 1964 national convention in Boulder, Colorado

Wallace occupied a specially designed on-campus house provided by the college. Colorado State purchased a large private home that had previously housed a sorority. Chi Chapter at North Carolina State sold its old home and moved into a university-financed house on the new fraternity row.

Rho Chapter at Rensselaer Polytechnic Institute dedicated one of the finest homes in the fraternity in impressive ceremonies. Rho undergraduates spurred the effort to get the new house started when they pledged their own money to the effort. "The Rensselaer Plan," as it has come to be known over the years, has proved to be a model for fund-raising in successful chapters.

And in the news, Charles Bassett II (Ohio State, 1951), was accepted into the third class of NASA astronauts; Washington State's Keith Lincoln (Washington State, 1959) was playing halfback for the American Football League's champion San Diego Chargers; and former baseball player John Berardino (Southern California, 1936) was starring as Dr. Steve Hardy in a new daytime drama, "General Hospital."

SCHOLARSHIP REACHES ALL-TIME HIGH

Dean Ben David (Ohio State, 1945), national scholarship commissioner, reported that the grades of 70 percent of Phi Tau chapters were above the all-men's averages on their campuses, ranking twelfth among the sixty national fraternities in 1962–63. The leading chapters in scholarship were at Franklin and Marshall, Transylvania, Lafayette, Colgate, and Nebraska Wesleyan.

America's involvement in the war in Vietnam had an enormous impact on Phi Kappa Tau, which began about the time the war started to escalate in 1964. Initially, because of increased college enrollment, the war's impact was positive; but by the end, the college fraternity would be one of the many institutions severely shaken by the antiwar and anti-establishment sentiments among the students in America's colleges and universities.

For its 1964 national convention, Phi Kappa Tau went to the campus of the University of Colorado, where past President Angelo was dean of men. The snapshot by Hugh C. Fowler (Colorado, 1945) that appeared on the cover of the *Laurel* following the convention told the story of the presidential contest. A rather sour-looking W. A. Hammond was passing the presidential gavel to the fraternity's new president, Lou Gerding, who was beaming. Dr. Hammond, who had visited all but nineteen of the fraternity's chapters, believed strongly that he needed to continue as president for another two years; but during his presidency, he had ruffled some feathers, and some on the National Council believed that while his travels to the chapters had been helpful, he had not provided the kind of leadership to the fraternity that it needed. Lou Gerding was not willing to postpone his run for president any longer. He believed that he was at the right point in his career to accept the responsibility, and he thought it would be especially appropriate to be elected president at the convention held at his alma mater, with eleven of his fellow Psi charter members in attendance. The political wrangling of the convention embittered Hammond, who was not accustomed to losing, though he vowed to continue his travels to the remaining chapters. Another Psi charter member, Ray Bushey, was general chairman of the convention and elected to the National Council along with John A. Edwards, Sr. (North Carolina State, 1950).

After the convention, Gerding appointed Councilor Mel Dettra to lead a committee to study the feasibility of a national leadership school. Dettra had directed leadership workshops at conventions and long been an advocate of holding a national leadership school as many other leading national fraternities had been doing for years.

Gamma Mu Chapter at Bradley University chartered in 1965

Populations of college men were expanding rapidly as many took educational draft deferments to keep from going to Vietnam. Secretary Anson appointed Field Secretary Tom Cunningham to a new position designed specifically to capitalize on the new opportunities for expansion. Bill Jenkins returned to the Central Office staff from military service in September 1964, and was named assistant national secretary. In May 1965, the Lambda Nu local was chartered as Gamma Lambda Chapter at Central Michigan University, and Gamma Mu was chartered at Bradley University in Peoria, Illinois. And under Cunningham's leadership, new colonies were in the works at eight more campuses.

And Phi Kappa Tau chapters continued to build and buy new chapter houses at an unprecedented rate. At Delaware, Alpha Gamma joined two identical houses on adjoining lots with a large pillared portico to form a single house. The new chapter at Northern Michigan bought a Victorian mansion in Marquette. Pi Chapter at the University of Southern California moved into a unique modern house on fraternity row, designed by Francis J. Heusel (Southern California, 1926); and another striking modern home was being built at the University of Kentucky for Kappa Chapter. Chapters at Kansas, Indiana, and Mississippi State all had ambitious building plans on the drawing board that would never be executed.

MACKINAC ISLAND CONVENTION

The Thirty-eighth National Convention at the Grand Hotel on Mackinac Island, Michigan, met in the midst of a great expansion boom. Delegates from Gamma Nu Chapter at the Rochester Institute of Technology and Gamma Xi at East Central State University in Oklahoma were attending their first convention as chartered chapters, and a large number of delegates from colonies added excitement to the convention.

At Mackinac, convention delegates voted to increase dues to fund a national leadership school, but they were not willing to make the increase effective until the following year, delaying the inaugural school until 1968. Two future national presidents, Mississippi attorney and 1961 Shideler Award winner Tom Stennis (Mississippi State, 1958) and Domain Chief Ray Clarke (Bowling Green, 1951), were elected to the National Council. Retiring National Councilor Warren Parker won the nomination and election for president over Arch Hammond, who was further frustrated by convention politics.

Jack Jareo, who had been editor of the *Laurel* in the late 1920s and headed the Stewart Howe alumni service in Champaign, Illinois, for many years, was appointed national alumni secretary and editor to relieve Anson of the responsibility for editing the magazine, which he had done "temporarily" for five years. The magazine's schedule had become irregular and had been a great source of criticism from Hammond and others.

During the biennium following the Mackinac convention, the fraternity was chiefly concerned with growth and expansion. Twelve new chapters were chartered in that period. The oldest local at the Fullerton campus of California State University became Gamma Omicron in September 1966. Zeta Phi Fraternity, founded by Korean War veterans at Youngstown State University in 1956, was chartered as

Gamma Pi Chapter during a January snowstorm in 1967. Nebraska Wesleyan alumni and undergraduates were instrumental in founding and nurturing a colony at Kearney State College (now Nebraska-Kearney), which was installed as Gamma Rho Chapter in ceremonies on April 1, 1967. Phi Kappa Tau became the eleventh national fraternity chartered at the University of California–Davis. The fraternity had been invited to expand at Davis, and Tom Cunningham was assisted by Dean Harold Hakes (Bowling Green, 1950), Davis' director of housing, in founding Gamma Sigma Chapter.

The first installation in the 1967–68 school year was Gamma Tau at Old Dominion University. The local society, Omega Phi Sigma, was five years old when the installation ceremonies were conducted on December 2, 1967. The next day, thirty-three undergraduates and eleven alumni of Gamma Sigma Fraternity were installed as Gamma Upsilon Chapter at Spring Hill College in Mobile, Alabama. The mother of Richard Lynch, a former president of the local who died while visiting Mexico, signed the charter for her son. In January 1968, Zeta Gamma Rho, a ten-year-old Northeastern University local, was installed as

Gamma Phi Chapter.

Dennis G. Smith (Mississippi State, 1962) founded the Phi Tau Delta local fraternity at Delta State University in Cleveland, Mississippi, with ten men in 1963. The local was chartered Gamma Chi of Phi Kappa Tau on February 25, 1968. Dr. Walter S. Corrie (Colgate, 1941), a member of the sociology faculty at Southwest Texas State University, held a reception in his home for participants in the chartering of the local Sigma Kappa Epsilon Fraternity as Gamma Psi Chapter of Phi Kappa Tau on April 20. Gamma Omega Chapter was installed at La Salle College in Philadelphia on

Delegates to the 1969 IMPACT at Georgetown College

April 27, 1968. The petitioning local, Sigma Phi Lambda, traced its history to November 1935. Iowa Wesleyan University became the home of Delta Alpha Chapter on May 19, 1968. One of the most successful chapters chartered during this era was Delta Beta Chapter at the University of Evansville. A local group named Sodalitas chose Phi Kappa Tau from twelve national fraternities and became the sixth national fraternity represented on the southern Indiana campus, when the charter was granted to forty-three men on May 28, 1968.

IMPACT INAUGURATED

The entire fraternity came to southern Indiana three months later for the first national leadership school at Indiana University in August. The new program was called "IMPACT," standing for imagination, management, programming, attitudes, communication, and training. The faculty of the three-day workshop was a combination of Phi Taus and outside experts including Sigma Chi John Pont, the Rose Bowl-bound head football coach at Indiana.

Mel Dettra, who had spent his entire term on the National Council working toward the program, chaired the IMPACT steering committee. He was assisted in that inaugural effort by Assistant National Secretary Bill Jenkins, who served as IMPACT administrator; Dr. Robert Mills (Kentucky, 1935), president of Georgetown College and IMPACT keynoter; Al Beretta (Hobart,

1957), coordinator of student services at Hobart; National Councilor Ray Clarke; 1965 Shideler Award winner Thomas L. Good (Illinois, 1962); Domain Chief Otto L. Schellin (Akron, 1947); and National Secretary Anson.

From Bloomington, the first IMPACT "graduating class" headed south to French Lick, Indiana, to the Thirty-ninth National Convention. While the IMPACT program in its idyllic campus setting was an enormously positive and uplifting event for the fraternity, the following convention laid open some long-festering problems underlying the successful façade.

In contentious discussions the convention approved three policy statements: (1) regarding membership selection, the fraternity is "opposed to infringement from any source on the right to selection of members"; (2) regarding the fraternity's relationship with universities, "its chapters and individual members pledge themselves to cooperate with college and university officials and to work only through legal and orderly means to bring and strive diligently to enhance the good name of their institutions"; and (3) stating the fraternity's opposition to the use, sale or possession of illegal drugs.

The convention grappled with a proposal to alter the Ritual. Past National President Gerding had chaired a Ritual review committee to consider changes to the existing initiation ceremony, because the National Council learned that members of the Colgate chapter had found portions of the Ritual objectionable to members who held religious beliefs other than Christianity. The resident council delegates took a very conservative view toward the efforts to change the Ritual and rejected the proposal resoundingly. Further, when it was learned that the resident council delegate from Alpha Upsilon at Colgate had not been initiated by the standard Ritual, his voting credentials were withdrawn. This action was one of the final steps in the eventual decision of the chapter to withdraw from Phi Kappa Tau and operate as a local fraternity. This issue was especially painful for National Secretary Anson, who, as an Alpha Upsilon alumnus, had worked hard to preserve the tenuous relationship between his chapter and the national fraternity.

Ohio State alumnus Melvin Dettra, Jr. was elected president. John Edwards was elected to the newly established vice president's position. Otto Schellin and Edward "Ted" Marye (Kentucky, 1948) were elected to the National Council.

Outgoing President Warren Parker had the unique opportunity to present a newly authorized past president's badge guard to all former presidents in attendance. The gold tetrahedron with a ruby at its apex was presented to Lou Gerding (1964–66), Harold "Hap" Angelo (1959–62), Roland Maxwell (1934–1959), F. R. Fletemeyer (1917–1919), and E. N. Littleton (1911). Calling it the "greatest honor in his life," Parker presented the final guard to the fraternity's first president, Taylor A. Borradaile.

VIETNAM *and* CAMPUS UNREST

Phi Kappa Tau was not functioning in a vacuum. It is instructive to understand the tensions in America during the summer of 1968. The war in Vietnam had continued to escalate since 1964; and being of draft age, college men were deeply affected by the prospect of going to a far-off unpopular war. The first known Phi Tau to die in the conflict was Capt. William W. Nichols, Jr. (Pennsylvania State, 1958), who was killed in a Viet Cong

ambush in October 1964. Lengthy reports on "our gallant Phi Taus" appeared frequently in *Laurels* of the era, and too many Vietnam deaths were listed in the obituaries. At the highest levels of the military, Secretary of the Navy Paul Ignatius (Southern California, 1938) and Marine Corps Commandant Leonard F. Chapman (Florida, 1932) were both involved in executing the war.

Generally, fraternities and many Phi Taus had been supportive of the war effort. Members of Beta Chi Chapter at Southern Illinois got national publicity when they ran from the campus to KXOK radio in St. Louis carrying a message: "It's about time, say the men

National Secretary Jack L. Anson presents the Borradaile Award to Gen. Leonard F. Chapman, Jr., commandant of the Marine Corps, in June 1968.

National President Melvin Dettra, Jr., signs the Delta Gamma charter at the University of Mississippi. Chapter founder F. Harrison "Buzz" Green is at far left. National Secretary Jack L. Anson and Assistant Secretary William D. Jenkins are at the right.

of Phi Kappa Tau Fraternity that publicity be given to the fact that there are college students who believe that it is important that we who are a part of SEATO [Southeast Asia Treaty Organization] HONOR our commitments and it's about time that our fighting men in Viet Nam know that there are students who appreciate the tremendous job they are doing."

Opposition to the war on the many of the nation's campuses was reaching a fever pitch, especially in the liberal arts institutions on the West Coast and in the Northeast. Three weeks after the murder of Martin Luther King, Jr., the radical Students for a Democratic Society occupied the office of Columbia University president Grayson Kirk. Phi Tau alumnus Kirk was forced to call in police after a five-day sit-in, and classes at Columbia were suspended on May 5. Presidential candidate Robert F. Kennedy was murdered June 5.

In addition, 1968 was a presidential campaign year, and the issues of the day were being argued in the political conventions that summer. The Democratic convention in Chicago had stirred massive demonstrations and rioting. A much calmer Republican convention engineered by Republican National Chairman Ray C. Bliss (Akron, 1938) nominated Richard Nixon, who would be elected in November.

As long-time National Chaplain Rev. Charles Spotts capsulized the struggle in one of his frequent *Laurel* messages: "You may not agree with their aims or their methods, but must listen to them. They are, in many cases, a voice for change, for change that is long overdue."

The last two years of the 1960s were, if nothing else, a time of change.

Remarkably, the 1968–69 school year was, on paper, one of the most successful in the fraternity's history. All-time records for numbers of pledges and initiates were set, and three new chapters joined the Phi Tau family. Frederick H. "Buzz" Green (Indiana and Mississippi, 1966), a field secretary initiated at Indiana University, is considered the founder of Delta Gamma Chapter at the University of Mississippi. He recruited the initial group that built the chapter that was chartered on March 23, 1969. A local fraternity, Kappa Tau, which was initially founded on November 15, 1945, by World War II veterans on the Bryant College campus in Providence, Rhode Island, became Delta Delta, Phi Kappa Tau's hundredth chapter. And the next week, a colony at St. Cloud State College (now University) became Delta Epsilon Chapter, the fraternity's first in Minnesota.

For the first time in the history of the fraternity, three undergraduates were invited to attend the meeting of the National Council, held immediately prior to the 1969 IMPACT at Georgetown College in Kentucky. The report of that meeting printed in the Fall 1969 *Laurel* is the first indication to the general membership that some serious problems were cropping up in the fraternity. The National Council was becoming concerned over a significant drop in scholarship and the alarming increase in the number of housing loans to chapters that were not being repaid on schedule. President Dettra also appointed another committee to consider changes to the Ritual in a continuing effort to resolve differences with the Colgate chapter.

ANGELO ENTERS CHAPTER ETERNAL

Past National President Harold E. Angelo died in September 1969 after a long illness. Only forty-five years old, Angelo had had an impressive career in both business and higher education, including an appointment as dean of Dartmouth's Amos Tuck School of Business, and a stint as dean of men at the University of Colorado. He was serving as executive vice president of the Colorado National Bank of Denver at the time of his death. Following his service as national president, he became active in affairs of the National Interfraternity Conference, serving as secretary, treasurer, and vice president. A large number of Phi Taus attended his Denver funeral.

Though the National Council had curtailed the expansion program, three charters were granted to colonies that had been working for two or three years to achieve chapter status. Delta Zeta Chapter was installed at Emporia State University in Kansas. Founder Borradaile, in his eighty-fifth year, attended the chartering of Delta Eta Chapter at Marshall University near his West Virginia home on April 18, 1970. Two hundred fifty attended the installation of Delta Theta Chapter at Georgetown College on April 25, 1970. College president Robert Mills, a Kentucky Phi Tau, welcomed the chapter to the campus. Kappa Theta Fraternity, a local society on the New Mexico Highlands University campus since 1931, was granted the Delta Iota charter on May 2.

Beta Kappa Chapter members at Oklahoma State University in a typical 1970s pose

William D. Jenkins accepted the executive director's position in 1971.

IMPACT 1970

The long-range planning committee chaired by National Councilor Ray Clarke introduced Phi Kappa Tau's membership development plan to the delegates attending the third IMPACT program at Southern Illinois University in 1970. In an effort to rethink the traditional "pledge program," the membership development plan was designed to help build the "total man." The plan included four "experience areas": (1) manpower recruitment, (2) membership orientation (rather than pledge training), (3) membership education, and (4) membership involvement. The plan encouraged use of the term "associate member" rather than "pledge" and a four-to eight-week orientation program. The program was hailed in the interfraternity world as a logical and progressive innovation. The concepts are still embraced twenty-five years later.

"I want to introduce my friend and fraternity brother, Zev Putterman… a drug addict." Those were the words used by Jack Anson to open one of the most effective presentations of the meeting to an absolutely hushed audience. W. Zev Putterman (Colgate and Syracuse, 1947) had been initiated into Alpha Upsilon Chapter at Colgate side by side with Jack Anson. In spite of a successful career in television, Putterman had become addicted to heroin in the 1960s. Recently recovered from his addiction, he openly shared his story in frank and direct terms. The undergraduates respected him as a peer, and the difficult issue of drug abuse that was devastating the campuses was confronted.

The most significant change to come from the Fortieth National Convention, which followed the IMPACT program in St. Louis, was the addition of three appointed undergraduates to the National Council to serve two-year terms without a vote. The first three to serve were Duane G. Merrill, Jr. (Southern California, 1970), Mark R. Shaw (Emporia State, 1970), and E. Michael Mastrandrea (Florida, 1969).

Thomas L. Stennis II, was elected national president and Ray Clarke vice president. Former Field Secretary Robert D. Leatherman, an attorney with the U. S. Department of Housing and Urban Development, and future National President and Executive Director John M. Green, an Omaha banker, were elected to six-year terms on the National Council. E. A. "Ted" Marye was elected to a four-year term, filling a vacancy. Domain Chief Robert Hampton and former Director of Chapter Development Thomas C. Cunningham were elected to fill the remaining two years in the terms of Stennis and Clarke.

In semantic changes, the positions of national secretary and assistant secretary were changed to executive director and associate executive director. Domain chiefs became known as domain directors and field secretaries were now chapter consultants.

ANSON RESIGNS, JENKINS IS REPLACEMENT

Executive Director Jack Anson enjoyed his new title for only three months. He resigned, effective November 30, 1970, to accept an appointment to a newly created position of executive director for the National Interfraternity Conference, the umbrella organization of national fraternities organized in 1909. Announcing Anson's resignation, Stennis observed that "the Jack Anson years have been of unequaled progress —our chapters have doubled, our membership has tripled, and our total assets have increased more than three-fold. To the post-1950 generations, Jack Anson and Phi Kappa Tau have become one and the same." William

D. Jenkins, who had been Anson's assistant since 1964, was immediately appointed acting executive director and was soon offered the position permanently.

CHALLENGES for PHI KAPPA TAU

Jenkins took over an organization with serious problems. The campus unrest had made its way to the Midwest. In one of the most poignant events of the period, four students were shot to death by the National Guard during a demonstration at Kent State University. One of the two young men killed was Jeff Miller, who following his older brother Russ (Michigan State, 1965), had pledged Alpha Alpha Chapter as a legacy in 1968, and later transferred to Kent State.

Even some of the traditionally strong chapters were experiencing tremendous difficulty. With the help of local alumni, Jenkins had personally conducted a major overhaul of Alpha Chapter, whose membership had gone from over one hundred to four, its smallest membership in history. At Michigan State, alumni closed the chapter and sold the house, investing the proceeds for the future.

W. Zev Putterman in an informal discussion at the 1971 IMPACT at Miami University; left to right: Tom Snyder, Art McClanahan, Jim Skovran, W. Zev Putterman

Taylor Borradaile autographs copies of the Golden Jubilee History *at the 1972 national convention in Miami, Florida.*

For years, the *Laurel* had been an organ of good news; problems and embarrassments were rarely discussed. So President Stennis' report on "The State of the Fraternity" in the spring 1971 issue must have come as a shock. "The 'state' of Phi Kappa Tau," he said, "might easily be considered one of transition." In language of the day, he intended to "tell it like it is." Discussing the challenges of the 1970s, he gave an honest evaluation of the financial problems confronting the fraternity:

"Chief...are the challenges of finance. The fiscal squeeze is being applied at all levels. Chapter rushing efforts have fallen off (pledge retention has fallen off even more), houses are not filled to capacity, accounts receivable are being permitted to sky-rocket, rents are not being paid on a timely basis and house corporations are reluctant to lower the boom, and over a period of years, the National Council and Executive Office have been too permissive with the chapters and various alumni organizations."

One economy measure was evident in that same issue of the *Laurel*. The magazine was down to eight pages, and it was the second consecutive issue without a color photo on the cover. The magazine's endowment fund of over $250,000 was nearly all invested in chapter loans, which were not being repaid. Only the generosity of the Phi Tau-run Lawhead Press, the magazine's publisher since 1930, allowed the *Laurel* to continue being published on credit. And that generosity was extended to the limit.

THREE NEW CHAPTERS

In spite of the challenges of the era, three new charters were granted in 1971. No additional chapters would be added until 1975. Delta Kappa Chapter at the University of Tennessee-Knoxville was chartered on January 23, 1971. Field Secretary "Buzz" Green had recruited the initial members of the colony in the fall of 1968. The Alban Club at Muskingum College in New Concord, Ohio, received the Delta Lambda charter on April 17, 1971. A colony since 1969, the Alban Club had been founded in 1925. On November 13, the Delta Mu charter was presented to members of the colony at the College of Santa Fe in Santa Fe, New Mexico.

During the fiftieth anniversary celebration at Xi Chapter at Franklin and Marshall, the Palm Award was presented to Dr. Charles Spotts, who had served the national fraternity as scholarship commissioner, member of the National Council, and, for the last twenty years, national chaplain. As chaplain, the Xi charter member had written inspirational messages in the pages of the *Laurel* in addition to overseeing the ritualistic work of the fraternity. President Stennis replaced Spotts with Frederick Johnson

(Colorado State, 1933), chaplain of Parkview Episcopal Hospital in Pueblo, Colorado. Johnson had entered the Episcopal priesthood as a second career after many years as a pharmacist.

Upsilon Chapter, which continued its strength at Nebraska Wesleyan through the 1970s, increased the capacity of their chapter house from thirty-nine to sixty with a $150,000 addition.

UNDERGRADUATES PROPOSE LEGISLATION

To save money, the 1972 IMPACT program was conducted in conjunction with the national convention at the Doral Country Club in Miami, Florida. Founder Borradaile, now walking with the help of two canes, was the convention's celebrity as undergraduates and alumni waited in line to purchase copies of *The Golden Jubilee History* autographed by Borradaile.

Undergraduates took the lead in making significant changes to fraternity policy. Future National President John F. Cosgrove (Florida, 1968), attending his second convention, led the effort to grant constitutional approval to the "little sister" organizations that were successfully operating in several chapters. A special membership card, badge, and initiation Ritual were designed for these women's auxiliary organizations. Resident council delegates finally gained full voting status for the three undergraduate members of the National Council. Domain Director James Heilmeier (Kent State, 1949) and Thomas C. Cunningham were elected to six-year terms on the National Council; Ray Clarke became president and Ted Marye vice president. Jack Jareo announced his retirement from a very successful six-year stint as editor of the *Laurel*, now in its second year in cost-saving tabloid format. Terry Leaman (Ohio, 1963) would succeed Jareo on February 1, 1973, with the new title of director of communications and public relations.

Capt. Bruce Archer is reunited with his wife after five years in a Vietnamese prison camp.

POW ARCHER RELEASED

Phi Taus at Rho Chapter finally got some good news from Vietnam as the United States was extricating itself from the long divisive war. Capt. Bruce Archer (Rensselaer, 1962) was released from a Viet Cong prisoner-of-war camp, where he had been held since his helicopter was shot down in 1968. Initially reported dead, his wife learned he was alive from a 1968 Christmas card. Rho advisor David Merow (Rensselaer, 1956) organized a letter-writing campaign to plead for his release when he learned about Archer's imprisonment in 1971. Archer was honored at Rho's homecoming celebration shortly after his return.

As a national fraternity, austerity was the order of the day for Phi Tau throughout the middle 1970s. The rapid decline in the number of men associated and initiated that came so quickly between 1969 and 1972 lev-

Taylor A. Borradaile at home in 1975

CONVENTION POSTPONED

The 1974 convention planned for Tan-Tar-A resort in Missouri's Ozark Mountains was postponed until 1975. President Clarke's public explanation blamed the postponement on the national energy shortage and the National Council's desire to hold a 1981 convention to celebrate the fraternity's seventy-fifth anniversary. While that was true, another important reality was that the fraternity could not afford it. IMPACT was now being conducted on a regional basis with an extremely tight budget and staffed with volunteer help from the revitalized domain director corps.

The spring of 1975 saw the installation of the only three chapters chartered between 1971 and 1982. The first two charters went to primarily commuter campuses in Ohio cities. Delta Nu Chapter was chartered at Wright State University in Dayton, and Delta Xi Chapter was installed at the urban Cleveland State University. Far from urban Ohio, the Delta Omicron charter went to a colony at Pan American University in Edinburg, Texas.

eled off, and an equilibrium was reached by the 1973–74 school year. Initiations, for example, reached a high of 1,724 in 1967–68. By the 1971–72 academic year, initiations had dropped to a low of 977 men. Climbing back to 1,105 initiates in 1973–74, that number would remain absolutely stagnant until the 1981–82 academic year. Though there was a general feeling of recovery, what really took place in the 1970s was a struggle to survive on a severely restricted budget and to find ways to reposition the organization for growth.

PHI TAU SPORTS STARS

A bright spot in the seventies was the athletic prowess of several Phi Tau alumni. Wendell Ladner (Southern Mississippi, 1969) was a standout in the American Basketball Association. Bill Mallory (Miami, 1954) was head coach of his alma mater's undefeated football squad that beat Florida in the Tangerine Bowl. Wes Stock (Washington State, 1954) was pitching coach for the Oakland A's in two World Series appearances.

The Tan-Tar-A convention of 1975 was memorable as the last one Founder Borradaile was to attend. Several lasting changes to the governance structure of the fraternity were made. The convention approved the creation of a system that allowed the vice president to automatically become president and finally permitted the election rather than appointment of the three undergraduate national councilors.

Raymond A. Bichimer (Ohio State, 1953) became the first representative of the Phi Kappa Tau Foundation to sit ex-officio on the National Council. Bichimer, who had been president of the foundation since 1971, had made tremendous strides to improve the relationship between the trustees of the foundation and the National Council.

Two past national presidents who had been key players in foundation activities since its formation were lost in the year following the 1975 convention. Dr. Henry Hoagland died in September 1975, and F. R. Fletemeyer died in 1976. Their loss dramatically changed the complexion of the board. Ewing Boles, the foundation's only remaining incorporator, had been chairman of the board since Bichimer became president.

Roland Maxwell presents the Maxwell Award to Dean Moors, president of Upsilon Chapter at Nebraska Wesleyan in 1977.

KEYSTONE CONVENTION DEDICATED *to* BORRADAILE

The 1977 national convention at Keystone, Colorado, was dedicated to Taylor Borradaile, who had died just before the convention at age ninety-two. As Phi Kappa Tau's only living Founder since 1958, Borradaile had been the link to the founding for an entire generation of Phi Taus. He had not missed a convention since he attended his first in 1951.

The delegates approved the first set of chapter standards to begin to hold under-performing chapters accountable. The campaign to get all chapters in compliance with the standards was called the "Borradaile Challenge."

Architect F. L. "Mac" McKinley acceded to the presidency, and Thomas Cunningham was elected vice president. Thomas Hendricks (Georgia Tech, 1961) was elected to fill the remaining two years of Cunningham's term. Johnny Johnson (Mississippi State, 1964) and Robert B. Mintz (Ohio State, 1971) were elected to six-year terms on the National Council in an open election, which included campaign speeches for the first time ever.

JENKINS RESIGNS

The big news of the convention came in the executive director's report when William D. Jenkins announced his intention to resign his position no later than June 1, 1978. The financial problems of the national fraternity had made the job an unpleasant one and Jenkins was ready to do something different. "I told myself that when the job was no longer fun, I'd look for something else to do." By 1977, that time had come. He ended up leaving sooner than he had anticipated, when a job opportunity became available in the spring of 1978.

CHAPTER HISTORIES

ΓΕ

GAMMA EPSILON CHAPTER
University of the Pacific
Stockton, California

Founded as Archania, 1854
Chartered as Phi Kappa Tau,
November 18, 1961

IN 1854 THOMAS H. LAINE and eleven other men founded the Archania Literary Society at the University of the Pacific. Early debates over slavery split the society in 1858, with the southern sympathizers maintaining the name Archania. Southern symbols such as the Confederate battle flag and a collection of bells representing women known as "belles" became a part of Archania's tradition. An impressive brick home was constructed in 1924, and an addition was built in 1961.

At the time of Archania's installation as Gamma Epsilon Chapter, it was the oldest local fraternity in America. The school's dean of students, Edward S. Betz, and Academic Vice President Dr. Samuel Meyer both joined the undergraduates in signing as charter members of Gamma Epsilon. At the installation banquet, Jack Anson presented the charter to President Rich Heil. National President Harold E. Angelo spoke at the banquet, as did his predecessor, Roland Maxwell.

Gamma Epsilon returned to its local status in 1978.

ΓΖ

GAMMA ZETA CHAPTER
University of Connecticut
Storrs, Connecticut

Founded as Phi Chi Alpha,
November 12, 1957
Chartered as Phi Kappa Tau,
December 3, 1961

PHI CHI ALPHA was an outgrowth of the pharmaceutical fraternity Phi Delta Chi, which had existed on the Connecticut campus since 1949. After two years of research, the local chose to affiliate with Phi Kappa Tau.

The installation was conducted on December 3, 1961, beginning with an afternoon tea at the chapter house, where the Gamma Zeta charter was signed. The installation banquet was at the Nathan Hale Hotel in Willimantic, Connecticut. Past National President Roland Maxwell and Jack Anson made brief remarks, and National President Harold E. Angelo gave a stimulating talk about the importance of maintaining the good reputation of the chapter. Chapter President Tim Salius accepted the Gamma Zeta charter.

Gamma Zeta Chapter became inactive in 1971.

ΓΗ

GAMMA ETA CHAPTER
East Carolina University
Greenville, North Carolina

Chartered as Phi Kappa Tau,
February 4, 1962

FIELD SECRETARY Roger Vaughn started the East Carolina colony in the spring of 1960. Seven men were in the original group. Three more were recruited in the 1960 fall rush, and an apartment was rented as a colony headquarters. When the colony outgrew the apartment, it rented a large space above a downtown Greenville shoe store for a chapter room, which was furnished with the help of a $500 loan from the national fraternity. An installation date was established when the colony had grown to thirty members.

The formal installation banquet was held in East Carolina's south dining hall on the evening of February 4, 1962. National Secretary Jack L. Anson presented the charter to Michael Wilkinson, president of the new Gamma Eta Chapter. The featured speaker was National President Harold E. Angelo, who discussed various aspects of responsibility. The colony's first president, Barney West, recounted the history of the group.

The charter had been signed earlier in the afternoon at a tea held at the Greenville Art Center.

ΓΘ

GAMMA THETA CHAPTER
Western Michigan University
Kalamazoo, Michigan

Founded as Beta Theta Upsilon
Chartered as Phi Kappa Tau,
April 13, 1962

MEMBERS OF WESTERN MICHIGAN local fraternity Beta Theta Upsilon worked for more than two years to attain chapter status in Phi Kappa Tau. The Gamma Theta charter was signed in ceremonies at the Western Michigan Student Center at 2:30 in the afternoon. From there, the crowd moved to the Southgate Inn for the installation banquet. Gale D. Dickinson (Michigan State, 1950), chairman of the Gamma Theta board of governors, was toastmaster. National Secretary Jack L. Anson delivered the main address, and Domain Chief J. Cullen Kennedy (Michigan, 1929) presented the charter to Gamma Theta President Andrew R. Rio. Past National President Frederick R. Fletemeyer made a special presentation of a copy of *The Golden Jubilee History of Phi Kappa Tau.*

At the time of the installation, visitors were able to see the new chapter house for Gamma Theta at 323 Stuart Street. House Corporation President Robert Zimmerman (Purdue, 1929) planned extensive renovations to the house over the summer to ready it for occupancy in the fall of 1962.

Gamma Theta became inactive in 1974.

Π

GAMMA IOTA CHAPTER
California State University–
Sacramento
Sacramento, California

Founded as Xi Theta Chi,
September 1946
Chartered as Phi Kappa Tau,
March 23, 1963

XI THETA CHI was founded by a group of World War II veterans attending Sacramento Junior College. When the school became Sacramento State College in 1947, Xi Theta Chi was the first fraternity to be recognized on the campus. Xi Theta Chi adopted a badge and coat of arms in the colors black and gold.

By the late 1950s, the college was encouraging the six local fraternities to consider national affiliations. Phi Kappa Tau began conversations with three locals and formally entered into a colony relationship on May 20, 1960.

Installation ceremonies took place on the Sacramento State campus on March 23, 1963. A loan from the national fraternity allowed the new chapter to purchase a 2-story house at 2231 "H" Street in Sacramento in 1965. Negotiations were handled by Ben Brewer (Southern California, 1947) who served as advisor and house corporation president for several years. Later, a single story house on a large lot was acquired. The chapter was living in this house when it became inactive in 1987 because of low membership.

ΓΚ

GAMMA KAPPA CHAPTER
C. W. Post College
of Long Island University
Greenvale, New York

Founded as Phi Tau, spring 1960
Chartered as Phi Kappa Tau,
February 29, 1964

IN THE FALL OF 1959, a group of men petitioned the Faculty Committee on Fraternities and Sororities for recognition. After a year of probation, official recognition by the college came in May 1961, with full voting privileges on the Interfraternity Council. With a membership of twenty-three, the group was granted colony status by Phi Kappa Tau in February 1962.

The Gamma Kappa charter was granted on February 29, 1964. A reception for the campus fraternities and sororities was held in the Pioneer Room of the school's south dining hall on the afternoon of the installation. The charter signing and installation banquet were held that evening at the Garden City Hotel. National President Dr. W. A. Hammond presided at the installation, and National Secretary Anson presented the charter to Gamma Kappa President Kenneth Uyl.

The chapter became inactive in 1974. An unsuccessful effort to revive the chapter by a group of undergraduates was begun in 1985. A second group formed in the spring of 1992 and was successful in returning the Gamma Kappa charter to C. W. Post on April 16, 1994. Past National President Ray A. Clarke and Director of Chapter Services Michael Reed presided at the installation.

ΓΛ

GAMMA LAMBDA CHAPTER
Central Michigan University
Mount Pleasant, Michigan

Founded as Lambda Nu,
May 1, 1963
Chartered as Phi Kappa Tau,
May 9, 1965

GAMMA LAMBDA Chapter had its beginnings in May 1963, when Lambda Nu Fraternity was founded in Warriner Hall. There were six initial members who built the group around the idea that hazing was not necessary for a successful fraternity. In the spring of 1964, Corresponding Secretary Jeff Rivard sent letters to potential national fraternities. A letter to National Councilor J. Cullen Kennedy (Michigan, 1929)

produced a visit from William D. Jenkins and Field Secretary Robert D. Leatherman (Akron, 1960), who installed Lambda Nu as a colony.

The installation took place on May 9, 1965. The charter was signed at an afternoon reception for members of the faculty, campus fraternities and sororities, and other alumni and friends. At the installation banquet, Jack L. Anson presented the charter to Gamma Lambda President James Maybaugh, and National President Lou Gerding gave the installation address.

The chapter closed early in 1989. Recolonization was begun in October 1990, with nineteen founders. The charter was granted to the new group on February 13, 1993. The charter was signed in the University Center ballroom, and the installation banquet was held at the Mount Pleasant Holiday Inn. Foundation Executive Vice President William D. Jenkins presided, and National Councilor Richard P. Harrison, Jr., gave the installation address. Executive Director John Green presented the charter to President James Bojack.

GAMMA MU CHAPTER
Bradley University
Peoria, Illinois

Chartered as Phi Kappa Tau,
May 16, 1965

IN THE FALL OF 1961, a group of friends living in Constance Hall and known around campus as the "connie cats" decided to start a new fraternity. Jeff Goetz had pledged Zeta Chapter before he transferred to Bradley, so under his influence, a Phi Kappa Tau charter became the group's objective. They officially became a colony on May 18, 1962. The colony rented a house at 1603 West Main Street in the summer of 1962, their home until the fall of 1964 when they rented a house on West Barker Street.

With the chartering requirements accomplished, Gamma Mu was installed on May 16, 1965. National Secretary Jack Anson presented the Gamma Mu charter to Chapter President Robert T. Otswald. Dean Edward M. King welcomed the chapter to the campus, and National President Lou Gerding gave the principal address.

The next fall, Gamma Mu moved to 1511 West Fredonia and soon rented the house next door as the young chapter grew. The chapter bought both of those properties over time, and they became known as the Red and Gold houses. They were demolished in 1983 to make way for a brand-new chapter house, which the chapter occupied in the fall of 1983.

GAMMA NU CHAPTER
Rochester Institute of Technology
Rochester, New York

Founded as Kappa Phi Omega,
November 1962
Chartered as Phi Kappa Tau,
April 2, 1966

KAPPA PHI OMEGA was born in the fall of 1962 to increase the Greek opportunities for men at Rochester Institute of Technology. The fraternity set about recruiting new members and becoming involved in campus activities. Kappa Phi Omega captured top fraternity scholarship honors in 1964–65. A chapter house was acquired and improved.

Having completed all of the chartering requirements, Gamma Nu was installed on April 2, 1966. At two o'clock in the afternoon, the chapter hosted a reception at the chapter house for members of the RIT faculty and administration, other fraternities, and Phi Tau dignitaries.

In a local banquet hall, Chapter President Gary Proud accepted the Gamma Nu charter. National President Gerding's address discussed the importance of the college fraternity system to the campus. When the RIT campus moved from downtown Rochester to its suburban campus in 1967, the fraternities gave up their private homes for modern on-campus residences.

GAMMA XI CHAPTER
East Central Oklahoma
State University
Ada, Oklahoma

Chartered as Phi Kappa Tau,
April 15, 1966

IN THE FALL of 1963, Tom Stubblefield, then pledged to Beta Kappa Chapter at Oklahoma State, obtained permission from Domain Chief F. L. "Mac" McKinley to investigate forming a colony at East Central State. In the 1964 spring semester, Stubblefield, Doyle Yarbourough, Monte Tull, and Ron Tucker, all members of Beta Kappa, transferred to East Central and formed a colony of Phi Kappa Tau.

The colony was installed as Gamma Xi Chapter on April 15, 1966. Following the afternoon charter signing, Dr. Edward James (Mississippi State, 1938) and his wife hosted a reception at their home. Dr. James was the first president of Alpha Chi Chapter, and his son became a charter member of Gamma Xi.

In the evening of April 15, National President Gerding gave the major address, and National Secretary Jack L. Anson presented the charter to Gamma Xi President Monte Tull.

GAMMA OMICRON CHAPTER
California State University–
Fullerton
Fullerton, California

Founded as Sigma Phi Omega,
fall 1960
Chartered as Phi Kappa Tau,
September 18, 1966

FIFTEEN MEN founded Sigma Phi Omega in the fall of 1960. Sam Cooper was the first president. The "Sigs" were the first Fullerton fraternity to acquire a chapter house in 1963, and the house boasted a separate study/library building, which was open twenty-four hours a day. The local became active in all facets of student life and, at the time of the installation, had the sophomore and junior class presidents and senior class vice president and treasurer among the membership.

Phi Kappa Tau's President Emeritus Roland Maxwell led the installing delegation as National President Warren Parker's representative. A charter signing, reception, and open house were held on the afternoon of September 18, 1966, and the installation banquet followed at the Saddleback Inn in Santa Ana. Gamma Omicron President Larry Birdwell accepted the charter from National Secretary Jack Anson. Director of Chapter Development Thomas C. Cunningham and Domain Chief Michael J. Raleigh also attended the installation.

ΓΠ

GAMMA PI CHAPTER
Youngstown State University
Youngstown, Ohio

Founded as Zeta Phi, 1956
Chartered as Phi Kappa Tau,
January 29, 1967

TWELVE VETERANS of the Korean War founded Zeta Phi Fraternity in 1956. The men were older than many students and they wanted to belong to a fraternity, but they were not willing to undergo the childish antics that were part of the existing fraternities' pledge programs. Before long, the group occupied a house on Park Avenue and adopted a constitution and the motto, "Cerebrum et Lacertus" (brains and brawn). Black and gray were the official colors.

By 1964 President Edward Knoop was promoting the idea of national affiliation, and Phi Kappa Tau became the leading candidate.

Director of Chapter Development Thomas C. Cunningham made a personal visit to Zeta Phi on May 5, 1965, and soon thereafter the group voted to work toward a Phi Kappa Tau charter.

The installation took place January 29, 1967, with National Councilor Melvin Dettra, Jr., taking the place of National President Warren Parker, who was caught in a Chicago snowstorm. Charter President Ronald L. Wasiluk accepted the Gamma Pi charter from National Secretary Jack L. Anson.

ΓΡ

GAMMA RHO CHAPTER
University of Nebraska at Kearney
Kearney, Nebraska

Chartered as Phi Kappa Tau,
April 1, 1967

THE NATIONAL FRATERNITY'S director of chapter development, Thomas C. Cunningham, established the Kearney colony on November 13, 1965. Don Hicks was appointed and later elected the first president. Twenty-five men had joined by the end of the first semester. A chapter home was established at 800 West 26th street in the fall of 1966 through the efforts of local alumni.

With the entire National Council present, the installation activities began with a luncheon at the St. John Motor Court, owned by Hart St. John (Nebraska Wesleyan, 1960), who was a member of the new chapter's board of governors and house corporation. The charter was signed at an afternoon reception at the chapter house, and the installation banquet followed at Grandpa's Steakhouse. National President Parker's address was titled "LSD— Leadership, Scholarship, and Devotion." National Secretary Jack L. Anson presented the Gamma Rho charter to Chapter President William Anderson.

The National Council, which was meeting in Kearney that weekend, was joined by representatives of chapters at Iowa State, the University of Kansas, and Nebraska Wesleyan, the latter presenting a Phi Tau flag to the new chapter as a gift of Upsilon Chapter.

ΓΣ

GAMMA SIGMA CHAPTER
University of California, Davis
Davis, California

*Chartered as Phi Kappa Tau,
April 29, 1967*

THE UNIVERSITY of California, Davis, invited Phi Kappa Tau to build a chapter on the campus after National Secretary Jack L. Anson's presentation to the faculty-student review board in 1965. Director of Chapter Development Thomas C. Cunningham built a colony of twenty-two men in the spring of 1966. Cunningham appointed Tom Arms as the colony's first president.

Andrew Henry, an assistant dean at the school, became a colony advisor and was later initiated. Dean Harold Hakes (Bowling Green, 1950) also served as an advisor and was instrumental in helping to equip the "B" Street chapter house acquired in 1967.

The colony was installed as Gamma Sigma Chapter on April 29, 1967. After a charter-signing ceremony and reception at the chapter house, the new chapter and visiting officers moved to the Caravan Inn in Sacramento for the black-tie installation banquet. Dean Hakes was toastmaster, and Jack L. Anson presented the Gamma Sigma charter to James Hall, the new chapter's president. National President Warren H. Parker addressed the scholastic value of a fraternity and its lifetime value in his remarks. A dance followed the installation banquet.

Gamma Sigma has been inactive since 1971.

ΓΤ

GAMMA TAU CHAPTER
Old Dominion University
Norfolk, Virginia

*Founded as Omega Phi Sigma,
May 1962
Chartered as Phi Kappa Tau,
December 2, 1967*

THIRTEEN STUDENTS from the Technical Institute, a two-year branch of Old Dominion, formed Omega Phi Sigma in May 1962 as a social club. The local occupied its first house and had grown to thirty men by the fall of 1964. Phi Kappa Tau accepted the group as a colony on February 8, 1965. Over the summer of 1967, the house was entirely remodeled and new living-room furniture installed.

Gamma Tau Chapter was officially born on December 2, 1967, when thirty-four men signed the charter in afternoon ceremonies. That evening, the installation banquet convened at the College Center. National President Warren H. Parker gave the installation address, and National Secretary Jack L. Anson presented the Gamma Tau charter to Frank O. Caudle, the new chapter's president.

Gamma Tau became inactive in 1972.

ΓΥ

GAMMA UPSILON CHAPTER
Spring Hill College
Mobile, Alabama

Founded as Gamma Sigma,
May 4, 1963
Chartered as Phi Kappa Tau,
December 3, 1967

CHARLES PASKERT and Arthur Rhyne are considered cofounders of Gamma Sigma local fraternity, the predecessor of Gamma Upsilon Chapter of Phi Kappa Tau. Gamma Sigma quickly made an impact on the social and intellectual life of the campus. As soon as the Spring Hill prohibition of national fraternities was lifted, Gamma Sigma searched for a national affiliation and officially became a Phi Kappa Tau colony on September 28, 1966. Domain Chief Thomas L. Stennis II, was instrumental in the colony's preparation for a charter.

The installation ceremonies were conducted on December 3, 1967. Thirty-three undergraduates and eleven alumni signed the Gamma Upsilon charter during an afternoon reception at the student center. Former President Richard Lynch's mother signed the charter for her son, who had died while working in Mexico.

At the installation banquet, Chapter President J. Allen Neuenschwander accepted the Gamma Upsilon charter from National Secretary Jack L. Anson. Gamma Sigma Founder Arthur Rhyne made congratulatory remarks, and Thomas L. Stennis II, gave the primary address.

ΓΦ

GAMMA PHI CHAPTER
Northeastern University
Boston, Massachusetts

Founded as Zeta Gamma Tau,
September 1959
Chartered as Phi Kappa Tau,
January 27, 1968

IN 1959 SIXTEEN Northeastern students formed Zeta Gamma Tau Fraternity, which was recognized by the university in 1961. The sixty members of Zeta Gamma Tau formally requested that Phi Kappa Tau grant them colony status. The Gamma Phi charter was granted on January 27, 1968. The chapter became inactive in 1976.

In the spring of 1986, roommates Greg Eakman and Doug Clinton started a twelve-member local fraternity on the Northeastern campus, adopting the name Phi Delta Nu. With the guidance of John Mullen and Mark Reed, members of Gamma Nu Chapter at the Rochester Institute of Technology, Phi Delta Nu decided to attempt to return the Gamma Phi charter to Northeastern. By January 1987, the group had doubled its membership and rented a seven-bedroom house. Executive Director John Meyerhoff visited the group on January 12, 1987, and officially established the group as Gamma Phi colony. The colony earned the Northeastern Fraternity of the Year Award and the Fraternity Man of the Year Award in May 1988.

The Gamma Phi charter returned to the Northeastern campus on May 31, 1988. Forty-seven men signed the charter at the Carl Ell Student Center, and the installation banquet took place at the Somerville City Club, where Executive Director John Green presented the charter to Gamma Phi founder and president, Greg Eakman.

The chapter was suspended for disciplinary reasons in 1995.

ΓΧ

GAMMA CHI CHAPTER
Delta State University
Cleveland, Mississippi

Founded as Phi Tau Delta, 1963
Chartered as Phi Kappa Tau,
February 25, 1968

DENNIS SMITH (Mississippi State, 1962) established local fraternity Phi Tau Delta when he transferred to Delta State. Ten men belonged to the original group founded in 1963. Dr. William F. LaForge (Southern Mississippi, 1956), head of the department of social science, was recruited immediately to chair the board of governors. Phi Tau Delta became a Phi Kappa Tau colony in the spring of 1965.

National Councilor Thomas L. Stennis II, headed the delegation of installing officers in National President Warren H. Parker's stead. Dr. LaForge was toastmaster at the installation banquet, where Stennis gave the principal address. Gamma Chi President Robert A. Quinn accepted the charter from National Secretary Jack L. Anson.

Gamma Chi became inactive in 1978 and was briefly reestablished in 1990 only to close again.

ΓΨ

GAMMA PSI CHAPTER
Southwest Texas State University
San Marcos, Texas

Founded as Sigma Kappa Epsilon,
November 1965
Chartered as Phi Kappa Tau,
April 20, 1968

SIGMA KAPPA EPSILON was founded by twenty-three men on the Southwest Texas State campus in November 1965. In its first month of existence, members of Beta Alpha Chapter at the University of Texas approached the local about affiliating with Phi Kappa Tau. After a personal visit from Assistant National Secretary William D. Jenkins, the local voted unanimously to pursue a Phi Kappa Tau charter.

On April 20, 1968, the Gamma Psi charter was signed during an afternoon reception at the home of Dr. Walter S. Corrie (Colgate, 1941), an associate professor of sociology at the school.

National Secretary Anson presented the charter to Gamma Psi President Bill Ramsey during the installation banquet at the Villa Capri Hotel in Austin. Past National President Lou Gerding gave the installation address, remarking that he was a charter member of Psi Chapter and had now participated in the installations of Alpha Psi, Beta Psi, and Gamma Psi Chapters.

Gamma Psi Chapter has been inactive since 1988.

ΓΩ

GAMMA OMEGA CHAPTER
La Salle College
Philadelphia, Pennsylvania

Founded as Committee of
Explorers, March 8, 1959
Adopted name Sigma Phi Lambda,
February 2, 1961
Chartered as Phi Kappa Tau,
April 27, 1968

TWENTY SPIRITED STUDENTS formed an organization to curb student apathy on March 8, 1959. The organization was clearly fraternal from the outset, but they first chose the name Committee of Explorers (COE).

When COE made it known that they intended to form a Greek-letter fraternity, alumni of the defunct local Sigma Phi Lambda approached the group asking them to revive the local, which had been closed since World War II. COE voted to adopt the aims, traditions, and name of Sigma Phi Lambda, which had originally been founded on November 14, 1935.

Sigma Phi Lambda became a colony of Phi Kappa Tau on February 5, 1968. The local was installed as Gamma Omega Chapter on April 27, 1968. Chapter President Paul E. Vignone accepted the charter, which had been signed by fifty-five undergraduates and three alumni. National Councilor Melvin Dettra, Jr., gave the evening's principal address following words from college officials and National Secretary Anson.

Gamma Omega's success was short-lived, and it became inactive in 1971.

ΔA

Delta Alpha Chapter
Iowa Wesleyan College
Mount Pleasant, Iowa

Chartered as Phi Kappa Tau,
May 19, 1968

THE IOWA WESLEYAN colony was established with twenty-six men in February 1967. Over the next year, members of the colony became deeply involved in the athletic, academic, and political activities of the campus.

The installation took place on May 19, 1968. Phi Kappa Tau's National President Warren H. Parker and Iowa Wesleyan's President Dr. Franklin H. Littel both participated in the ceremonies.

The president of the new Delta Alpha Chapter accepted the charter from National Secretary Jack L. Anson.

Delta Alpha became inactive in 1984 because of low membership.

ΔB

Delta Beta Chapter
University of Evansville
Evansville, Indiana

Founded as SODALITAS, 1967
Chartered as Phi Kappa Tau,
May 26, 1968

NINETEEN MEN founded a local group in 1967 called SODALITAS, a Latin word translated to mean "society of persons with common interests and common goals." Phi Kappa Tau was selected from a list of twelve national fraternities for affiliation. It was a happy coincidence that the group's faculty advisor, Evansville swimming coach James S. Voorhees (Illinois, 1952), was a member of Phi Kappa Tau. Coach Voorhees had been a Shideler Award winner in 1955.

Forty-three men signed the Delta Beta charter, the fraternity's ninety-eighth. Following the charter signing, the installation banquet was held at the Evansville Ramada Inn. National President Warren H. Parker give the installation address, university President Dr. Wallace Billingsley Graves welcomed the new chapter to the campus, and National Secretary Jack L. Anson presented the charter to Delta Beta President Robert S. Howe.

For many years, Delta Beta's chapter house was a large residential home on Lincoln Avenue. In 1985 the chapter moved to a newly built home on campus, which was financed by the university. The house, which holds forty-eight men, is on a Greek square with two other fraternities.

ΔΓ

Delta Gamma Chapter
University of Mississippi
Oxford, Mississippi

Chartered as Phi Kappa Tau,
March 23, 1969

THE UNIVERSITY OF MISSISSIPPI invited Phi Kappa Tau to colonize on the campus in March 1967. On May 11 Director of Chapter Development Thomas C. Cunningham officially formed a colony from a group that F. Harrison "Buzz" Green had put together earlier in the school year. Green is considered the chapter's founder.

The Delta Gamma charter was signed on the afternoon of March 23, 1969. National President Melvin Dettra, Jr., gave the principal address at the installation banquet at the Oxford Holiday Inn. National Secretary Jack L. Anson presented the Delta Gamma charter to Chapter President Peter Lauer.

The chapter obtained a small house near the campus that served as a chapter house until 1984, when Delta Gamma moved into its newly constructed thirty-six-man home. The construction of the house was made possible primarily by the hard work of alumni Brad Rainey and Pat Patterson.

148

ΔΔ

DELTA DELTA CHAPTER
Bryant College
Smithfield, Rhode Island

Founded as Kappa Tau,
November 15, 1945
Chartered as Phi Kappa Tau,
May 10, 1969

THE BRYANT LOCAL fraternity, Kappa Tau, was founded by twenty-seven men on November 15, 1945. A constitution and bylaws were approved two months later at a meeting in the old Bryant library. The local came near extinction in 1951, but successful recruitment in 1952 averted the crisis, and the chapter gained strength through the 1950s and 1960s.

Kappa Tau was installed as Delta Delta Chapter on May 10, 1969, when thirty-four undergraduates and twenty-seven alumni signed the charter. National President Melvin Dettra, Jr., was the primary speaker at the installation banquet, and National Secretary Jack L. Anson presented the fraternity's one hundredth charter to Delta Delta President David J. Paire.

In 1971 the campus was moved to Smithfield from Providence. Dur-ing the change of campuses, it was decided not to continue affiliation with Phi Kappa Tau because of the uncertainty of the new surroundings and a reduction in membership. The fraternity reclaimed the Kappa Tau name on March 3, 1990, when they became a colony of Phi Kappa Tau.

The charter was returned in installation ceremonies on May 14, 1994. Past National President Thomas C. Cunningham and William D. Jenkins, executive vice president of the Phi Kappa Tau Foundation presided at the rechartering.

ΔΕ

DELTA EPSILON CHAPTER
Saint Cloud State University
Saint Cloud, Minnesota

Chartered as Phi Kappa Tau,
May 17, 1969

THE COLONY AT Saint Cloud State was founded by thirty men recruited by Field Secretary Larry Jones (Colorado State, 1963) on February 25, 1968. The colony occupied a house on the banks of the Mississippi at 201 Ramsey Place in the fall of 1968. The colony membership had grown to forty-eight by the time of the installation.

Colony members signed the Delta Epsilon charter on Saturday afternoon, May 17, 1969. The installation banquet and dance took place that evening at the Atwood Memorial College Center on the campus. Past National President Warren H. Parker gave the principal address, and National Secretary Jack L. Anson presented the Delta Epsilon charter to Chapter President William Nord. Gary Baumann, who would later join the national fraternity's staff, was named the 1968–69 Mr. Phi Tau at the banquet. Delta Epsilon became inactive in 1979 but has recently returned to the campus.

National Vice President Stephen Brothers and Assistant Executive Director Craig Little returned the Delta Epsilon charter in ceremonies held the weekend of April 29–May 1, 1994. Three of the chapter's original charter members took part in the installation.

ΔΖ

DELTA ZETA CHAPTER
Emporia State University
Emporia, Kansas

Chartered as Phi Kappa Tau,
March 14, 1970

DIRECTOR OF CHAPTER Development Thomas C. Cunningham selected twelve men through an interview process to form the nucleus of a colony in November 1967. Tucker Kehoe was the first president. The colony acquired a small lodge for meetings and social functions in 1968, then bought a house the next year.

Phi Kappa Tau became the eighth national fraternity chartered on the

Emporia State campus, then known as Kansas State Teachers College. The installation ceremonies took place on March 14, 1970, culminating more than two years of organizational work. The college's president, Dr. John E. Visser, was the guest of the new chapter at the afternoon charter signing and reception. Domain Chief John M. Green traveled from Omaha for the festivities.

National President Melvin Dettra Jr., presided at the installation banquet that evening, and National Secretary Jack L. Anson presented the newly signed charter to Delta Zeta President Mark Shaw.

The chapter became inactive in 1977.

ΔH

DELTA ETA CHAPTER
Marshall University
Huntington, West Virginia

Founded as Beta Nu,
October 1966
Chartered as Phi Kappa Tau,
April 18, 1970

WHEN THE MARSHALL Interfraternity Council decided the campus needed more fraternities in the fall of 1966, six men founded Beta Nu Fraternity. After a visit from Assistant National Secretary William D. Jenkins in April 1967, Beta Nu voted to seek a charter from Phi Kappa Tau. That fall, the colony purchased a house at 1638 Sixth Avenue and raised the funds to equip its new home.

Phi Kappa Tau's 103rd charter was presented to the former Beta Nu Fraternity on April 18, 1970, during an installation banquet at the Hotel Frederick. The Delta Eta charter was signed earlier that day at the chapter house. Founder and Mrs. Taylor A. Borradaile were the honored guests of the entire installation, with Founder Borradaile affixing his signature to the Delta Eta constitution and making characteristically brief remarks at the banquet. National President Melvin Dettra, Jr., gave the main installation address.

Despite its auspicious beginning, the chapter became inactive within a year.

ΔΘ

DELTA THETA CHAPTER
Georgetown College
Georgetown, Kentucky

Chartered as Phi Kappa Tau,
April 25, 1970

GEORGETOWN COLLEGE President Dr. Robert Mills (Kentucky, 1935) encouraged Phi Kappa Tau to enter Georgetown, and a colony was founded on May 17, 1968. The colony grew steadily and was invigorated by IMPACT–1969, held on the campus in August. The colony won the Interfraternity Council scholarship cup in both 1969 and 1970 and built a membership of thirty-four men.

More than 250 persons attended a reception at the Georgetown Student Center preceding the signing of the Delta Theta charter on April 25, 1970. Chapter President Carl Hensley accepted the Delta Theta charter from National Secretary Jack L. Anson at the installation banquet that evening. Georgetown Dean of Men James Bergman welcomed the chapter to the campus, and IFC Vice President John Sturm brought greetings from the rest of the campus Greeks. National President Melvin Dettra, Jr., gave the installation's principal address.

In the fraternity, Delta Theta's most notable alumnus was Dr. W. Joseph Joiner, who had been elected national vice president of Phi Kappa Tau in 1989 and was in line to become national president before his untimely death.

ΔI

DELTA IOTA CHAPTER
New Mexico Highlands University
Las Vegas, New Mexico

Founded as Kappa Theta, 1931
Chartered as Phi Kappa Tau,
May 2, 1970

SERVICE, SACRIFICE, and loyalty were the founding principles of Kappa Theta Fraternity in 1931. The local built a reputation as a campus leader. Early in 1968, Kappa Theta decided to end its nearly forty years as a local and become affiliated with Phi Kappa Tau.

The installation took place on May 2, 1970. Chapter President Jim Pendergrass accepted the Delta Iota charter, which had been signed earlier that afternoon, on behalf of the new chapter. National President Melvin Dettra, Jr., gave the principal address of the evening at the Flamingo Inn. Former Field Secretary Dr. John S. Johnson (Lawrence, 1935), assistant to the Highlands president and chapter advisor, was the master of ceremonies for the installation banquet.

By 1975 the new chapter had become inactive.

ΔK

DELTA KAPPA CHAPTER
University of Tennessee
Knoxville, Tennessee

Chartered as Phi Kappa Tau,
January 23, 1971

FIELD SECRETARY F. Harrison "Buzz" Green recruited a nucleus of eight men during the week of September 22, 1968. A month later, nineteen men participated in the formal beginning of the colony. The university made the former Pi Kappa Phi house at 1800 Lake Avenue available as a chapter house.

Thirty colony members signed the Delta Kappa charter in the Heritage Room of the Carolyn P. Brown Memorial University Center. National President Thomas L. Stennis II, and acting Executive Director William D. Jenkins were joined in the festivities by board of governors members Robert B. Bernhard (Cornell, 1959), Philip W. Hyatt (Auburn, 1954), and Joseph A. Setaro (Southern Mississippi, 1956).

Delta Kappa President Gary Pack accepted the newly signed charter at the installation banquet in Gatlinburg, Tennessee. Stennis challenged the new Delta Kappa men to make their chapter something they would be proud of as alumni. The chapter's winter formal dance followed the banquet.

ΔΛ

DELTA LAMBDA CHAPTER
Muskingum College
New Concord, Ohio

Founded as the Alban Club,
February 13, 1925
Chartered as Phi Kappa Tau,
April 17, 1971

THIRTEEN MEN FOUNDED the Alban Club at Muskingum College on January 13, 1925. The name of the Scottish Highlander "Alban" was chosen because of the Scottish descent of the founders and their admiration for the faith, originality, and friendliness of the early Scottish Presbyterians. Albans Gary McCollim and William Strohm guided the search for a national affiliation, and in 1969 the Alban Club became a colony of Phi Kappa Tau. By early 1971, the charter requirements were achieved, and an installation date was set for April.

The charter signing and the installation banquet were held on April 17, 1971. National President Thomas L. Stennis II, led the Phi Kappa Tau delegation that included Executive Director William D. Jenkins, National Vice President Ray A. Clarke, past National President Melvin Dettra, Jr., Domain Director James K. Heilmeier, Administrative Assistant John Mankopf, and Editor Jack W. Jareo. Muskingum officials included Dr. William P. Miller, the acting president, and Paul Napier (Bethany, 1931), associate dean of admissions, among others. Chapter President Robert B. Riley accepted the Delta Lambda charter on behalf of the new chapter, making Phi Kappa Tau the second national fraternity on the Muskingum campus.

Delta Lambda Chapter is housed in a modern college-owned home in a wooded setting on the campus edge.

DELTA MU CHAPTER
College of Santa Fe
Santa Fe, New Mexico

Chartered as Phi Kappa Tau,
November 13, 1971

DELTA MU CHAPTER at the 1,300-student College of Santa Fe was installed on November 13, 1971. Members of the Santa Fe colony signed the Delta Mu charter at an afternoon ceremony. College President Cyprian Luke, and Dean of Students Alfred Kane joined the receiving line for the postsigning campus reception.

National President Thomas L. Stennis II, gave the primary address at the installation banquet. Executive Director William D. Jenkins presented the charter to Chapter President John B. Kelleher. Domain Director and past National President Lou Gerding, Administrative Assistant John Mankopf, and National Councilor Robert D. Leatherman rounded out the national fraternity's delegation.

Extremely low membership forced the chapter into inactive status in 1982.

DELTA NU CHAPTER
Wright State University
Dayton, Ohio

Chartered as Phi Kappa Tau,
March 1, 1975

UPON THE RECOMMENDATION of Dr. Russell E. Hay (Miami, 1937), Director of Chapter Development Gary Baumann (St. Cloud State, 1969) formed a colony of thirty-two men on October 14, 1973. Dr. Hay, a member of the Wright State faculty served as the first board of governors chairman and The Rev. Nicholas R. A. Rachford (Cincinnati, 1964) was the chapter advisor. The colony quickly became the largest fraternity on the campus and became active in student activities and community service projects. In the spring of 1974, colony members assisted in the clean-up after the tragic Xenia, Ohio, tornadoes.

The Delta Nu charter was signed on the afternoon of March 1, 1975, in the Presidential Dining Room at Wright State's University Center. National President Ray A. Clarke presided at the installation banquet at the Miami Valley Golf Club that evening. Executive Director William D. Jenkins presented the charter to colony President Richard B. Ruef who had transferred from Ohio State where he had joined Gamma Chapter.

Greek organizations are not housed at Wright State but a long-awaited Greek housing project is currently on the drawing board.

DELTA XI CHAPTER
Cleveland State University
Cleveland, Ohio

Chartered as Phi Kappa Tau,
April 5, 1975

A CLEVELAND STATE colony was formed by Director of Chapter Development Gary Baumann on November 25, 1973. Past National President Melvin Dettra, Jr. and National Councilor James Heilmeier assisted in the initial organization of the fifteen-man colony. Dettra served as the first chairman of the board of governors.

The April 5, 1975, installation ceremonies began with the Delta Xi charter signing in the Panel Hall of the university's Fenn Tower. Cleveland State's President Dr. Walter B. Waetjen welcomed the new chapter to the university during the installation banquet that evening at the Wickliffe Holiday Inn. National President Ray A. Clarke gave the principal address following the presentation of the charter to Chapter President Glen A. Oches.

Though Cleveland State is primarily a commuter school, the chapter in 1983 occupied a historic home once owned by John Brough, governor of Ohio in the Civil War. This arrangement lasted only about a year.

The chapter is currently inactive.

DELTA OMICRON CHAPTER
Pan American University
Edinburg, Texas

Chartered as Phi Kappa Tau,
April 12, 1975

FIFTEEN MEN came together to form a colony on the Pan American campus on May 2, 1973. The group was organized by Gary Baumann, the fraternity's director of chapter development. Phi Kappa Tau was the fifth national fraternity to come to the school.

Members of the colony quickly assumed leadership roles on the campus including the presidencies of the Interfraternity Council, Greek Council and the Pan American University Student Association.

Donald Wright (Nebraska Wesleyan, 1959) and Dr. Donald Walker (Centre, 1948) formed the initial board of governors.

Installation ceremonies took place on April 12, 1975. A 2:00 p.m. reception and charter signing was held on campus in the University Center Ballroom. National President Ray Clarke presided and Executive Director William D. Jenkins presented the Delta Omicron charter to Edward O. Ghelardini at the installation banquet at the La Cucaracha Restaurant in Reynosa, Mexico. The chapter is currently inactive.

CHAPTER SEVEN

REFOCUS & RENEWAL

John W. Meyerhoff (Colgate, 1961) was the right man for the job of executive director in the spring of 1979. A navy veteran, Meyerhoff had been head basketball coach at Brevard College in North Carolina for six years, where his record was 121–79. To the executive director's position, he brought a coach's enthusiasm and the experience of managing the tight budget of a junior college basketball team— exactly the right skills for Phi Kappa Tau.

The fraternity had been without an executive director since Bill Jenkins' departure a year earlier. A team of volunteers and staff members kept the Oxford office running in the meantime. National President McKinley oversaw the executive office's administration, Vice President Cunningham worked with director of field operations Greg Hollen (Maryland, 1975) to supervise chapter services, and National Councilor Tom Hendricks oversaw the tenuous financial situation. At least, the absence of an executive director freed up some room in the budget for chapter support.

"Coach" Meyerhoff, as he soon became known around the fraternity, also gained the nickname "El Cheapo," which he accepted as a badge of honor in his efforts to rebuild the financial strength of the national fraternity. One of his first tests was to coordinate a national convention, which would be the first fraternity convention he ever attended.

1979 CONVENTION

To keep costs low, the 1979 national convention was held on the campus of the University of Tennessee in Knoxville. Nebraska Wesleyan pledge brothers Tom Cunningham and John Green became the only president and vice president team to come from the same pledge class in the same chapter. Two other future national presidents were elected to six-year terms on the National Council. Harold Short, chairman of the Flatiron Companies in Boulder, Colorado, and winner of the 1940 Shideler Award, would become president in 1983. The ambitious young president of the Miami, Florida, Bar Association, John Cosgrove, would assume the national presidency at the 1985 convention.

An extremely moving and memorable part of the 1979 convention program was the appearance of Eileen Stevens, whose son, Chuck Stenzel, had been killed in a hazing incident at an Alfred University local fraternity just eighteen months earlier. Mrs. Stevens described the painful path that led to her realization that her son's death from alcohol poisoning and exposure was a result of fraternity hazing. She was just beginning to speak out to seek support for her fledgling Committee to Halt Useless College Killings (C.H.U.C.K.). National fraternities had initially been wary of Mrs. Stevens, fearing she was on an antifraternity crusade. "I am not antifraternity, absolutely not," she explained, "I am anti-abuse." Two standing ovations indicated that Phi Kappa Tau had made the right decision in being the first national fraternity to invite her to speak. Since that time, she has returned to Phi Kappa Tau events several times and has spoken to almost every national fraternity and sorority and on hundreds of college campuses.

A convention tradition was established with the debut of the Rump Club which was established as an informal organization to encourage

1976 Shideler Award recipient Ed Lowry (center) relaxing with Beta Beta Chapter brothers at the University of Louisville

Mrs. Eileen Stevens shares the story of her son's death with the 1979 national convention.

alumni attendance at conventions. Primarily geared toward former national officers who no longer had an official role to play in the conventions, the club was named for England's powerless seventeenth century Rump Parliament.

The Knoxville convention kicked off a year that would finally show signs of a turnaround for Phi Kappa Tau. The popularity of fraternities was clearly on the rise. No single reason accounted for the change in attitude; but observers of the trend pointed to the new conservatism, the "preppy" craze, and the *National Lampoon's* 1978 hit movie, *Animal House*, whose impact was as much blessing as curse.

CHAPTER REVIVALS

Alpha Sigma Chapter at Colorado State and Alpha Pi Chapter at the University of Washington were both revived in the spring of 1980. Indicative of a new emphasis on scholarship, newly appointed Educational Director Dr. Monroe Moosnick (Transylvania, 1953), Theta Chapter's long-time faculty advisor, reinstated the national fraternity's scholarship award for the chapter with the best grades in the fraternity. The trophy had not been awarded since 1966.

DIAMOND JUBILEE

By the time the Diamond Jubilee convention was called to order to celebrate the fraternity's seventy-fifth anniversary at Miami University in July, 1981, the initiation trend line was on its way up. The 1980–81 year had seen an increase of two hundred initiations over the previous year, the first increase in nearly ten years.

An attitude of optimism and enthusiasm permeated the entire Diamond Jubilee convention. Jack Anson presided at the dedication of the fraternity's anniversary gift to Miami University. Sometimes called Phi Tau Park, the circular grouping of stone benches surrounds a bronze marker with the inscription, "Phi Kappa Tau, 1906–1981, presented on the Diamond Anniversary of its founding at Miami University on March 17, 1906," encircling the coat of arms. The park, which was designed by architecture student Bert Elliott (Miami, 1978), is within sight of the old North

Phi Kappa Tau Foundation Trustees J. Oliver Amos and Raymond A. Bichimer chat at the dedication of the Phi Tau Park in 1981.

Dorm (now Elliott Hall) and the site of Old Main, the buildings that had figured so prominently in the fraternity's founding. National President Thomas C. Cunningham presented the gift to Miami University President Paul G. Pearson. As a living link to the Silver and Golden Jubilees held on the Miami campus, Hugh C. Nichols gave the dedicatory address. Nichols was honorary co-chairman of the Diamond Jubilee along with Ewing Boles, and he had served as general chair-

man of both the 1931 and 1956 gatherings. He had attended his first convention in 1920 and received the Palm Award at the awards banquet later in the convention.

In regular convention business, the delegates approved the first-ever national undergraduate dues of $25 per man per year and elected domain director and former chapter consultant Walter G. "Sonny" Strange (Auburn, 1970) and Seattle architect Robert G. Aldridge (Washington, 1954) to the National Council.

Raymond Bichimer was elected vice president to succeed John Green at the 1983 convention.

Former National Councilor Richard C. Lennox was joined by his son, Richard K. Lennox (Miami, 1954) and grandson Michael W. Lennox (Purdue, 1979) at the convention banquet. The Lennoxes were thought to be the only current three-generation Phi Tau family. Also attending the banquet was Cary S. Miller, one of two living Foundation Members who had been present at the founding March 17, 1906. The Non-Fraternity Association's first secretary, Robert L. Meeks, sent greetings but was unable to attend.

The fraternity's revitalization continued with the rechartering of Beta Alpha Chapter at the University of Texas–Austin over the weekend of February 5–7, 1982, exactly thirty-nine years after the original chartering.

In April two new Kentucky chapters were installed as Delta Pi Chapter at Murray State University and Delta Rho at Eastern Kentucky University. Delta Sigma Chapter became the first national fraternity on the Webber College campus in Babson Park, Florida.

THE BOLES CHALLENGE

One of the most important meetings ever held in the history of Phi Kappa Tau occurred in December 1982 at the venerable Columbus Club in Columbus, Ohio. At that meeting, Chairman of the Board of Trustees of the Phi Kappa Tau Foundation, Ewing

T. Boles, told members of the executive committee of the foundation and officers of the fraternity that he would personally match any gift to the Phi Kappa Tau Foundation up to one million dollars. Boles' dramatic announcement, often referred to as the "Boles

Challenge," started a flurry of activity. By the end of that luncheon meeting, the groundwork was laid for what would become a capital campaign titled "The Decision for Phi Kappa Tau." The initial goal was two million dollars, just enough to meet Boles' challenge, but it soon became apparent that the two-million-dollar goal could be exceeded and, it was raised to three million.

The foundation had been talking about a major fund-raising campaign for a number of years. Boles, who had made the foundation his life's work, realized that he could jump-start the process by making an attention-getting pledge. The key to success in the campaign, consultants told the trustees, was to identify a group of major prospects who could be approached for significant "leadership gifts" and to assemble a volunteer corps who had the clout and willingness to ask.

The all-star steering committee, with Boles as honorary chairman, included Foundation President Dan L. Huffer (Ohio State, 1961), National President John M. Green as chairman of the current officers committee, and Thomas L. Stennis II, as chairman of the past presidents' committee. Attorneys Lawrence L. Fisher (Ohio State, 1960) and Raymond A. Bichimer headed the heritage gifts committee. Past National President Thomas C. Cunningham chaired the official family committee, former Executive Director William D. Jenkins chaired the former staff committee, past National President Melvin Dettra, Jr., was the

general alumni chairman, and John Meyerhoff chaired the effort to get undergraduate chapters to make pledges. National Councilors Harold H. Short, Ross E. Roeder, and John F. Cosgrove were all at-large members of the steering committee.

Another key to the success of the campaign was Boles' ability to persuade Jack Anson to postpone his just-announced retirement from the National Interfraternity Conference to serve as campaign director on a part-time basis. Anson opened an Oxford campaign office at the National Headquarters and spent two days a week there on campaign business. He was assisted by J. Luke Strockis (California State–Long Beach, 1977), who also had responsibility for the alumni relations and development work of the fraternity.

The bronze marker at the center of the Phi Tau Park

The Phi Tau Park was the fraternity's memorial gift to Miami University at the Diamond Jubilee in 1981.

National officers and chapter members in an "Old West" pose during the rechartering of Beta Alpha Chapter at the University of Texas–Austin in 1982

GULFPORT CONVENTION, 1983

Evaluations of the Forty-sixth National Convention, held at a branch of the University of Southern Mississippi on the gulf coast, were in near unanimity on several points: the food was awful, the banquets were crowded, the humidity was unbearable, the dormitory accommodations were spartan, and the convention was one of the best in history. "At least that's what former Grand Secretary R. K. Bowers thinks and he's attended

40 of the 46 [Phi Kappa Tau conventions]," reported the *Laurel*. No particularly important legislation was passed, but two events stand out in almost every delegate's mind.

One was a shrimp boil hosted by past National President Tom Stennis and his family at their Gulfport home, Stenhaus. The outdoor party, complete with New Orleans Dixieland music, gave the whole convention a genuine taste of southern hospitality.

And the event that no one who attended will ever forget was the announcement of the "Decision for Phi Kappa Tau." Most of the delegates had no idea about the behind-the-scenes work that had gone into the campaign. The well-orchestrated announcement struck strong emotional chords. A multimedia presentation called "Phi Kappa Tau: Mirroring an American Century," produced by Luke Strockis, preceded the actual announcement of

"Reach for the stars" was the theme of Ewing T. Boles' dramatic speech at the 1983 national convention.

the Boles Challenge. Campaign director Jack Anson introduced Boles and revealed his one-million-dollar challenge publicly. Anson explained to the awed crowd of 275 that Boles' gift was the largest ever made to a fraternity or fraternity foundation in the more than two-hundred-year history of Greek-letter organizations and that $2.26 million toward the three million dollar goal had already been pledged.

But the star of the show was the eighty-eight-year-old Boles himself. His inspiring talk, interrupted many times by ovations, was completely extemporaneous and overtook the audience. He raised his enormous hand high above his head, exhorting the crowd to "reach for the stars" as he explained his incredible loyalty to Phi Kappa Tau by saying that "no matter how much I do for Phi Kappa Tau, I can never repay it for all it has done for me."

BOLES NAMED HONORARY FOUNDER

For Bole's lifetime of service to Phi Kappa Tau and his tremendous generosity, the National Council hit upon a unique and appropriate way to honor him. In addition to naming the National Headquarters building for him, he was named an honorary founder of Phi Kappa Tau, to be forever remembered in the same breath as Douglass, Boyd, Shideler, and Borradaile.

In the convention's officer elections, Harold Short was elected national vice president, putting him in position to succeed Raymond Bichimer at the 1985 convention. Jack Anson and Ross Roeder were elected to six-year terms on the National Council. Domain Director and former staff member Greg Hollen was elected to fill an unexpired term.

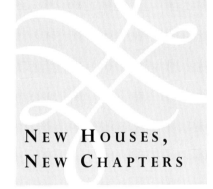

NEW HOUSES, NEW CHAPTERS

No Phi Tau chapter had built a new chapter house since Alpha Phi Chapter at the University of Akron completed its new home in 1973. With the dedication of its new house on October 1, 1983, Gamma Mu Chapter at Bradley University started a new trend. The $300,000 home was designed for a capacity of forty-four men, with ample space for dining and chapter activities. Soon after the completion of the house, Gamma Mu's

Hugh C. Nichols was honorary chairman of the Diamond Jubilee and general chairman of the Silver and Golden Jubilee celebrations.

membership topped the sixty mark for the first time in its history.

The fraternity continued to grow, with three charterings in the spring of 1984. Alpha Kappa Sigma, a local society founded at California State Polytechnic University in Pomona, California, in 1958, became Delta Tau Chapter on May 5, and the Delta Upsilon charter was granted to a colony at the University of Tennessee

at Martin. Beta Rho Chapter at the University of California–Los Angeles, inactive since 1959, was rechartered on June 3, 1984.

For the second October in a row, a new chapter house was dedicated. The 1984 dedication came at the University of Mississippi's Delta Gamma Chapter. A handsome thirty-six-man house boasted a large paneled living room, basement party room, and dining facilities for one hundred.

McConnell Elected to U.S. Senate

In the fall 1984 elections, A. Mitchell "Mitch" McConnell (Louisville, 1961) pulled off a surprising victory in a race for one of Kentucky's U. S. Senate seats. A series of television commercials, now studied in political science classes, used late in the campaign, helped McConnell defeat longtime Senator Dee Huddleston by a slim margin. He was the only

Republican to unseat an incumbent Democrat in U.S. Senate races around the country.

Phi Kappa Tau held a victory dinner for McConnell at the Kentucky Center for the Performing Arts in Louisville. Several of McConnell's classmates, Beta Beta Chapter founder Morton Walker, and a large number of undergraduates turned out to congratulate him. While the *Laurel* reported that McConnell was the fraternity's first U. S. Senator, that was incorrect. The late Hugh Morris (Delaware, 1930) had represented Delaware in the U.S. Senate many years earlier.

"Decision" Exceeds Goal

The "Decision for Phi Kappa Tau" officially closed on December 31, 1984, after a general appeal to all members and chapters. The three-million-dollar goal was exceeded by over $230,000, making the drive the most successful of any Greek letter organization in history. For his extraordinary leadership and generosity, Ewing Boles was given the National Interfraternity Conference's Gold Medal at its

1985 annual meeting. The Gold Medal, the highest possible award for a fraternity man, had been given to Ronald Reagan, Tau Kappa Epsilon, in 1983, and Boles received the honor along with Barry Goldwater, a member of Sigma Chi.

The Tau Chapter charter was returned to a colony at the University of Michigan on December 1, 1984, in ceremonies at the chapter house and the Michigan Union. In January 1985, Delta Phi Chapter was installed at the University of Arkansas in Fayetteville, the first chapter in that state. Later that spring, Delta Chi Chapter was installed at the University of Rochester in New York, joining Gamma Nu as the second chapter in that city.

SCOTTSDALE, 1985

For the first time since 1977, Phi Kappa Tau returned to a resort hotel for its Forty-seventh National Convention in 1985. Former Grand Secretary R. K. Bowers represented Epsilon Chapter's graduate council for the forty-first time since he attended his first national Phrenocon convention in 1915. It would be his last.

Senator Mitch McConnell spent a portion of his August Senate recess with the convention delegates in Scottsdale, making the principal address at the Awards Banquet, where he also received the Borradaile Award. Resident council delegates were delighted to spend informal moments with McConnell around the Registry Resort's pool.

President Short passed the gavel to John Cosgrove for the next biennium, and Walter "Sonny" Strange was elected vice president of the fraternity. Two outstanding domain directors, Dr. W. Joseph Joiner II (Georgetown, 1973) and Greg Hollen, were elected to six-year terms on the National Council.

Executive Director John Meyerhoff presents the Delta Psi charter to Chapter President Jeffrey Soldo.

Two New Houses, Three New Chapters

Fall 1985 saw the dedication of a second new chapter house in Mississippi in as many years. Beta Epsilon Chapter moved into the house, whose design had been unveiled at the Gulfport convention in 1983. House Corporation President and Deep South Domain Director Steve Nelson (Southern Mississippi, 1973) cut the ribbon on the forty-eight-man chapter house on November 2, 1985. At the same time, Beta Chapter repurchased the historic home it had been forced to sell in 1978 after fifty-eight years. Astute local alumni had retained a first right of refusal when the house was sold, and fortunately, the chapter had regained enough strength to exercise its option when the new owner decided to sell.

The Delta Psi charter was presented at the black-tie installation ceremonies attended by 206 at Rider College on March 15, 1986. Rider chemistry professor Dr. Richard Beach (Muhlenberg, 1952) was instrumental in guiding the colony as advisor.

In April 1986, a large number of Michigan State alumni turned out to witness the return of Alpha Alpha's charter. Alpha Alpha alumni enthusiastically supported the effort to rebuild their chapter, which had been closed since 1972.

After an absence of forty-seven years, Omega Chapter officially returned to the University of Wisconsin in Madison on November 15, 1986. Two transfer students, Daniel Schleck (Coe, 1983) and James Heinritz (Lawrence, 1983), helped lead the effort to reopen the chapter, which had been closed since the Great Depression. An original Omega charter member, Paul Elfers (Wisconsin, 1924), contributed $5,000 to a housing fund at the time of the rechartering.

NIC Gold Medal to Anson

Jack Anson added another significant honor to his long résumé when he received the National Interfraternity Conference's Gold Medal, becoming the third Phi Tau to receive the award. Roland Maxwell was the first in 1959, and Ewing Boles (nominated by Anson) was the 1984 winner. It was a tribute to Jack's standing in the interfraternity community that he was nominated for the award by a member of another fraternity. In accepting the award at the NIC's annual meeting in St. Louis, he explained his lifetime of devotion to college fraternities, saying simply, "I believe in the American college fraternity and its ideals."

On March 28, 1987, after a long struggle as a colony, the Gamma Gamma charter was returned to St. John's University in Queens, New York.

The Northeast Missouri State colony earned the Delta Omega charter in ceremonies at Kirksville, Missouri, on May 2, 1987, and the following day at College Station, Texas, the Epsilon Alpha charter was granted to Phi Kappa Tau's Texas A&M colony.

*National President Harold Short,
the 1940 Shideler winner, presents
the award to Scott Gindlesberger in 1987.*

MEYERHOFF RESIGNS

The Epsilon Alpha ceremony was the final one for both National President Short and Executive Director Meyerhoff. Short's term would end at the upcoming convention, and Meyerhoff had submitted his resignation in April to be effective June 30, 1987, so that he could relocate to the western New York area where he had spent part of his youth and college years.

The eight years of the Meyerhoff executive directorship had seen a significant turnaround in Phi Kappa Tau's national organization. The national fraternity's income had grown by 300 percent; the number of functioning chapters and colonies had grown from seventy to ninety-five, and the fraternity's foundation completed the most successful capital campaign in the history of Greek-letter organizations; and the National Headquarters building was completely restored and redecorated.

JOHN GREEN IS NEW EXECUTIVE DIRECTOR

When the search for a new executive director began, a former national president probably did not enter anyone's mind as a potential candidate. But the idea did occur to John Green. President of his family's Wauneta Falls Bank in tiny Wauneta, Nebraska, for several years, he was ready for a career change.

National President John F. Cosgrove signs the Epsilon Gamma charter at Trenton State College.

His Phi Tau credentials were impeccable. He had been a domain chief, served two terms on the National Council, and then served as national vice president and president. And he is probably the only Phi Tau to have spent his honeymoon at a fraternity convention (at the Grand Hotel on Mackinac Island in 1966).

Though Green accepted the offer of employment sometime in the summer of 1987 and assumed the executive director's role at the 1987 convention, it took him until November to finally begin in Oxford full-time.

KING'S ISLAND CONVENTION

At the 1987 convention at the King's Island amusement park near Cincinnati, the most significant piece of legislation approved by the delegates was the removal of recognition for little sister programs. While the structure of the various programs around the country varied greatly, there was concern that in too many chapters the distinction between a fraternity member and a little sister was blurred when both paid dues, pledge fees, or other assessments that ran through the chapter's books. In order to preserve the single-sex status of the college fraternity, it seemed wise to abandon the problematic little sister programs entirely.

Minor revisions also were made to the Ritual.

Cleveland Mayor George V. Voinovich (Ohio, 1956), who had orchestrated Cleveland's renaissance from "mistake on the lake" to All-American City, received the Borradaile Award and was principal speaker at the convention awards banquet held at the College Football Hall of Fame. The awards banquet location was especially appropriate for two other award winners. A second Borradaile Award went to Alpha's William G. Mallory, now head football coach at Indiana University, and the Shideler Award was presented to Scott Gindlesberger (Mount Union, 1984), a magna cum laude Mount Union graduate and Division III All-American quarterback for the Mount Union Purple Raiders.

John Cosgrove was installed as the fraternity's president, and Walter "Sonny" Strange was elected vice president. New graduate members of the National Council were John D. Good (Ohio, 1947) and Stephen Brothers (California–Berkeley, 1966).

RAPID EXPANSION

While John Green had signed several charters as national president, the Epsilon Beta charter was his first as executive director during installation ceremonies at the West Virginia Institute of Technology at Montgomery in November 1987.

Epsilon Gamma became Phi Kappa Tau's 123rd chapter during installation ceremonies at New Jersey's Trenton State College on January 30, 1988.

Gamma Phi Chapter was officially reopened at Northeastern University in Boston, when forty-seven members signed the new Gamma Phi charter on May 31, 1988.

One of John Cosgrove's great priorities was to reinstate the national leadership school that had been so successful during the years Cosgrove had been an undergraduate at the University of Florida. Twenty years after the first national IMPACT, the Leadership Academy was born.

FIRST LEADERSHIP ACADEMY

National Council member Dr. W. Joseph Joiner served as dean of the first Leadership Academy at Miami University in August 1988. Each chapter was asked to send three delegates, and more than three hundred men participated in that first academy. With the financial support of the Phi Kappa Tau Foundation, the per-delegate cost was kept to a minimum, and top-notch speakers brought an air of professionalism that was never possible in the regional IMPACT programs.

The first academy was also the forum for the introduction of the fraternity's new risk-management policy. In an increasingly litigious society, things that used to be considered pranks or chalked up to "boys being boys" were becoming liability exposures. And no fraternity advocate could justify the illegal use (and abuse) of alcohol or dangerous hazing stunts that were too often a part of fraternity life. No wonder fraternity chapters were becoming more and more difficult to adequately insure. For all of those reasons—and because it was the right thing to do—Phi Kappa Tau adopted strict policies regarding alcohol, hazing, and other potential risks. The most significant (and controversial) aspects of the new policy had to do with alcohol.

The new policy strictly prohibited the purchase of alcohol with chapter funds, the bulk purchase of alcohol (kegs), and the underage use of alcohol on chapter property.

The policy also strictly prohibited (and defined) hazing and sexual abuse and required a number of educational programs. While the policy has been a constant challenge to enforce, it has gone a long way to keep insurance available and affordable for Phi Kappa Tau's chapters.

The Virginia Wesleyan colony was granted the Epsilon Delta charter on December 10, 1988, in Virginia Beach. After four years as a colony, the Beta Theta charter was returned to the Kansas colony, officially reopening Beta Theta, which had been a casualty of the early 1970s. Dr. Alan Pickering, the chapter's first president in 1948, participated in the ceremonies.

Two of the original Beta Mu charter members attended their chapter's rechartering at Kent State University on March 18, 1989. The chapter had been closed since 1969.

Alpha Theta Chapter at the College of William and Mary was rechartered on April 8, 1989, with original charter member M. Carl Andrews (William and Mary, 1926) in attendance.

The William Paterson colony, which had been working for four years to achieve chapter status, earned the Epsilon Epsilon charter on April 15, 1989.

VANCE IS FOUNDATION EXECUTIVE

The Phi Kappa Tau Foundation hired Carl D. Vance (Miami, 1967) as its first full-time administrator in 1989. In 1986 Jack Anson opened a foundation office in the century-old home, which had served Alpha Chapter as its first chapter house in 1909, across Campus Avenue from the fraternity's National Headquarters. He traveled from his home in Indianapolis to man the office two days a week until Vance came on board.

Phi Kappa Tau and Delta Gamma facilitators at an early TEAM Discovery weekend

New Orleans, 1989

By the time Walter "Sonny" Strange introduced his ambitious set of goals and objectives for his presidency during the final banquet of the fraternity's 1989 convention in New Orleans, every delegate had a sense that he had helped shape the fraternity's future.

During the convention's business sessions, several projects initiated by President John Cosgrove were completed. A completely revised constitution and statutes prepared by past President Harold Short's constitution review committee was adopted after considerable discussion and debate. The chapter standards first approved in 1977 were expanded to include three tiers: minimum, median, and superior. New scholarship standards, requiring chapters to exceed the all-men's average on their campus by .10 grade points, also were adopted.

Long-time Hawkeye Domain Director Tom Hazelton (Coe, 1975) and Wendell Smith (Michigan State, 1953) were elected to six-year terms on the National Council, and Jack Anson was elected national vice president by acclamation. After a prolonged and spirited ovation, a teary-eyed Anson told the delegates that this was the greatest honor he had received since his invitation to join Phi Kappa Tau at Alpha Upsilon Chapter in 1947.

Unfortunately, Jack Anson did not live long enough to become national president. He died of a heart attack on September 15, 1990, after a successful recovery from prostate-cancer surgery. Anson had been providing tremendous leadership in the area of alumni relations, and his death left a leadership void in the national fraternity that would not easily be filled.

Anson would have succeeded President Strange at the 1991 convention in Long Beach, California. Without a clear successor, Strange expressed his desire to serve two more years as president. The convention consented and also asked John Cosgrove, the immediate past president, to continue in that role on the National Council. W. Joseph Joiner was elected vice president to succeed Walter Strange at the 1993 convention. Elected to six-year terms on the National Council in Long Beach were former Chapter Consultant Richard P. Harrison, Jr. (Ohio, 1979) and National Chaplain Rodney E. Wilmoth (Nebraska Wesleyan, 1957).

The fraternity's financial advisor, Donald E. Snyder, Sr. (Cornell, 1949), chaired a committee that recommended the establishment of a five-dollar annual fee to be paid by each of the fraternity's undergraduate

National President Walter G. Strange, Jr., outlines his presidential objectives at the 1989 convention in New Orleans.

members for a housing-loan fund. The plan was heartily endorsed by the convention.

Attending the 1991 convention for the first time as voting delegates were brothers from two new chapters in the State College of New York system at Buffalo and Oswego. Epsilon Zeta and Epsilon Eta chapters were both chartered in the fall of 1989. The New York chapters were joined by delegates from the new Epsilon Theta Chapter, which was chartered at San Francisco State in May 1990.

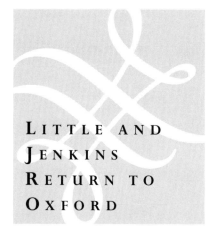

LITTLE AND JENKINS RETURN TO OXFORD

Two former members of the fraternity staff returned to Oxford in 1991.

Former chapter consultant Craig Little (Ohio State, 1980), who had been fraternity advisor at the University of Oklahoma since 1986, returned to the fraternity staff in a newly created assistant executive director position. He assumed responsibility for convention and Leadership Academy planning and also developed a cooperative venture with the women of Delta Gamma called TEAM (together everyone accomplishes more) Discovery.

Organized on a regional basis, these weekend-long workshops in rustic settings are focused on team building, leadership development, and goal setting.

Former fraternity Executive Director William D. Jenkins succeeded Carl Vance as executive vice president of the Phi Kappa Tau Foundation, with responsibility for grant management as well as fund-raising.

On September 20, 1992, National Vice President W. Joseph Joiner died following a lingering illness, almost exactly two years after Jack Anson had died holding the same office. Joiner was only thirty-eight years old. The National Council appointed Rodney Wilmoth as Joiner's replacement, and C. Brent DeVore (Ohio, 1961), president of Otterbein College, was asked to fill Dr. Wilmoth's unexpired term to assure that the National Council would be at full strength at the 1993 national convention at the Innisbrook Resort in Florida. But one more tragedy was to beset the National Council. Walter "Sonny" Strange was

too ill to attend the 1993 convention, and he died a short time after the convention on October 3.

Past President John F. Cosgrove substituted for Strange at the Epsilon Iota chartering at Barry University, near Cosgrove's Miami, Florida, home in April 1993. Strange had been able to attend the long-awaited Maryland rechartering in May.

At the final banquet of the 1993 convention, the new national president, Rodney Wilmoth, a United Methodist minister, spoke eloquently about his objective of drawing together the leadership so devastated by the untimely deaths that had interrupted the clear vision that Anson, Joiner and Strange had brought to the fraternity.

The convention drew to a close with a dramatic announcement. Ewing Boles had died at age ninety-seven in November 1992. It was no secret that Boles had made significant provision for the Phi Kappa Tau Foundation in his will. But until that evening, only the trustees of the foundation knew that he had left $3.7 million in trust

Delegates to the Inaugural Leadership Academy at Miami University

for the benefit of the foundation. Incredibly, he alone had seen to it that the financial future of the fraternity he loved so much was assured.

The words to the "Brotherhood Song," the traditional capstone to Phi Kappa Tau conventions, had special meaning that night.

After those tragic losses, the following biennium brought some significant births. Five new chapters were chartered beginning with Epsilon Kappa at Rutgers just six weeks after the 1993 convention. In the southeast, charters were signed at Longwood College in Virginia and Pembroke State in North Carolina in April 1994 and at Clemson in South Carolina in April 1995. A colony at Pace University in New York became Phi Kappa Tau's newest chapter, Epsilon Xi, in May 1995.

The Brotherhood Song

WE ARE BROTHERS NOW AND EVER

UNTIL THE DAY WE DIE.

AND WHEN THAT TIME COMES ROLLIN' 'ROUND

AND WE BID OUR LAST GOOD-BYE

THERE IS ONE THING SURE AND CERTAIN

LET US BOW OUR HEADS IN AWE

WE'LL MEET AGAIN IN HEAVEN, SURE

IN THE NAME OF PHI KAPPA TAU.

TOWARD the SECOND CENTURY

The 1995 convention in Washington, DC, looked toward a new millennium and Phi Kappa Tau's second century with the visionary report of the blue ribbon "Phi Tau 2000 Com-

mittee," headed by Otterbein College President C. Brent DeVore, a member of the National Council. C. William Crane (Georgia, 1980) and Joseph J. McCann, Jr. (Spring Hill, 1974) were elected to terms on the National Council that will end in 2001.

A poignant cap to the first ninety years of Phi Kappa Tau came just as the manuscript for this new history was being completed early in 1996. Astronaut Leroy Chiao (California-Berkeley, 1979), on his second space shuttle mission, secretly carried with him a small token of an earthly connection—

the jeweled National President's badge which Stephen Brothers will wear and pass down to Vice President Greg Hollen. Even Founder Taylor Borradaile, who always claimed Phi Kappa Tau was "working out just the way I planned it," would have to admit that as Phi Kappa Tau entered its tenth decade, it had come a long way from that chilly afternoon in Old Main.

CHAPTER HISTORIES

ΔΠ
DELTA PI CHAPTER
Murray State University
Murray, Kentucky

Chartered as Phi Kappa Tau,
April 17, 1982

DIRECTOR OF EXPANSION Ken Boyle (Muhlenberg, 1975) recruited the twenty-one initial members of the Murray State colony in January 1980.

Dr. William Batsel (Transylvania, 1968), a psychology professor, became the first colony advisor, and Ross Meloan (Murray State, 1980), assistant to the vice president for student development, was recruited as an advisor and eventually initiated. The group became quite active on campus and posted the highest grade-point average of all of the campus fraternities.

A large residential home on a wooded lot was acquired on a lease/purchase option in the summer of 1980, and in the fall the colony participated in its first formal rush. By the time the charter requirements were met, the colony had retained its high grade-point average and was involved in all aspects of student life.

The Delta Pi charter was presented on April 17, 1982, in ceremonies attended by Executive Director John Meyerhoff, past National President Edward A. (Ted) Marye, and Bluegrass Domain Director William F. Brasch (Louisville, 1967). Thirty-four brothers signed the charter, which was presented to the new chapter's president, Jim Peck.

Delta Pi became inactive in 1987.

ΔΡ
DELTA RHO CHAPTER
Eastern Kentucky University
Richmond, Kentucky

Chartered as Phi Kappa Tau,
April 18, 1982

RICHMOND ATTORNEY W. Joseph Joiner and transfer student Brian Bellairs (Georgetown, 1978) started the colony at Eastern Kentucky, which was recognized by the interfraternity council in the spring of 1981. After one semester, the colony had a membership of twenty-three and had the second highest grade-point average among the campus fraternities.

Maintaining its high grades, the colony became involved in philanthropic, social, and athletic activities at Eastern Kentucky and reached a membership of thirty-one, which completed its set of chartering requirements.

The Delta Rho charter was presented in the university's Powell Building on April 18, 1982. Past President Edward A. (Ted) Marye gave the principal address, and Executive Director John Meyerhoff passed the charter to Chapter President Doug Lefler. Capt. James Hardin (Mississippi, 1970), who had served as faculty advisor to the colony, received recognition for his help.

ΔΣ
DELTA SIGMA CHAPTER
Webber College
Babson Park, Florida

Chartered as Phi Kappa Tau,
May 1, 1982

DR. AL STRICKLAND (Indiana, 1980) began to develop a colony at Webber College in the spring of 1981 by holding a series of meetings to determine if men on campus were interested in forming a fraternity. A core group of six men volunteered during these meetings, and seventeen more joined in the fall. George Ledak (Indiana, 1980) received a graduate assistantship from the national fraternity to work with the colony. His leadership helped the group to accomplish its chartering requirements.

On May 1, 1982, the Delta Sigma Chapter became the fourth chapter in Florida and the first Greek organization on the Webber campus. An impressive group of dignitaries attended the ceremonies. Joining National President John M. Green and Executive Director John W. Meyerhoff were past Grand Secretary R. K. Bowers, National Councilor John F. Cosgrove, and Domain Director Jerry Curington (Florida, 1969). Members of the board of governors were Hubbard Biggs (Florida, 1940), James Crawford (Florida State, 1957), and Thomas Freeman (Florida State, 1949).

Meyerhoff presented the charter to Chapter President Bill Lyman, and Souhail Sabbagh and Robert Oliver presented the chapter with a contribution of $50,000 toward a housing fund on behalf of the Sabbagh family.

Delta Sigma is currently inactive.

DELTA TAU CHAPTER
California State Polytechnic University
Pomona, California

Founded as Alpha Kappa Sigma, 1958
Chartered as Phi Kappa Tau,
May 5, 1984

IN 1957 a like-minded group of students rented a two-story house near downtown Pomona and soon became known as "the Park Avenue boys." Under the leadership of Richard Rand, the group moved to

larger quarters and adopted the name Association for Kellogg Spirit, or Alpha Kappa Sigma. When the university lifted a ban on fraternities in 1964, the group became known as Alpha Kappa Sigma Fraternity. The current chapter house was first occupied in the fall of 1970.

By the time the brothers of Alpha Kappa Sigma decided to affiliate with a national fraternity in 1981, the local was the oldest and most respected fraternity on the campus. Alpha Kappa Sigma officially became a colony on February 26, 1981. Three years of work toward a Phi Kappa Tau charter culminated in the installation ceremonies at Kellogg West on the Cal Poly campus.

Corey Wilson, winner of the 1985 Shideler Award compiled a detailed ninety-five-page history of Alpha Kappa Sigma which was first distributed in 1985.

DELTA UPSILON CHAPTER
University of Tennessee–Martin
Martin, Tennessee

Chartered as Phi Kappa Tau,
May 26, 1984

FRANK ZEIGLER, Scott James, and transfer student Mike Smith, who had been a founder of Delta Pi Chapter at Murray State University, quietly built a group of fifteen men who petitioned Phi Kappa Tau for colony status on April 1, 1982. At that time, the group also went public with their intentions to form a chapter of Phi Kappa Tau. The *Laurel* editor, Tim W. Collins (Transylva-

nia, 1978), traveled to Martin to associate the colony members. Initially denied recognition by the campus interfraternity council, the national fraternity assisted in an appeal that finally gained recognition for the group in 1983.

The colony found a potential chapter house, which was owned by the mayor of Martin, but even the mayor's help could not overcome a zoning restriction that precluded the chapter from making the house its home.

With chartering requirements accomplished, the Delta Upsilon Chapter was installed in May 1984. An inability to retain sufficient membership forced the young chapter to close in 1989.

DELTA PHI CHAPTER
University of Arkansas
Fayetteville, Arkansas

Founded as Chi Gamma Phi,
March 1983
Chartered as Phi Kappa Tau,
January 19, 1985

TWELVE MEN founded Chi Gamma Phi Fraternity at a March 1983 meeting in Yocum Hall on the University of Arkansas campus. A handshake and motto were adopted, and David Wise was elected the first president. The search for a national fraternity to affiliate with began immediately. In the process, David Wise attended Phi Kappa Tau's 1983 convention in Gulfport, Mississippi. After a visit from Executive Director John Meyerhoff and Domain Director Alan Nordean

(Oklahoma State, 1967), the group unanimously selected Phi Kappa Tau from among five national fraternities hoping to enter the university. Dr. David Kessinger (Long Beach State, 1973) and Dr. Robert Davis (Ohio State, 1953) assumed advisory roles with the colony. Cleman Neff (Oklahoma State, 1953) became the first chairman of the board of governors.

In the fall of 1984, the chapter acquired its first home at 20 South Hill Avenue, where they remained until a larger house was rented in the fall of 1986.

Installation ceremonies took place in Fayetteville on January 19, 1985, with National President Raymond A. Bichimer and Executive Director Meyerhoff signing the Delta Phi charter along with the charter members.

ΔΧ

Delta Chi Chapter
University of Rochester
Rochester, New York

Chartered as Phi Kappa Tau, February 23, 1985

THE IDEA OF A NEW Rochester fraternity was first discussed in 1983 by Michael S. Morgioni, David Molyneux, Joe Bouchard, and John McLaughlin, who was a member of Phi Kappa Theta Fraternity from the University of New Hampshire. Rochester's director of Greek affairs, Lou Stark, recommended that the group affiliate with one of the national fraternities that had expressed a desire to come to the campus.

A core group of fourteen interested students met with representatives from national fraternities Chi Phi, Sigma Phi Epsilon, and Phi Kappa Tau. Unanimously, they elected to affiliate with Phi Kappa Tau, and the colony began regular weekly meetings. In December 1983, Director of Expansion K. Steven Lilly (Evansville, 1980) visited from National Headquarters and established plans for recruitment, financial management, and public relations. By the fall of 1984, a board of governors was established, and the colony became heavily involved in campus activities and philanthropy.

Thirty-nine members signed the Delta Chi Chapter's charter on February 23, 1985.

ΔΨ

Delta Psi Chapter
Rider College
Lawrenceville, New Jersey

Founded as Fraternity Expansion Group, April 20, 1983
Chartered as Phi Kappa Tau, March 15, 1986

BEGUN AS A FRATERNITY expansion group on the Rider campus, the Phi Kappa Tau colony was officially established on December 3, 1984, with thirty-five members. The group's purpose from the outset was to develop a fifth Rider fraternity that would enhance the social, academic, intellectual, and cultural life of its members.

Dr. Richard Beach (Muhlenberg, 1952), a Rider chemistry professor, assumed the role as chapter advisor and has provided outstanding leadership to the group ever since.

In 1985 the group successfully petitioned to gain its own on-campus housing, and the group soon grew to fifty-six members. Dr. Beach was instrumental in negotiating a $25,000 inter-chapter loan from Eta Chapter's house corporation to equip a complete commercial kitchen in the chapter house.

National President Harold Short presided at the black-tie installation ceremonies on March 15, 1986. Executive Director Meyerhoff presented the charter to the new Delta Psi Chapter's president, Jeff Soldo.

ΔΩ   ΕΑ   ΕΒ

Delta Omega Chapter
Northeast Missouri State
University
Kirksville, Missouri

*Chartered as Phi Kappa Tau,
May 2, 1987*

PHI KAPPA TAU'S first Missouri chapter traces its history to the spring of 1985 when sixteen men, mostly members of the football team, formed a group interested in forming a new fraternity. After a personal visit from Executive Director John W. Meyerhoff, the group chose to affiliate with Phi Kappa Tau from the three national fraternities it was considering.

Over the summer, the group decided to disband, thinking the road to chartering would be too difficult. Leadership Consultant Charles T. Ball (Miami, 1982) visited the campus in the first days of the fall semester and persuaded colony leaders to reconsider. Leadership Consultant Gregory J. Naso (Coe, 1982) worked extensively with the young colony as it began to develop.

The colony had a membership of fifty-three by the time the Delta Omega charter was signed on May 2, 1987. Meyerhoff was joined in the chartering ceremonies by former Executive Director William D. Jenkins and National President Harold H. Short. Toby Timion was the charter president.

Delta Omega's chapter house is owned and managed by the national fraternity.

Epsilon Alpha Chapter
Texas A&M University
College Station, Texas

*Chartered as Phi Kappa Tau,
May 3, 1987*

SEVEN MEN FORMED the nucleus of the Texas A&M colony when it was founded in February 1983. In the four years of development toward chapter status, the colony became actively involved in intramural sports and philanthropic activities.

Over one hundred people attended the black-tie charter banquet at the College Station Hilton. National President Harold Short and Executive Director Meyerhoff came to College Station from Kirksville, Missouri, where the Delta Omega Chapter had been chartered the day before. Harry Fontenot III, the only colony founder who was still an undergraduate, was the master of ceremonies for the installation banquet. Forty-six new Phi Taus had signed the Epsilon Alpha charter which was presented to Joe Canella, the chapter president.

Epsilon Beta Chapter
West Virginia Institute of
Technology
Montgomery, West Virginia

*Chartered as Phi Kappa Tau,
November 21, 1987*

CHARLES "SPEEDIE" TACKETT, who had been a member of an unsuccessful colony at the Florida Institute of Technology, joined with fourteen other men to found the Phi Kappa Tau colony at the West Virginia Institute of Technology in the fall of 1984. Tackett was the first president.

In the fall of 1985, four brothers moved into the first unofficial house at 1006 Third Avenue. The colony continued to grow slowly, and work was begun on fulfilling chartering requirements. By the fall of 1987, the colony began to grow more quickly and purchased its first home at 810 Third Avenue from Father Jacob, a retired Catholic priest, for $70,000.

The installation ceremonies took place on November 21, 1987. At three in the afternoon, the Epsilon Beta charter was signed in the WVIT Center ballroom. An installation banquet was held at the Saint George Orthodox Church in Charleston that evening. John Green presented the first charter since becoming executive director to Chapter President Perry Murphy, who also was serving as an undergraduate National Councilor. WVIT President Dr. Robert Gillespie welcomed the chapter to the campus, and National President John F. Cosgrove gave the main address of the evening.

ΕΓ
EPSILON GAMMA CHAPTER
Trenton State College
Trenton, New Jersey

*Chartered as Phi Kappa Tau,
January 30, 1988*

IN 1985 TIM GALLAGHER, Ken Novak, Bert Lundberg, and Greg Septer resigned their memberships in a local fraternity with the intention of bringing a new national fraternity to Trenton State. They contacted Phi Kappa Tau and found the headquarters staff eager to discuss expansion with them.

On March 14, 1986, Executive Director John W. Meyerhoff and Director of Chapter Services Eric P. Kelly (Colorado, 1980) visited the group, which had grown to twenty-three members. The first fourteen members were initiated on May 7 and ten more on October 17. Steady growth continued through 1987, and the chartering requirements were achieved.

The colony officially became Epsilon Gamma Chapter on January 30, 1988. The charter was signed in the Trenton State Student Center prior to the installation banquet. Executive Director John W. Meyerhoff presented the charter to President George Trillhaase. National President John F. Cosgrove and Trenton State College President Dr. Harold Eickhoff both made inspirational remarks. Founder Tim Gallagher was toastmaster.

ΕΔ
EPSILON DELTA CHAPTER
Virginia Wesleyan University
Virginia Beach, Virginia

Chartered as Phi Kappa Tau,
December 10, 1988

In September 1986, a group of men who belonged to the local fraternity Sigma Chi Delta petitioned Phi Kappa Tau to become a colony of the fraternity. The petition was approved, and the group became an official colony. By the end of 1987, the group had grown to thirty-three members and associates. Advisor Dave Kennedy and Dean David Buckingham helped the colony fulfill the chartering requirements.

The Epsilon Delta charter was signed and presented on December 10, 1988. Thirty-two men participated in the signing in the Virginia Wesleyan chapel along with National President John Cosgrove and Executive Director John M. Green. The installation banquet and dance were held at the beach front Holiday Inn in Virginia Beach.

ΕΕ
EPSILON EPSILON CHAPTER
William Paterson College
Wayne, New Jersey

*Chartered as Phi Kappa Tau,
April 15, 1989*

GLENN CIRAPOMPA (Bethany, 1985) was the founder of the William Paterson colony during the fall semester of 1985. There were thirteen men in the original group. The colony grew steadily and worked to complete their chartering requirements over the next four years.

On April 15, 1989, the colony finally earned its charter as Epsilon Epsilon Chapter, Phi Kappa Tau's 125th. The charter banquet was held at the Ramada Inn in East Hanover, New Jersey, with Peter Maes serving as toastmaster. National Vice President Walter G. (Sonny) Strange presided, and Executive Director John M. Green also delivered remarks to the charter members and guests.

Chapter President Kevin Sullivan accepted the charter on behalf of the new chapter.

EZ   EH   EΘ

EPSILON ZETA CHAPTER
State University College–Buffalo
Buffalo, New York

*Chartered as Phi Kappa Tau,
October 14, 1989*

WITH THE GUIDANCE of former Executive Director John W. Meyerhoff, a small group of men, who had been part of an unsuccessful Zeta Beta Tau colony, formed the Buffalo colony in October 1987. The group began to participate in campus activities, philanthropy, and recruitment.

In the spring of 1989, the colony formed a board of governors and with the assistance of Executive Director John Green, the colony was able to secure its own residence hall for its first chapter home.

Completing all the chartering requirements, the installation ceremony took place on October 15, 1989. John Green and National President Walter G. (Sonny) Strange were present for the charter signing, and the Epsilon Zeta chartering formal capped the weekend.

EPSILON ETA CHAPTER
State University College–Oswego
Oswego, New York

*Chartered as Phi Kappa Tau,
November 11, 1989*

GREG MONTAGUE (Georgia Tech, 1988) transferred to Oswego and set out to bring Phi Kappa Tau to the campus. He gathered a group of students, who were recognized by the college on October 23, 1987. In November Montague and forty interested men asked to be recognized by Phi Kappa Tau as a colony. The colony approval came on April 30, 1989, when thirty men were associated.

Forty-three undergraduates and four alumni signed the Epsilon Eta charter on November 11, 1989, at the Eis House in Mexico, New York. Chapter Advisor Thomas Shelberg signed the charter along with board of governors members Peter Gabrial (Rochester Tech, 1983) and Chet James (Westminster, 1989). National President Walter G. (Sonny) Strange presided. Executive Director John M. Green presented the charter to Chapter President Robert Beattie.

EPSILON THETA CHAPTER
San Francisco State University
San Francisco, California

*Founded as Alpha Sigma Chi,
April 1988
Chartered as Phi Kappa Tau,
May 10, 1990*

IN THE SPRING semester of 1988, thirteen men gathered in a hot, cramped residence hall room on the sixth floor of Mary Park Hall. Their goal was to lay the foundation for a fraternity experience that would unite a group of friends into a strong brotherhood and give a group of focused leaders the opportunity to make a significant impact on the San Francisco State University campus.

From the founding of their local fraternity, Alpha Sigma Chi, the brothers were committed to cultural and racial diversity. From the very first meetings, the group believed that the strengths of each brother and his contributions to the fraternity experience allowed all the brothers and the organization to grow. The strength of the new organization was its focus on high ideals and the brothers' commitment to one another.

Starting with Phillip Cainfichi who had the initial vision for starting an organization, all of the men in the chapter worked for its betterment. After reviewing literature from several national fraternities, the group met with Reed Anderson (California–Berkeley, 1966), who shared the idea of the innate worth of each individual and the history of the national fraternity. The membership was impressed that many of the principles important to Alpha Sigma Chi were equally important to Phi Kappa Tau. The match was a natural one.

With targeted recruitment efforts and a united team effort, the group of thirteen grew to fifty-five. On May 10, 1990, the colony was installed as the Epsilon Theta Chapter. Two years of hard work, fund-raising and service to the campus and community, had paid off.

The legacy left by the thirteen founders continues to play an important part in the development of San Francisco State University students. What began as a group of men wanting to make a difference, has continued to grow and change, each new group of students building on the initial framework. The founding principle remains constant, "Together we are stronger, than if we stood alone…"

EPSILON IOTA CHAPTER
Barry University
Miami Shores, Florida

Chartered as Phi Kappa Tau,
April 17, 1993

THE BARRY COLONY was installed as Phi Kappa Tau's 129th chapter on April 17, 1993, after a year and a half. The installation festivities began with the Red Carnation Ball the night before the installation banquet. Parents and other Barry students were invited to take part in the celebration.

The charter was granted at a banquet held at the Miami Airport Marriott. Past National President John Cosgrove presided and was assisted by William D. Jenkins, executive vice president of the Phi Kappa Tau Foundation. The charter was presented to John Evans Bruner and Victor L. Higbee, who served as banquet toastmaster.

Brand new Epsilon Iota Chapter announced the formation of a scholarship in the name of Luis Daniel Valdez, the first chairman of the colony's board of governors.

EPSILON KAPPA CHAPTER
Rutgers University
New Brunswick, New Jersey

Chartered as Phi Kappa Tau,
September 18, 1993

JASON FARELLA (Rider, 1990) transferred to Rutgers in the fall of 1990 and soon located William Aprea (Georgia Tech, 1991) and Mark Tekrony (Kentucky, 1987). Together, they attempted to form a Phi Kappa Tau colony on the Rutgers campus. By the spring of 1992, the group had grown to twenty-nine. Domain Director Jeff Brittingham (Delaware, 1980) met with the group in August to discuss the steps to chartering. The group officially became a colony on October 21, 1992. Jason Farella was the first president.

A house at 121 Hamilton Street was rented and occupied on June 1, 1993, and the petition was completed by the middle of August. At the 1993 national convention, the colony won the Fletemeyer prize as the outstanding colony in the fraternity. The group had progressed through the colony development process in less than eleven months.

The installation was held at the Somerset Holiday Inn, with 170 persons gathered for the event on September 18, 1993. Past National President John Cosgrove presided as Epsilon Kappa was chartered, the 130th chapter in Phi Kappa Tau.

EΛ

EPSILON LAMBDA CHAPTER
Longwood College
Farmville, Virginia

Chartered as Phi Kappa Tau,
April 9, 1994

THE LONGWOOD COLONY was founded September 18, 1992, after an invitation from the school to start a group there. The colony built an excellent reputation on the campus, electing three Student Government presidents and completing outstanding philanthropic work.

By the spring of 1994, the colony had achieved the chartering requirements and the installation date was set for April 9, 1995, after nineteen months as a colony. The Epsilon Lambda charter was signed in the Longwood Rotunda and the members of the new chapter hosted a reception in their chapter room after the signing.

The installation banquet was held at the Longwood Center for the Visual Arts that evening. Chapter President Darrell Wells accepted the charter from Executive Director John M. Green and William D. Jenkins gave the primary address representing National President Wilmoth who was unable to attend. Wells later joined the national fraternity staff as director of expansion.

EM

EPSILON MU CHAPTER
Pembroke State University
Pembroke, North Carolina

Founded as Sigma Phi Sigma
Chartered as Phi Kappa Tau,
April 22, 1994

MEMBERS OF SIGMA PHI SIGMA local fraternity formed the Pembroke colony on October 14, 1991. The colony immediately became involved in a wide array of campus activities and received a community service award from the Chamber of Commerce.

The colony accepted the Epsilon Mu charter on April 22, 1994, after three years of work and development. Installation ceremonies took place at the Prince Charles Radisson Hotel in Fayetteville, North Carolina. Past National President Ray A. Clarke represented National President Wilmoth, giving the keynote address. Phi Kappa Tau Foundation Executive Vice President William D. Jenkins and Director of Expansion Robert Reece represented the national fraternity's professional staff. Reece presented the Epsilon Mu charter signed by thirty founders to Chapter President Sean Bagwell.

Following the singing of the Brotherhood Song, the black-tie installation festivities concluded with a dance.

EN

EPSILON NU CHAPTER
Clemson University
Clemson, South Carolina

Chartered as Phi Kappa Tau,
April 1, 1995

THE CLEMSON COLONY was established on February 6, 1994, and was chartered after fourteen months of hard work.

Colony members were initiated on March 30–31, 1995, and the installation ceremony took place on the evening of March 31. National President Rodney Wilmoth presided at the ceremonies held at the Peachtree Plaza in Atlanta. In addition to the newly initiated members, the Epsilon Nu charter was signed by fraternity staff members Rob Reese, Steve Hartman, and Greg Blaisdell; Clemson's Director of Greek Affairs Mandy Hayes; and Board of Governors Chairman Tom Abrams.

Epsilon Xi Chapter

Pace University
Pleasantville, New York

Chartered as Phi Kappa Tau,
May 5, 1995

IN THE SPRING of 1993, eight men, who were not satisfied with the fraternities at Pace University, founded an organization of their own. Those first eight were David Zwickel, Dave Kennedy, John McNeill, Andy Daniello, Greg Purna, Isaac Kashanian, Mike Sumberac, and Dave Thomas. Through Upstate Domain Director Jeff Lawton (State University College–Oswego, 1990), the group learned about Phi Kappa Tau. Two additional groups joined the original eight to form the Pace colony in December 1993.

Pace colony became Epsilon Xi Chapter, the fraternity's 134th, on May 5, 1995. The installation was held on the Pace University campus. Past National President Thomas C. Cunningham presided along with Executive Director John M. Green. The charter was presented to Epsilon Xi Chapter President John McNeill.

APPENDIX

National Convention Sites and Dates

Ohio University, Athens OH	October 21–22, 1911
Ohio University, Athens OH	February 24, 1912
Ohio University, Athens OH	March 6–7, 1914
Ohio State University, Columbus OH	May 21–22, 1915
Centre College, Danville KY	December 21–22, 1915
Mount Union College, Alliance OH	December 21–22, 1916
University of Illinois, Champaign IL	December 20–22, 1917
Mount Union College, Alliance OH	January 11–12, 1919
Mount Union College, Alliance OH	September 19–20, 1919
Claypool Hotel, Indianapolis IN	October 14–16, 1920
Ohio State University, Columbus OH	September 1–3, 1921
Chicago Beach Hotel, Chicago IL	September 1–3, 1922
Phoenix Hotel, Lexington KY	August 30–September 1, 1923
Hotel Tuller, Detroit MI	August 28–30, 1924
Muehlebach Hotel, Kansas City MO	August 27–28, 1925
West Baden Springs Hotel, West Baden IN	August 24–28, 1926
Bigwin Inn, Ontario, Canada	August 25–27, 1927
West Baden Springs Hotel, West Baden IN	August 23–25, 1928
Phoenix Hotel, Lexington KY	August 22–24, 1929
Grove Park Inn, Asheville NC	August 28–30, 1930
Silver Jubilee—Oxford OH	August 26–28, 1931
No quorum—Adjourned, Oxford OH	August 21, 1932
No quorum—Adjourned, Oxford OH	June 26, 1933
Purdue Memorial Union, West Lafayette IN	August 29–31, 1934
Council met as convention, Oxford OH	August 24, 1935
Nittany Lion Inn, State College PA	August 27–29, 1936
Troutdale in the Pines, Evergreen CO	June 25–28, 1938
French Lick Springs Hotel, French Lick IN	August 27–28, 1940
Hotel Spink, Lake Wawasee IN	June 25–28, 1947
Elms Hotel, Excelsior Springs MO	January 24–29, 1949
Bedford Springs Hotel, Bedford Springs PA	January 20–23, 1951
French Lick Springs Hotel, French Lick IN	June 24–27, 1953
Golden Jubilee—Oxford OH	June 27–30, 1956
Huntington Sheraton Hotel, Pasadena CA	June 18–21, 1958
Shawnee Inn, Shawnee-on-Delaware PA	June 27–30, 1960
Grove Park Inn, Asheville NC	June 20–23, 1962
University of Colorado, Boulder CO	June 24–27, 1964
Grand Hotel, Mackinac Island MI	August 25–31, 1966
French Lick Sheraton Hotel, French Lick IN	August 25–26, 1968
Chase Park Plaza, St. Louis MO	August 26–28, 1970
Doral Country Club, Miami FL	August 15–18, 1972
Tan-Tar-A Resort, Osage Beach MO	August 25–28, 1975
Keystone Lodge, Keystone CO	August 13–17, 1977
University of Tennessee, Knoxville TN	August 21–25, 1979
Diamond Jubilee—Oxford OH	July 29–August 1, 1981
USM Gulf Park, Long Beach MS	August 9–14, 1983

The Registry Resort, Scottsdale AZ	August 14–18, 1985
Kings Island Inn, Kings Mill OH	August 11–15, 1987
The Fairmont Hotel, New Orleans LA	August 8–12, 1989
Hyatt Regency, Long Beach CA	August 7–10, 1991
Innisbrook Resort, Tarpon Springs FL	August 3–8, 1993
JW Marriott, Washington DC	July 29–August 3, 1995

National Presidents

Taylor A. Borradaile (Miami)	1906–1907
Harvey C. Brill (Miami)	1907–1908
Wilmer G. Stover (Miami)	1908–1909
Alexander R. Paxton (Miami)	1909–1910
Edward E. Duncan (Miami)	1910–1911
Ernest N. Littleton (Miami)	1911
H. A. Pidgeon (Ohio)	1911–1912
C. R. Ridenour (Ohio)	1912–1913
Dr. William H. Shideler (Miami)	1913–1914
Robert C. Webber (Ohio)	1914–1915
Eckley G. Gossett (Ohio State)	1915
S. Frank Cox (Centre)	1915–1916
Ewing T. Boles (Centre)	1916–1917
Frederick R. Fletemeyer (Illinois)	1917–1919
Henry E. Hoagland (Illinois)	1919–1920
Dr. Edgar Ewing Brandon (Miami)	1920–1923
John V. Cotton (Centre)	1923–1925
Dr. Harry A. Taylor (Nebraska Wesleyan)	1925–1928
Dr. Isaac Miles Wright (Muhlenberg)	1928–1930
W. Massey Foley (Miami)	1930–1934
Roland W. Maxwell (Southern California)	1934–1959
Harold E. Angelo (Mississippi State)	1959–1962
Dr. William A. Hammond (Miami)	1962–1964
Louis C. Gerding, Jr. (Colorado)	1964–1966
Warren H. Parker (Nebraska Wesleyan)	1966–1968
Melvin Dettra, Jr. (Ohio State)	1968–1970
Thomas L. Stennis II (Mississippi State)	1970–1972
Ray A. Clarke (Bowling Green)	1972–1975
Edward A. Marye, Jr. (Kentucky)	1975–1977
F. L. McKinley (Oklahoma State)	1977–1979

Thomas C. Cunningham (Nebraska Wesleyan)	1979–1981
John M. Green (Nebraska Wesleyan)	1981–1983
Raymond A. Bichimer (Ohio State)	1983–1985
Harold H. Short (Colorado State)	1985–1987
John F. Cosgrove (Florida)	1987–1989
Walter G. Strange, Jr. (Auburn)	1990–1993
Dr. Rodney E. Wilmoth (Nebraska Wesleyan)	1993–1995
Stephen Brothers (California–Berkeley)	1995–1997

Presidents of the Phi Kappa Tau Foundation

Dr. W. A. Hammond (Miami)	1945–1962
Ewing T. Boles (Centre)	1962–1964
Dr. W. A. Hammond (Miami)	1964–1966
Ewing T. Boles (Centre)	1966–1971*
Raymond A. Bichimer (Ohio State)	1971–1981
Dan L. Huffer (Ohio State)	1981–1986
Frederick E. Mills (Ohio State)	1986–

Ewing Boles was named Chairman of the Board in 1971 and retained that position until his death.

National Secretaries/Executive Directors

Roger C. Smith (Miami)	1911–1913
Eckley G. Gossett (Ohio State)	1913–1915
G. Floyd Cooper (Ohio)	1915–1916
Alexander C. Kerr (Ohio)	1916–1917
Ralph K. Bowers (Mount Union)	1917–1929
Richard J. Young (Miami)	1929–1961
Jack L. Anson (Colgate)	1961–1970
William D. Jenkins (Bowling Green)	1971–1978
John W. Meyerhoff (Colgate)	1979–1987
John M. Green (Nebraska Wesleyan)	1987–

Shideler Award Recipients

William E. Cromer Alpha–Miami University	1938
Herman E. Taylor Pi–University of Southern California	1940
Harold H. Short Alpha Sigma–Colorado State University	1940

Louis Liebl, Jr.
Rho–Rensselaer Polytechnic Institute — 1941

Dana Sherwood Jones
Beta–Ohio University — 1942

Wallace R. Steffen
Alpha Omega–Baldwin–Wallace College — 1947

Harold S. Burt
Zeta–University of Illinois — 1948

R. Douglas Trezise
Alpha Alpha–Michigan State University — 1949

John E. Fulker
Alpha–Miami University — 1950

John L. Myers
Beta Tau–Bowling Green State University — 1951

John D. Ray
Alpha Lambda–Auburn University — 1953

Gene A. German
Alpha Alpha–Michigan State University — 1954

Thomas S. Nichols
Alpha–Miami University — 1955

James S. Voorhees
Zeta–University of Illinois — 1955

James G. Jones
Alpha–Miami University — 1956

James J. Kaster
Alpha Psi–University of Texas–El Paso — 1957

Henry R. Adler
Beta Tau–Bowling Green State University — 1958

Richard E. Truchses
Eta–Muhlenberg College — 1959

Colin A. Heath
Alpha Delta–Case Western Reserve University — 1960

Thomas L. Stennis II
Alpha Chi–Mississippi State University — 1961

Thomas J. Scott
Kappa–University of Kentucky — 1962

Lawrence H. Westerfield
Kappa–University of Kentucky — 1963

Lawrence L. Fisher
Gamma–Ohio State University — 1964

Thomas L. Good
Zeta–University of Illinois — 1965

John E. Sullivan
Pi–University of Southern California — 1966

Oscar F. Westerfield
Kappa–University of Kentucky — 1967

Forrest S. Kuhn, Jr.
Beta Beta–University of Louisville — 1968

Tom Lockhard
Gamma Mu–Bradley University — 1969

James M. Harvey
Gamma Chi–Delta State University — 1970

Chris R. Youtz
Alpha Lambda–Auburn University — 1971

Thomas D. Creighton
Upsilon–Nebraska Wesleyan University — 1972

Jay E. Smith
Pi–University of Southern California — 1973

Robin L. Feuerbacher
Alpha Zeta–Oregon State University — 1974

Karl S. Bourdeau
Eta–Muhlenberg College — 1975

Edwin J. Lowry, Jr.
Beta Beta–University of Louisville — 1976

Stephan M. Nelson
Beta Epsilon–Southern Mississippi — 1977

David L. Arlington
Gamma Nu–Rochester Institute of Technology — 1978

Patrick McGrath III
Alpha Eta–University of Florida — 1979

Gregory C. Stangle
Alpha Kappa–Washington State University — 1980

Gary R. Bergman
Phi–Bethany College — 1981

Robert L. Chiles
Beta Beta–University of Louisville — 1982

Daniel F. Atherton
Theta–Transylvania University — 1983

Steven C. Krohn
Beta Epsilon–Southern Mississippi — 1984

Corey L. Wilson
Delta Tau–Cal. State Polytechnic Univ.–Pomona — 1985

Lincoln D. Zehr
Upsilon–Nebraska Wesleyan University — 1986

Scott R. Gindlesberger
Epsilon–Mount Union College — 1987

Vincent Forte
Beta Epsilon–Southern Mississippi — 1988

Paul D. Hrics
Epsilon–Mount Union College — 1989

Jeffrey Zaniker
Lambda–Purdue University — 1990

182 Patrick Griffin
Zeta–University of Illinois 1991

Paul Cramer
Gamma Alpha–Michigan Tech 1992

Scott Wagner
Beta–Ohio University 1993

Rodney Harl
Nu–University of California, Berkeley 1994

Brent Cutshall
Upsilon–Nebraska Wesleyan University 1995

Palm Award Recipients

1938	Dr. William H. Shideler (Miami, 1906)
1938	Dr. Edgar Ewing Brandon (Miami, 1906)
1938	Ewing T. Boles (Centre, 1914)
1938	Dr. Henry E. Hoagland (Illinois, 1916)
1938	Dr. Harry A. Taylor (Nebraska Wesleyan, 1923)
1946	Dr. William A. Hammond (Miami, 1910)
1947	Robert M. Ervin (Centre, 1920)
1947	Paul T. Gantt (Franklin & Marshall, 1921)
1947	Ralph W. Beach (Delaware, 1929)
1949	Clifford C. Beasley (Florida, 1931)
1951	Ray A. Bushey (Colorado, 1924)
1952	Homer J. Dana (Washington State, 1927)
1953	Peter F. Good (Ohio, 1924)
1958	Ernest N. Littleton (Miami, 1909)
1958	Louis C. Gerding (Colorado, 1924)
1963	Roland W. Maxwell (Southern California, 1922)
1964	John B. Maran (New York, 1924)
1968	Reid A. Morgan, Jr. (Auburn and Washington, 1951)
1968	Harold E. Angelo (Mississippi State, 1942)
1968	Ben E. David (Ohio State, 1945)
1971	Jack L. Anson (Colgate, 1947)
1971	Warren H. Parker (Nebraska Wesleyan, 1931)
1971	Frederick R. Fletemeyer (Illinois, 1916)
1972	Dr. Paul H. Dunn (Mississippi State, 1938)
1977	John F. Mankopf (Coe, 1965)
1977	Thomas L. Stennis II (Mississippi State, 1958)
1979	William D. Jenkins (Bowling Green, 1957)
1981	Hugh C. Nichols (Miami, 1920)

1988	Melvin Dettra, Jr. (Ohio State, 1945)
1988	Ray A. Clarke (Bowling Green, 1951)
1990	Edward A. Marye, Jr. (Kentucky, 1948)
1990	Raymond A. Bichimer (Ohio State, 1953)
1991	Paul A. Elfers (Wisconsin, 1924)

Maxwell Award Recipients

1961	Upsilon–Nebraska Wesleyan University
1963	Theta–Transylvania University
1965	Upsilon–Nebraska Wesleyan University
1967	Upsilon–Nebraska Wesleyan University
1969	Upsilon–Nebraska Wesleyan University
1971	Rho–Rensselaer Polytechnic Institute
1975	Chi–North Carolina State University
1977	Upsilon–Nebraska Wesleyan University
1979	Eta–Muhlenberg College
1980	Rho–Rensselaer Polytechnic Institute
1981	Beta Epsilon–University of Southern Mississippi
1982	Beta Epsilon–University of Southern Mississippi
1983	Alpha–Miami University
1984	Zeta–University of Illinois
1985	Iota–Coe College
1986	Rho–Rensselaer Polytechnic Institute
1987	Theta–Transylvania University
1988	Gamma Alpha–Michigan Tech. University
1989	Gamma Alpha–Michigan Tech. University
1990	Alpha Rho–Georgia Institute of Technology
1991	Gamma Mu–Bradley University
1992	Beta–Ohio University
1993	Beta Beta–University of Louisville
1994	Beta–Ohio University
1995	Theta–Transylvania University

Taylor A. Borradaile Award Recipients

| 1968 | General Leonard Chapman (Florida, 1932) former Commandant of the U. S. Marine Corps |
| 1969 | Smith L. Rairdon (Ohio State, 1922) former Executive Vice President of Owens-Illinois, Inc. |

1970   Richard W. Ervin, Jr. (Florida, 1926)
        Chief Justice of the Florida Supreme Court

1971   Morris Jobe (Akron, 1938)
        President of Goodyear Aerospace

1972   Dr. John R. Dunning (Nebraska Wesleyan,
        1926) former Dean of the Graduate School of
        Engineering, Columbia University

1973   J. Oliver Amos (Miami, 1928)
        President of Amos Press

1974   Wesley G. Stock (Washington State, 1954)
        Chief Pitching Coach, Oakland Athletics

1975   Bruce K. Brown (Illinois, 1917)
        Director and Consultant, Ingram Corporation

1976   Dr. Grayson L. Kirk (Miami, 1921)
        President Emeritus, Columbia University

1977   Raymond C. Bliss (Akron, 1938)
        former Chairman, Republican National
        Committee

1978   Jack A. Soules (Ohio State, 1946)
        Dean, Cleveland State University

1979   Paul L. Newman (Ohio, 1943)
        Actor, Race-car Driver, Philanthropist

1981   William N. Liggett (Miami, 1939)
        Chairman and CEO, First National Bank of
        Cincinnati

1982   Dr. Ernest H. Volwiler (Miami, 1911)
        former Chairman of Abbott Laboratories,
        inventor of Pentothal

1983   William F. Kerby (Michigan, 1928)
        Chairman and CEO, Dow, Jones & Co.,
        and publisher, *The Wall Street Journal*

1984   Paul A. Elfers (Wisconsin, 1924)
        former Executive Vice President,
        Fisher Controls, International

1985   A. Mitchell McConnell, Jr. (Louisville, 1961)
        U. S. Senator, Kentucky

1986   George V. Voinovich (Ohio, 1956)
        Mayor of Cleveland, Ohio

1987   William G. Mallory (Miami, 1954)
        Head Football Coach, Indiana University

1988   Norman W. Brown (Ohio State, 1950)
        Chairman, Foote Cone & Belding
        Communications, Inc.

1989   Dr. Ernest F. Nippes, Jr. (Rensselaer, 1935)
        Professor of Metallurgical Engineering,
        Rensselaer Polytechnic Institute

1990   Donald S. Frederick (Miami, 1928)
        former Vice President Rohm & Haas,
        developer of Plexiglas

1991   Gen. Carl E. Mundy (Auburn, 1955)
        Commandant, U. S. Marine Corps

1992   Richard W. Vomacka (Middlebury, 1965)
        Leader in emergency medicine

1993   Robert E. Holmes (Ohio, 1941)
        former Chief Justice, Ohio Supreme Court

1995   Paul E. Raymond (Coe, 1923)
        Retired educator and attorney

INDEX

193